Advance Praise for D

'The book fuses together heritage conservation and history in a very impressive manner ... It will enrich the understanding of those interested in the history not only about these buildings but also more widely about historical monuments and their preservation' – Rudrangshu Mukherjee, Chancellor and Professor of History at Ashoka University

'The first real attempt to bring historical sites and buildings of the past within the reach of the masses ... Interestingly, all the "facts" are laid before you without taking a particular position when dealing with controversies surrounding the sites and their afterlife. A must-read for all' – Syed Ali Nadeem Rezavi, Professor of History at Aligarh Muslim University and author of *Fathpur Sikri Revisited*

'Monuments are a window into our heritage and past. Given the increasing interest in history and reliance on non-academic sources, it is imperative to locate the monuments in their larger historical contexts. This is where Shashank Shekhar Sinha scores, and authoritatively. From the conception of the monuments to their afterlives, Sinha skilfully connects the dots for the viewers and the readers, in accessible language. His multilayered, multidimensional history of three imperial cities and six World Heritage Sites offers an excellent academic–public interface for the study of monuments, the cities in which they are located, and their extended geocultural connections' – Rana Safvi, author of *The Forgotten Cities of Delhi* and *Shahjahanabad*

'A book to be read several times, in different ways — a guide to six UNESCO World Heritage Sites, a work on the history of Sultanate and Mughal architecture and urbanism, and a survey of the important scholarly debates in history and conservation, rendered in an easy-to-read form' — Swapna Liddle, author of *Connaught Place and the Making of New Delhi*

DELHI
AGRA
FATEHPUR SIKRI

Shashank Shekhar Sinha is an independent researcher and, currently, Publishing Director at Routledge (South Asia), Taylor & Francis Group. He has previously taught history at undergraduate colleges in the university of Delhi for almost a decade. A public historian and the author of *Restless Mothers and Turbulent Daughters: Situating Tribes in Gender Studies*, his writings are recommended readings at various universities and institutions. He has been part of key academic committees of the Indian Council of Social Science Research (ICSSR) and the Indian Council of Historical Research (ICHR).

He publishes regularly in academic journals and books as well as popular media outlets. His articles on the UNESCO World Heritage Sites in *Frontline* magazine have been received well and he also features on programmes related to history and heritage on television channels like Rajya Sabha TV, News18 and NDTV 24X7, among others.

Forthcoming in the series

Buddhist Monuments of India
Temples of South India

For Ben

MAGNIFICENT HERITAGE SERIES

Towards newer explorations

DELHI AGRA

MONUMENTS, CITIES AND CONNECTED HISTORIES

FATEHPUR SIKRI

Shashank
10 . III . 2023

SHASHANK SHEKHAR SINHA

MACMILLAN

First published 2021 by Macmillan
an imprint of Pan Macmillan Publishing India Private Limited,
707 Kailash Building
26 K. G. Marg, New Delhi – 110 001
www.panmacmillan.co.in

Pan Macmillan, The Smithson, 6 Briset St, Farringdon, London EC1M 5NR
Basingstoke and Oxford
Associated companies throughout the world
www.panmacmillan.com

ISBN 978-93-89104-10-3

Copyright © Shashank Shekhar Sinha 2021

All rights reserved. No part of this publication may be reproduced, stored in or introduced into a retrieval system, or transmitted, in any form, or by any means (electronic, mechanical, photocopying, recording or otherwise) without the prior written permission of the publisher. Any person who does any unauthorized act in relation to this publication may be liable to criminal prosecution and civil claims for damages.

1 3 5 7 9 8 6 4 2

This book is sold subject to the condition that it shall not, by way of trade or otherwise, be lent, re-sold, hired out, or otherwise circulated without the publisher's prior consent in any form of binding or cover other than that in which it is published and without a similar condition including this condition being imposed on the subsequent purchaser.

Typeset in Joanna MT Std by Manmohan Kumar
Printed and bound in India by
Replika Press Pvt. Ltd.

For my three sisters, Jyotsna, Arpana and Rashmi, and their most caring respective halves, Ravi Sinha, Satish Chandra and Sanjay Sinha

CONTENTS

List of Figures and Maps	x
A Note on the Series	xi
How to Read This Book	xiii
Prologue: A Tale of Three Imperial Cities	xvii
Introduction: Monuments, Cities and Connected Histories	1
1. The Qutb Minar and its Monuments	69
2. Humayun's Tomb	99
3. The Agra Fort	128
4. Fatehpur Sikri	158
5. The Taj Mahal	191
6. The Red Fort	224
Author's Note	256
Endnotes	265
Index	282

LIST OF FIGURES AND MAPS

IMAGES

Introduction	between pages 12 and 13
1. The Qutb Minar and its Monuments	between pages 80 and 81
2. Humayun's tomb	between pages 108 and 109
3. The Agra Fort	between pages 135 and 136
4. Fatehpur Sikri	between pages 165 and 166
5. The Taj Mahal	between pages 199 and 200
6. The Red Fort	between pages 230 and 231

All photographs are taken by the author, other than those credited otherwise.

SITE MAPS

The Qutb Minar complex	72-73
Humayun's tomb complex	104-05
The Agra Fort complex	132-33
Fatehpur Sikri	162-63
The Taj Mahal complex	196-97
The Red Fort complex	228-29

A NOTE ON THE SERIES

Departing from existing studies on the subject, this series looks at heritage sites and the cities in which they are located in their larger geographical, sociocultural and historical contexts. It brings together latest and complex academic research from across disciplines, including history, archaeology, architecture, art history and heritage studies and presents it in an accessible form. Addressing the gap between the academic and popular understandings of history, the series discusses how stereotypes, assumptions and myths come into being around monuments and their builders, and how they impact our reading of the related historical periods.

Each volume in the series provides a multilayered and multidimensional account of the evolution of monuments, their architectural details, the life and times of rulers who built them, their afterlives, anecdotes and folklore surrounding them as well as debates and controversies related to the heritage sites. They also contain comprehensive, illustrated and self-sufficient chapters on the UNESCO World Heritage Sites in the respective geocultural region.

The books in the series will form essential reads for teachers, students and scholars of history, archaeology, architecture, art history, heritage studies and tourism and hospitality. Authoritative and accessible, they will be indispensable for tourists, foreign and domestic, and heritage enthusiasts. Finally, architects, conservationists, policymakers, think tanks and organizations working on monuments and heritage cities will also find these volumes very useful.

HOW TO READ THIS BOOK

The book is divided into three parts – a substantive prologue about the six UNESCO World Heritage Sites (Qutb Minar, Agra Fort, Humayun's tomb, Fatehpur Sikri, Taj Mahal and Red Fort) in the context of the rise of three imperial cities related to the Delhi Sultanate and Mughal India; a detailed introduction which discusses the larger geocultural and historical contexts in which the three imperial cities came into being and how their settlements and monuments developed; and six chapters on the individual World Heritage Sites.

HOW MUCH TIME DO YOU HAVE AND WHAT DO YOU WANT TO KNOW

You can choose to read the book in the following ways depending on how much time you have and how much you want to know:

If you have enough time and want to get a comprehensive idea of the larger geocultural and historical contexts within which the three cities and their monuments developed, then you should read the complete book.

If you have less time and want to know more about the six UNESCO World Heritage Sites and how they relate to the three imperial capitals of medieval India, then read the prologue (A Tale of the Three Imperial Cities) and the six individual chapters.

If you have still less time and want to learn about some specific sites and their builders and their times, then read the chapters along with the relevant portions of the introduction (Monument, Cities and Connected Histories). The introduction follows a chronological framework and all the headings are clearly laid out.

If you don't have much time and want to know only about some specific site(s), then just read the individual chapter(s) connected with the site(s). The individual chapters are designed to be self-sufficient and standalone resources.

WHAT TO EXPECT IN THE CHAPTERS

The six chapters of this book bring together in a concise format, a multilayered and multidimensional history of these World Heritage Sites. They incorporate the latest research on the subject and modern controversies surrounding the sites. Any person who chooses to read any chapter should have, in around thirty pages, accessible yet authoritative information.

All chapters follow a consistent format and include the following components:

- Circumstances leading to the construction of the heritage site
- Information on the design and layout
- Site map and photographs of monuments. Some photographs have been labelled to give a better idea of what commonly referred architectural motifs look like.
- Graphic account of all monuments at a site including their evolution, histories, architecture, functions, myths, folklore and connected human stories.
- Boxes containing interesting trivia and key insights
- Afterlife of the site: What happened to the site after the primary builders left the scene?

- One section connected with the most controversial/debated/ discussed aspect of the World Heritage Site appears towards the end of each chapter. These include:
  - How Delhi's first Friday Mosque became the 'Might of Islam' mosque (Qutb Minar)
  - How the tomb complex was restored in the 21st century (Humayun tomb)
  - How 'Somnath Gate' ended up being in the Agra Fort (Agra Fort)
  - Was shortage of water the reason for the decline of Sikri? (Fatehpur Sikri)
  - How the idea of the Black Taj and other myths came into being (The Taj Mahal)
  - How the Red Fort became a site of India's Independence Day celebrations (Red Fort)
- The chapters also contain mini stories about the development of certain architectural features or practices/icons associated with royalty.
  - The chapter on Qutb Minar discusses the evolution of arches and domes.
  - The chapter on Humayun's tomb has stories on the evolution of tombs in Islam, *char bagh* (four-fold garden) and the deployment of the concept of *hasht bihistht* or a design representing an irregular octagon (an allusion to eight gates of the 'Garden of Paradise') in tomb architecture. It also covers the conversation between red sandstone and white marble in Sultanate and Mughal architecture.
  - The chapter on Agra Fort explores the evolution of *jharokha darshan* and the Diwan-i Aam ('Hall of Public Audience')

besides glass-art technique or *ayina kari* (elements of which are seen in the Shish Mahal).

- The chapter on Fatehpur Sikri shows how the layout of a new city borrowed on the idea of a Mughal camp which formed a mobile mini city in itself.
- The chapter on Taj Mahal discusses how an improvised tomb garden came to symbolize the 'Garden of Paradise' on earth. It also explores the evolution of architectural features like the dome, the minaret and the *jilaukhana* or the forecourt.
- The chapter on Red Fort shows how the concept of irregular octagon came to influence the design of the palace-fort. It also discusses how the emperor's seat in the Diwan-i Aam evolved to reflect his exalted status alongside the stories of the famous peacock throne and the Koh-i-Noor diamond.

PROLOGUE
A Tale of Three Imperial Cities

Delhi and Agra are among the most densely populated cities in the world. They have also always been the seats of power and empires, along with Fatehpur Sikri, for more than a millennium, and ongoing excavations reveal settlements from much earlier times. No wonder the monuments of Delhi and Agra figure on the itinerary of every tourist – foreign or domestic. While some tourists come specifically to see Delhi and Agra, many arrive primarily to see the Taj Mahal but do not leave without visiting the six UNESCO World Heritage Sites – Qutb Minar, Humayun's tomb and the Red Fort in Delhi and the Agra Fort, Fatehpur Sikri and the Taj Mahal in the Agra–Sikri region. Even though Fatehpur Sikri is not a part of the Agra district administration, its proximity to both the cities often makes it a part of the sightseeing tour packages. Sikri forms an integral part of the experience of Delhi and Agra, and the Mughal empire. Over a period, these six heritage sites of the three imperial capitals have become preferred tourist destinations of India. They consistently figure in the list of top ten monuments that attract most tourists – international and domestic – and generate most revenues.

For the foreign tourists not as familiar with Indian history, visits to these six World Heritage Sites mostly form their first encounter with the country's rich cultural heritage, their introduction to the exotic world of the Delhi Sultanate and the Mughals. For domestic tourists who are perhaps relatively more familiar with India's history, such trips help them revisit, perhaps revise, their understanding of these monuments and personalities or prominent events linked with them from their school textbooks.

Monuments, however, always offer a lot more. They tell us multiple stories not just about the specific history of the individual monuments but also of the cities they belong to and the larger historical period they represent. These monuments, identified by the UNESCO as World Heritage Sites, have larger connected histories which also include their afterlives and the popular, sometimes political, constructions of their pasts. Unpeeling these layers of history can be a lot more informative, engaging and interesting if done in a way in which these connect with the visiting public. And, this is one of the key features of this book and the series. This book has been crafted for tourists, general readers, history enthusiasts and even teachers and students of related courses so that detailed academic research is distilled in an attractive and accessible format. But this series of books goes beyond that; it also looks at the myths, folklore and popular histories surrounding the sites.

IS THIS BOOK ANY DIFFERENT

Despite their strongly connected pasts and present, most books on Delhi, Agra and Fatehpur Sikri are either city-centric and deal with an individual city or are monument-centric and focus only on individual monuments or heritage sites. So far, there is no single book which discusses the connected histories of these three cities and of the monuments within them. Comprising a detailed introduction and six self-sufficient chapters – one on each World

Heritage Site – this book also provides an illustrated history of almost 500 years of the medieval and early modern period, from around the 12th century to the 18th century. It brings together different perspectives and the latest research from archaeology, architecture, history, art history and heritage studies, but presents them in a simple and accessible language. So, the volume provides a multidimensional and multilayered account of the evolution of Delhi, Agra and Fatehpur Sikri and their monuments, examining the role of diverse factors including the Indian and Central Asian political and cultural influences, local power dynamics, role of the Sufi saints, political economy, dynastic and individual ambitions, migrations and invasions and attempts at repairs and restorations in later times.

The six individual chapters of this book bring together in a concise format, the comprehensive and multilayered history of the six World Heritage Sites of Delhi, Agra and Fatehpur Sikri. After discussing the circumstances leading to the construction of the sites, these chapters take the readers on a graphic historical tour of the monuments discussing their evolution, their architectural styles, related anecdotes as well as myths and folklore surrounding them. Simultaneously, they also make the readers aware of the debates and controversies surrounding the sites and their individual monuments. Finally, they also explore the afterlife of the heritage sites – what happened to the sites once the primary builders or sponsors left the scene? In this sense, the book goes beyond the 18th century and brings the history of the monuments to near modern times.

DELHI, AGRA, FATEHPUR SIKRI: SHIFTS OF THE IMPERIAL CAPITAL

This book is also an exploration of the capital cities of north India along with the UNESCO heritage monuments. These monuments are from the long historical period of the 12th century to 18th century, which marked the transition of power from Rajput states to the Delhi Sultanate to the Mughals. The Delhi Sultanate – lasting from the late 12th to early 16th century – saw a succession of dynasties who were either Turks or Afghans, including the Mamluk Turks, Khaljis, Tughlaqs and Lodis. The Lodis in turn gave way to the Chaghtai or Timurid Mongols who came to be popularly known as the Mughals in the mid-16th century. The Mughals were replaced by the British colonial power in the 18th–19th centuries. The British ruled India till the country secured its independence in 1947.

Delhi remained the capital of the Sultanate from around the late 12th century to early 16th century. The capital shifted to Agra under the Lodis. The Mughals, by and large, preferred to rule from Agra till around the mid-17th century when emperor Shah Jahan (r. 1628–58/66) brought the seat of power back to Delhi. It would however be wrong to say that only Delhi or Agra remained imperial capitals in this entire duration – it moved to other places as well, though temporarily. The key to understanding this conundrum is to understand the movements of the rulers – either of the Delhi sultans or of the Mughal emperors. When the rulers moved, their courts moved and with them the courtiers, administrative machinery and service providers. And, most ambitious rulers remained mobile either to acquire new territories or quell revolts in the acquired territories. Some temporarily moved for better weather or repose. Most architectural constructions took place when the rulers stayed at a place for a relatively longer time.

During the period of the Delhi Sultanate, the capital once temporarily shifted to Daulatabad in the Deccan, presently Aurangabad, in Maharashtra. The Deccan was the final frontier for ambitious rulers based in Delhi–Agra. Their approaches differed, though. The Delhi sultan Alauddin Khalji (r. 1296–1314) sent imperial campaigns also aimed at securing booty or tribute. Muhammad bin Tughlaq (r. 1325–51) preferred to conquer the region and he also created a co-capital in Daulatabad to rule Deccan/peninsular India better. After the reign of Muhammad bin Tughlaq, the sultans let go off their control of the Deccan and chose to concentrate on north India, which broadly came to be known as Hindustan. With the disintegration of the Delhi Sultanate, peninsular India saw the emergence of Deccani sultanates, which later gave a tough time to the Mughals. Akbar and Jahangir mostly tried to manage Deccan from Agra, which was strategically better located for the purpose than Delhi. Jahangir also stayed in tents during his Deccan operations. Over a period, the Mughal encampments had become well-equipped mobile cities and served like on-field capitals. In the chapter on Fatehpur Sikri, we will discuss how such encampments inspired the construction of Mughal palaces and imperial establishments. Towards the late 17th–early 18th century, Aurangzeb stayed in such encampments in the Deccan for a very long time, trying to save a disintegrating empire from the older Deccani sultanates and the emerging Marathas.

Under the Mughals, the capital also moved to places like Fatehpur Sikri and Lahore. The Mughal emperor Akbar's decision to shift the imperial seat to Fatehpur Sikri also had a spiritual component: his proximity to the Sufi saint Salim Chishti. However, Lahore (now in Pakistan) served an important strategic purpose. The Mughal empire had expanded to include Afghanistan, Badakshan and surrounding areas. Besides, the rise of the Safavid empire in Central Asia necessitated a continuous watch. Emperors like Akbar (r. 1556–1605), Jahangir (r. 1606–28) and later

Aurangzeb (r. 1658–1707) therefore stayed for longer periods in Lahore.

Despite occasional changes in the imperial seats, the rulers kept coming back to the strategic Delhi–Agra axis along the river Yamuna. For those migrating from the politically unstable areas of Central Asia of the 10th–12th centuries, Punjab and Delhi offered a land of opportunities, particularly for those looking eastwards. Mahmud of Ghazni's invasions had shown that the mountain passes in the north-west were not invincible and Punjab–Multan could serve as a springboard for campaigns in north India. Later, Muhammad of Ghuri and the early Turks used Punjab as a base to launch their attacks on the Rajputs in north India.

But why was the Delhi–Agra axis so important? Control over Delhi offered a continuous command over the vast Gangetic plains, right up to the Bay of Bengal. The later move to Agra offered direct control over the rich agricultural tract between the rivers of Ganga and Yamuna, the doab; better connectivity to trade routes of the subcontinent and enhanced commercial prospects; and strategic access to Rajasthan, Gwalior, Malwa, Gujarat and later, the Deccan. River Yamuna, which connected Delhi and Agra, offered huge possibilities for transport and communication.

THE CONNECTED HISTORIES OF DELHI AND AGRA

Little do the visitors to Delhi and Agra realize how much the histories of the two cities intersect. They are sometimes referred to as twin imperial cities or capitals. For a small but significant period, Fatehpur Sikri near Agra too became a third imperial capital of the region. These connections became established in the 16th century, when the Lodi rulers from Delhi shifted their capital to Agra. The city was probably under the control of the

Rajputs or Jats, an agricultural community, before passing under the control of the Delhi Sultanate.

The city of Delhi mostly developed as a series of settlements which were planned as capital cities by successive rulers and dynasties over time. These have coalesced into a continuous overarching megacity of the present time. With the establishment of the Sultanate, Delhi's first 'Red Fort', the Lal Kot, (not to be confused with the prominent Red Fort built later by the Mughals) became the site of the first Muslim settlement in north India. Located in the arid spurs of Delhi Ridge in modern Mehrauli, this erstwhile Rajput citadel gave way to what presently constitutes the Qutb Minar complex. This complex and the eponymous Qutb Minar, which is a UNESCO World Heritage Site, forms a major tourist centre of attraction and is discussed in a chapter in this book. Known as the original 'Old Delhi', the imperial-residential area around the Qutb remained the seat of the Delhi sultans till Alauddin Khalji decided to build a new fortified city, Siri, around what are now known as the Siri Fort and Shahpur Jat village. Frequent Mongol invasions were making Delhi vulnerable at a time the Sultanate was trying to extend imperial control over Rajasthan, Malwa, Gujarat and send campaigns to south India. The Khaljis were replaced by the Tughlaq dynasty whose soldier-founder, Ghiyasuddin Tughlaq (r. 1320–25), established a new settlement called Tughlaqabad, on the southern end of the ridge in Delhi, between modern Badarpur and Faridabad. It is said that a curse by the Sufi saint Nizamuddin Auliya led to the abandoning of the new city before it was fully populated. The next sultan, Muhammad bin Tughlaq, not only extended the Sultanate's control over Deccan and peninsular India, he also fortified the area between Qutb and Siri and called it

Jahanpanah ('The Refuge of the World'). But Muhammad bin Tughlaq's reign also saw the beginning of the disintegration of the Sultanate; it had become too large and unwieldy by now. His successor, Firuz Shah Tughlaq (r. 1351–88), tried to maintain control over north India and let the Deccan and other areas go. He also did something most ambitious sultans would do: find a new settlement. Located on the banks of the river Yamuna, this new city was called Firuzabad. Henceforth, all future settlements of Delhi would adjoin the Yamuna rather than the rocky Aravalli ridge – Salim Garh, built by the rulers of Sur dynasty; Dinpanah ('Refuge of the Faithful'), built by the Mughal emperor Humayun; Humayun's tomb, built by emperor Akbar; and Shahjahanabad, built by Akbar's grandson, Shah Jahan.

The shift to Agra came at a critical point in the career of the Sultanate which had started disintegrating under the Tughlaqs. Sindh and Multan in the west, Bengal in the east and states in Rajasthan and the Deccan broke away. And, the governors of Malwa, Gujarat and Jaunpur declared their independence. A Mongol invasion in 1398, led by Timur Lane, gave a death blow to an already weakened Delhi. Sikander Lodi (r. 1489–1517), the second ruler of the Lodi dynasty, re-established imperial control over parts of north India and shifted the capital of the Sultanate from Delhi to Agra. The shift, it was hoped, would strengthen Sultanate's fragile control over the crucial Ganga–Yamuna doab and bring more resources by way of agriculture and trade. It would also help them recover parts of central India. An old brick Rajput structure, called the Badalgarh Fort, became the imperial seat of the Lodis and, later, the Mughals. With the shift of the imperial seat to Agra, Delhi receded into the ranks of a provincial city for a while. However, it continued to remain important spiritually and symbolically as the foundational centre of Muslim rule in north India. The Lodis continued to build their tombs and mosques in Delhi and these can be seen in places currently known as Lodi Gardens, Green Park, South Extension I and II, Defence Colony and Mehrauli.

After defeating the last Lodi sultan Ibrahim Lodi in the First Battle of Panipat (1526), Babur, the Mongol ruler from Ferghana valley, laid the foundations of what came to be known as Mughal rule in India. One of the first things he did was to ask his son Humayun to rush to Agra to take control of the Lodi imperial treasury. Babur, however, stayed in Delhi to celebrate and perhaps consolidate and legitimize his victory. He visited the tombs of Sufi saints Bakhtiyar Kaki and Delhi sultans like Balban and Alauddin Khalji, alongside the Qutb complex, and other buildings, pools, gardens and landmarks of Delhi. Interestingly, he also had his name proclaimed as the sovereign in the mosques of Delhi. Soon after, he left for Agra and preferred to rule from there. During his short reign (1526–30), he built gardens in Agra modelled on the ones in Kabul. Upon Babur's death in 1530, his son Humayun was coronated at the Agra Fort, which had been wrested from the Lodis. However, the second Mughal emperor (r. 1530–40; 1555–56) chose Delhi to lay the foundations of his new city called Dinpanah or the 'Refuge of the Faithful'. Humayun chose a site located on the banks of the river Yamuna, close to the Sufi saint Nizamuddin Auliya's hospice. This city project was carried forward by the Afghan ruler, Sher Shah Suri under the name of Shergarh. Founder of the Sur dynasty, he defeated Humayun in successive battles (1539–40) and brought Delhi and Agra under Afghan control. Humayun had to live in exile till he regained the throne in 1555. Remains of Dinpanah and Shergarh can still be seen in the Purana Qila complex near the Delhi Zoo. Some Sur constructions can also be seen around the Qutb complex in the vicinity of the tomb of Sher Shah Suri's favoured Sufi saint, Bakhtiyar Kaki.

Akbar, Humayun's son and successor, occupied the first Mughal fort in Delhi, the Dinpanah by defeating the Surs and other independent chieftains. However, he preferred to rule from Agra, a decision also motivated by an unsuccessful assassination attempt on his life during his visit to Delhi in 1564. But Akbar did not neglect his father's constructions in Delhi. Asserting control over Humayun's legacy, he ordered the building of a magnificent mausoleum (c 1562–71) near Nizamuddin Auliya's hospice, known as Humayun's tomb – a structural complex which is now a UNESCO World Heritage Site and is explored in a chapter in this book. Akbar also provided large Afghan-style tombs for his wet-nurse Maham Anga and her arrogant son, Adham Khan, in Delhi. Located near the Qutb complex, Adham Khan's tomb is situated on the top of a wall that once enclosed the Lal Kot. In his imperial seat Agra, Akbar rebuilt the old Badalgarh fort located on the banks of Yamuna. The right bank of the river, in the direction of the flow. was earmarked for the residences of the nobility. Gradually, *havelis* (mansions) and habitations began to develop along the right bank. Thanks to consolidation of Mughal rule under Akbar and his wide-ranging administrative and economic reforms, imperial Agra began to grow, in size, wealth and influence. It also began to emerge as a major commercial hub in north India.

Akbar decided to shift the capital to Sikri, 45 kilometres from Agra, protected by the spiritual realm of the Sufi saint Salim Chishti by whose blessings he had an offspring and successor. With the Mughal conquest of Gujarat in 1572–73, Sikri began to be known as Fatehpur Sikri which meant, 'City of Victory'. This planned city is a UNESCO World Heritage Site and forms a separate chapter of this book. Over the next thirteen to fourteen years (1571–85), the new capital saw Akbar trying to integrate a population with diverse socio-religious inclinations. Political uncertainties in the north-west, arising out of the death of his brother Mirza Hakim in 1585, led Akbar to shift his capital to Lahore where he stayed till 1598. When he came back, the Deccan was embroiled in warfare and Akbar decided to shift to Agra, rather than returning to Sikri. Akbar died in 1605 after striking a truce with his rebellious son Salim, who had been named after the Sufi saint Salim Chishti. Salim ascended the throne at Agra under the name Jahangir or 'Seizer of the World'.

The new emperor Jahangir spent a lot of time in Lahore, Agra and Kashmir. However, the Delhi connect always remained important. Jahangir's predecessor Akbar had paid a visit to Delhi's holy places in 1576. Shah Jahan also made visits to the tomb of Nizamuddin Auliya much before Delhi became the capital again. Mughal emperors would also visit Delhi for hunting purposes. The area around Dinpanah and Nizamuddin Auliya's tomb remained important on the trade map as it lay on the highway connecting Agra and Lahore. A huge rest house, Azimganj Sarai, came up at this site – it lies between the Delhi Zoo and the Sunder Nursery today, and is being restored. Agra's location had however become strategically important to deal with the upheavals in the Deccan from the time of Jahangir. His reign saw Agra growing along the Yamuna. *Havelis*, streets, houses, bazaars and shops developed along the right bank along with gardens which came up on both sides of the river.

During the early decades of the 17th century, Agra had emerged as a major commercial hub and exchange centre for goods manufactured in the subcontinent. It had surpassed Delhi in many ways. The town was buzzing with the presence of domestic and foreign traders, merchants, middlemen or agents, financiers, money changers, insurers and transporters. *Sarais*, workshops and markets began dotting the city. By the time Jahangir's successor, Shah Jahan, ascended the throne, Agra had become known as 'a wonder of the age' and 'one of the biggest cities in the world'. He changed the name of Agra to Akbarabad, 'the city of Akbar', to honour his grandfather. Shah Jahan's reign (1628–58/66) is known for its imperial grandeur and golden period for architecture. He renovated Agra Fort by adding three new marble palace courtyards and, when his beloved wife Mumtaz Mahal died, he built the iconic Taj Mahal in Agra in her memory. The monument is still regarded as one of architectural wonders of the world. In this book, the Taj Mahal is explored as the most famous UNESCO World Heritage Site of the Indian subcontinent, which is visited by millions of visitors every year. During Shah Jahan's time, gardens with buildings along the Yamuna became a common building form, though the left bank remained primarily occupied with imperial ones. Agra also became a great literary and cultural centre. The city, however, developed as a long, narrow strip. Unlike Delhi, which saw successive ambitious sultans build respective settlements or cities at different places – generally moving away from the dry Aravalli spurs in the south towards the river Yamuna in the north-east – Agra developed linearly along the river. The length of the city far exceeded its breadth and Agra became progressively congested with buildings and encroachments to remain an imperial capital. The city was restrictive for Shah Jahan's grand building plans and stately processions.

In 1639, the emperor decided to build a new capital in Delhi and leave behind a lasting impression of his reign. Besides being the centre of Muslim rule in north India, Delhi had always remained an important pilgrimage destination. Soon, a new capital, Shahjahanabad came into being on the banks of Yamuna in Delhi. The Red Fort was its Qila-i-Maula ('Exalted Fort'). This palace-fort is now considered a UNESCO World Heritage Site and will be discussed in a chapter in the book. The Red Fort stood at the juncture of two principal commercial streets/avenues – one headed towards the iconic Chandni Chowk and the other towards modern Daryaganj. The 17th-century Mughal capital soon became a big commercial hub and attracted traders and businesspersons from different parts of the world. This 'Walled City' is now known as 'Old Delhi' in comparison to the 'New Delhi' built by the British in the beginning of the 20th century.

With the shift of the imperial seat to Shahjahanabad and the Red Fort in Delhi, Agra began to progressively lose its sheen. Aurangzeb, Shah Jahan's son and successor, ruled from Shahjahanabad but also held courts at Agra. It was at the Agra Fort that he kept Shah Jahan imprisoned till the latter's death in 1666. Aurangzeb also met the prominent Maratha leader Shivaji at this fort. After 1680, Aurangzeb left Delhi to deal with political troubles in the Deccan and, like Jahangir, lived and held courts in tent cities. After Aurangzeb's death (1707), his successor Bahadur Shah spent his five-year reign trying to pacify rebellions at different places and could never stay in the Red Fort.

With Bahadur's Shah death, began a period (1712–61) when the Mughal emperors would remain static at Delhi. The Deccan seceded from the empire, but Delhi remained populous and saw the construction of some monuments and garden houses. The imperial authority however lapsed into the hands of powerful nobles, regents, military commanders and provincial governors. These kingmakers ruled in the name of the emperors. The emperors' and Delhi's imperial authority was also eroded by the invasions of Nadir Shah (1739) and Ahmad Shah Durrani (1757); Maratha occupation (1757–61); and the Third Battle of Panipat (1761). The post-1761 period gave some respite to Delhi, but it also saw the Mughal emperor Shah Alam II (r. 1759–1806) trying to reconstitute imperial authority in Bengal rather than in Shahjahanabad and giving away important political and economic concessions to the English East India Company. And then, there was another Maratha occupation of Delhi in 1785. The imperial authority of the emperors of Hindustan was now limited to Delhi as they successively lost territories to competing powers, externally and internally.

Both Delhi and Agra came under the control of the English East India Company when Lord Lake defeated the Marathas in 1803. Agra was incorporated in the North Western Provinces while Delhi was put under a British Resident, who constantly encroached on the diminishing powers of the Mughal emperor. The Red Fort, however, remained the centre of social and cultural life in Delhi. The coming together of the Europeans and Mughal Delhi resulted in what is known as the Delhi Renaissance – a period characterized by the new scientific learning and intellectual activities of the Delhi College (now the Zakir Husain College) and its Oriental and English departments. This period of intellectual and cultural efflorescence was soon disrupted by one of the most formidable challenges to the British rule in the 19th century, the 1857 rebellion. The rebellion reiterated the symbolic importance of Delhi as the capital of Hindustan and the Mughals as the rulers of Hindustan. The rebels asked the last emperor Bahadur Shah Zafar to assume the leadership of the 1857 rebellion. And the Red Fort emerged as the headquarters of the rebel government. After the suppression of the rebellion, the Queen of England was proclaimed the Empress of India, ending the rule of the East India

Company. The British restated the aura and imperial symbolism of Delhi by holding the three Imperial Durbars in 1877, 1903 and 1911 in the city and not in Calcutta, the seat of the British government. In the opening decades of the 20th century, the colonial government decided to build their last imperial capital in Delhi, the New Delhi, a little away from Yamuna and south of Shahjahanabad. This was to serve as the new capital of colonial India and, after 1947, independent India. As the book goes into production, there are plans afloat to further rebuild and redevelop New Delhi, particularly the Parliament building (formerly Council House) and the central vista lying between India Gate and the Rashtrapati Bhavan (formerly Viceroy's House).

THE WORLD HERITAGE SITES

Of the six World Heritage Sites being discussed in the form of dedicated chapters in this book, only one, the Qutb Minar complex, belongs to the Delhi Sultanate and the remaining five to Mughal period. Interestingly, the Qutb complex saw architectural interventions by all prominent dynasties of the Sultanate – the Turks, the Khaljis, the Tughlaqs and the Lodis. Of the remaining five, three – Agra Fort, Humayun's tomb and Fatehpur Sikri – were primarily built during the time of the Mughal emperor Akbar, though Agra Fort was substantively rebuilt by his grandson Shah Jahan. Akbar's reign is particularly known for integration of people, cultures and architectural styles and this reflects prominently in the Agra Fort and Fatehpur Sikri. The last two sites, Taj Mahal and the Red Fort, were built during the time of Shah Jahan, whose reign is known as the 'classical period' of Mughal architecture and Persian influences.

If one were to further analyse these sites, the Qutb complex forms a site of the earliest Muslim settlement in north India. It therefore has remains of a mosque, minarets, tombs, graves and a madrasa (college/school for Islamic instruction) built by different dynasties. Of the three forts – Agra Fort, Fatehpur Sikri and the Red Fort – the first served as a one of the strongest bastions in the period of early consolidation of the Mughal rule. Gradually, settlements came to be built around it. Fatehpur Sikri was built as a new imperial city in the 16th century and its 'Imperial Complex' still has remains, in reasonably good state, of palaces, imperial establishments and waterworks. The city also formed an important Sufi centre and its 'Sacred Complex' still physically demonstrates the spiritual realm of Shaikh Salim Chishti. The Red Fort at Delhi was built as the palace-fort of the 17th-century Mughal capital Shahjahanabad. This Mughal bastion continued to remain important for the social and political life of Delhi even after the disintegration of the empire. It came to centrestage once again during the 'Great Indian Rebellion' (1857–58). The Red Fort also emerged as the symbolic centre of the anti-colonial resistance in the 1940s. Once the British rule ended, the fort became embedded in the national iconography as the site of India's Independence Day celebrations.

Finally, two of the six World Heritage Sites are tombs – Humayun's tomb and the Taj Mahal. Known as the 'Precursor to the Taj', the former introduced elements of classical Persian architecture and the idea of a monumental tomb garden which also symbolized a Quranic paradise. Its recent restoration has brought the monument prominently back on Delhi's tourist map and in debates related to conservation. This idea of the paradise tomb garden first introduced in Delhi was perfected and taken to its classical form in Agra, in the form of the Taj Mahal. Voted as one of the 'New Seven Wonders of the World', the Taj has continuously dominated the city's cultural landscape since its construction. It also remains one of the iconic representations of India. It might be worthwhile to highlight the other thread that physically and organically connects Delhi and Agra – the river Yamuna, which flows through both the cities. Four of these sites, Agra Fort, Humayun's tomb, Taj Mahal and the Red Fort, were built on the banks of the river as part of a conscious plan. Occupying an important position in India's sacred geography, the now feeble Yamuna once formed the lifeline of two leading political formations of their time – the Delhi Sultanate, especially its later phase, and the Mughal empire.

INTRODUCTION
Monuments, Cities and Connected Histories

Killi tau dhilli bhayi
Tomar bhaya mat hiin

(The nail has become loose
The Tomar's wish will not be fulfilled)

The name 'Delhi' is popularly traced to this lore about the *dhilli killi* or the 'loose nail' which refers to the oldest artefact in the Qutb Minar complex, the iconic iron pillar. Standing firm in the courtyard of the congregational mosque in the Qutb complex, this 1,600-year-old rust-free pillar otherwise bears proud testimony to the significant advances India had made in the field of metallurgy and casting in ancient times. The legend related to the pillar is mentioned in the epic *Prithviraja Raso* composed by Chand Bardai, the court poet of the legendary Rajput king Prithviraja Chauhan. The period between 1000–1200 CE is known for the emergence and proliferation of several clan- or lineage-based Rajput states in north India. Attachment to land, family and honour were some of the key characteristics of these clans and they were mostly warring with or claiming superiority over each other. They claimed descent from *suryavanshi* (old solar) or *chandravanshi* (lunar) families of the warrior class, *kshatriyas*. And they built fortresses on an unprecedented scale and patronized Hinduism and Jainism. Of the various Rajput clans,

2 DELHI, AGRA, FATEHPUR SIKRI

the two important ones associated with the early medieval history of Delhi include the Tomars and Chauhans. It is important to appreciate their presence not only to understand the later history and building activities of the Turks, Afghans and Mughals in Delhi and the shift of the capital city between Delhi and Agra but also to appreciate the UNESCO World Heritage Sites better.

RAJPUTS AND THE EMERGENCE OF DELHI

As the story goes, a Brahmin once narrated the tale of an iron pillar to Tomar king Anangapala, also known as Bilhan Deo. His rule would be stable, the Brahmin prophesied, till the iron pillar stood firm. It was rooted deep in the ground and rested on the hood of Vasuki, the mythical serpent king who supports the world from below. A curious Anangapala, however, ordered the pillar to be dug up, and when the base of the pillar finally emerged, it was found smeared in Vasuki's blood. A nervous king ordered the pillar to be reinstalled. However, despite efforts, the pillar could not be fixed – it remained loose – *dhilli killi*. The story signified that instability had set in under the reign of the Tomar king, leading to the entry of the Turks in the region to shape the next era of Delhi. Interestingly, a short 11th-century inscription on the iron pillar credits Anangpala Tomar with establishing Delhi.

Former governors of the Pratihara dynasty – who had succeeded the illustrious Gupta dynasty – the Tomars became independent and ruled from Hariyanaka country with its capital, 'Dhillika', as Delhi was then known.[1] Some fortifications and structures built by the Tomars in the Badarpur–Surajkund area of Delhi still survive. Excavations at Anangpur fort in this area have revealed several artefacts, including coins, pottery, utensils and stone sculptures belonging to the Rajput era. Anangpur village in Badarpur is possibly named after one of the Tomar kings, Anangapala I or II.

One of these kings is also credited with the construction of the stone masonry dam nearby. Surajkund reservoir in the vicinity is likewise attributed to another Tomar king, Suraj Pal.[2]

Anangpal II built a fortified citadel called the Lal Kot or 'Red Fort' after shifting his base to the arid Mehrauli region of Delhi in mid-11th century CE (Fig. 1). Though this is a different 'Red Fort' than the prominent one built later by Mughal emperor Shah Jahan, now a UNESCO World Heritage Site, the building of this fort is important in the development of Delhi and its architectural heritage. The ruler probably also built a tank known as the Anangtal, located close to the Qutb Minar. Water required for the construction of later Delhi sultan Alauddin Khalji's unfinished Alai Minar in the Qutb complex was brought from the Anangtal. The Tomars are therefore regarded as builders of some of the earliest surviving waterworks in Delhi.[3]

The Tomars and their successors, Chauhans, are also known to have issued coins of silver and copper carrying motifs of bull and horseman which are also called Nandi and Rajput horseman coins. These coins were probably minted in Delhi and have been referred to as 'Dilliwala' or 'Dhillika' in the early medieval texts.[4] Inscriptions belonging to 13th and 14th centuries have been found in and around Delhi at Palam, Sonepat and Naraina indicating that the control of the region – also known as 'Yoginipura' and 'Dhilli' – passed from Tomars to Chauhans to 'Shakas' or 'Turushka'. Both 'Shakas' or 'Turushka' are terms used for the subsequent rule of Delhi sultans.[5]

RAJPUTS, TURKISH CONQUEST AND THE FOUNDATION OF THE DELHI SULTANATE

While the Tomars were consolidating their hold over Delhi, the Chauhans or Chahamanas were extending their control in Ajmer and surrounding areas. During the 12th century CE, the Chauhan king Vigraharaja IV, who is known as Visala Deva in the bardic accounts, defeated the Tomars and captured Dhillika.[6] Inscriptions on the Delhi–Topra pillar, currently located within the Firuz Shah Kotla complex in Delhi, discuss his reign and his conquest of the region lying between the mountain ranges of the Himalayas and the Vindhyas. Vigraharaja's nephew Prithviraja III, also referred to as 'Rai Pithora', is the most famous of the Chauhan Rajputs.[7] He remains the hero of many legends and bardic accounts including the hagiographic epic *Prithviraja Raso*, which also mentions the *dhilli killi* story. The epic narrates stories of the numerous battles of the Chauhan kings, including his victory over Muhammad of Ghur in the First Battle of Tarain (1191) as well as his romantic liaisons with Samyogita – daughter of his rival, Jaichand, the king of Kannauj.

Rai Pithora conquered many small states in Rajasthan and defeated the Chandela Rajputs of Bundelkhand. Subsequently repulsed by Bhima II, the ruler of Gujarat, Rai Pithora turned his attention towards Punjab and the Gangetic valley and started challenging the Ghurid possessions in the region. A war between him and the Turks, represented by Muhammad Ghuri, soon became inevitable. We will pick up the story from here in a while, but in order to understand the emergence of the Delhi Sultanate in the 1200s, it is important to discuss the background of the Turks.

The Turks were original inhabitants of Central Asia and Western China, more specifically the region around the Altai Mountains. They had migrated to the Transoxiana, the region between rivers Amu Darya (Oxus) and Syr Darya (Jaxartes), in 11th century CE. These Turks were recruited by the Iranian rulers of the region and the Baghdad-based Abbasid Caliphate (750 to 1258 CE) as mercenaries, slaves and palace guards, and gradually converted to Islam. Towards the end of the ninth century CE, the Abbasid

Caliphate started disintegrating and the Islamized Turks started emerging as main contenders of power. As the centralized rule weakened, provincial governors started becoming independent. They accepted the nominal suzerainty of the Caliph in return for his letter of approval. Soon, these new rulers started assuming ambitious titles like 'Amir' or later 'Sultan'.

The situation emerging in the Islamic heartland was a particularly complicated one marked by tension and strife between Muslim sects, Islamicized Turks and non-Muslim Turks, Muslims and non-Muslims, and between the infant Muslim states. The Samanids (Iranian by descent) came to power in these circumstances, towards the end of ninth century CE. They ruled over Transoxiana, Khurasan and parts of Iran. However, they had to continuously deal with the Turkish incursions from Central Asia. The Samanids were replaced by the Ghaznavid kingdom founded by a Turkish slave,[8] Alaptgin. Based in Ghazni, it became the new defender of the Islamic lands against the continued Turkish incursions from Central Asia. Its most famous ruler, Mahmud of Ghazni (998–1030 CE), was a great champion of the Iranian spirit and Persian language and culture. Under Mahmud of Ghazni, the Turks were not only becoming Islamized but also Persianized and it was this culture that they brought to India, two centuries later.

For two hundred years, before Qutbuddin Aibek established the Delhi Sultanate, military and political engagements went on in the region between the Turks and other kingdoms. Mahmud of Ghazni first conquered Punjab and Multan and his subsequent raids involved plundering of temples and cities in India. He conducted raids of Nagarkot in Punjab Hills, Thanesar (near Delhi), Kannauj and Mathura in 1018 and Somnath in 1025. Historians differ on the motives behind Mahmud's campaigns and raids in India. Some say he wanted to spread Islam. Others argue that his plunders were aimed at financing his campaigns in Central Asia which alternated with his raids on India. Still others are of the opinion that he wanted to establish a permanent outpost in Punjab. However, most agree on one point – Mahmud did not have any serious long-term territorial interest in India. But his campaigns did have some long-term implications. The Ghaznavid conquest of Punjab and Multan had clearly shown that the mountain chains in the north-west were not unsurmountable. It also exposed the fault lines in the political situation in north India. The Punjab-Multan region was to later serve as a springboard for Muhammad Ghuri's campaigns in north India and the Gangetic heartland.

In 1173, Shahabuddin Muhammad, also known as Muizuddin Muhammad bin Sam or Muhammad Ghuri, ascended the throne in Ghazni while his brother was ruling in Ghur. In 1178, he tried to capture Gujarat by marching across the Rajputana desert but was repulsed by the Gujarat ruler, Bhima II. Ghuri now turned his attention towards Ghaznavid possessions in Punjab and conquered Peshawar (1179–80) and Lahore (1186). By 1190, he was looking at Delhi and the Gangetic doab while Prithviraja, moving from the Ajmer region, was trying to extend control in the Ghurid Punjab and the doab region.

Muhammad Ghuri and Prithviraja Chauhan first clashed over Tarbarhinda (Bhatinda) in what is known as the First Battle of Tarain (1191). Ghuri lost the battle and was pushed back further into Punjab. He however regrouped his forces and defeated Prithviraja in the Second Battle of Tarain (1192). The Turkish cavalry, strengthened by the introduction of iron stirrups and a new type of harness, played a decisive role in the confrontations between the Turks and north Indian rulers. Fast-moving armed men shooting arrows from superior-bred Arabian horses had brought with themselves a new type of warfare, in which Rajputs were found severely wanting. Soon Delhi, Ajmer and parts of eastern Rajasthan came under Turkish control.

The conquest of Delhi by Muhammad Ghuri, based in the central Afghan region of Ghur (hence described as Ghuri), marked the establishment of the Delhi Sultanate. After the Second Battle of Tarain, Ghuri returned to Ghazni leaving the affairs of India in the hands of his trusted slave and commander-in-chief, Qutbuddin Aibek. Between 1192 and 1206, when Ghuri died, Aibek expanded the Turkish conquests to include the Ganga–Yamuna doab, Bundelkhand and parts of central India, Gujarat, Bihar and Bengal. Meanwhile Ghuri, who had been pursuing his Central Asian dream, lost to the Khwarizm empire in a battle in 1203. With this ended the Central Asian prospects of the Ghurid empire. The next few decades saw the development of a Turkish state based exclusively in India.

TURKISH CONQUEST STRENGTHENS TRADE AND BRINGS SUFISM

The Turkish campaigns were not only about political conquests but they also strengthened India's commercial and cultural relations with countries in Central and West Asia. Delhi was to emerge as a centre for trade, commerce and religious exchange as well as become a political capital under Aibek and his successors. India's interactions with Islam and Muslims did not begin with the advent of the Turks. Arab Muslim merchants had played an important part in India's commerce with West Asia, Southeast Asia and China between the 8th and 10th centuries. They traded in Indian fabrics, incenses and spices. The Pratihara rulers of western and north India traded in Arabian horses despite their hostile relations with the Arab rulers of Sindh. The Arabs had become so important for overseas trade that the Rashtrakuta rulers of the Deccan encouraged Muslim traders to settle in their domains and build mosques. Likewise, an Arab settlement had come up in Malabar. Indian traders and merchants had also been visiting Iran and Iraq.

Islam did not have a pronounced political impact initially. In fact, one notices a lot of cultural inter-borrowing. The Arab conquest of Sindh at the beginning of eighth century CE did not lead to any major political or cultural changes. Rather, some works on astronomy and mathematics got translated into Arabic including Aryabhata's treatise *Suryasiddhanta*. Likewise, Indian physicians, philosophers, mathematicians and master craftsmen had also been visiting the Abbasid court which majorly patronized science and learning. Islam established itself in Punjab and Sindh between the 9th and 10th centuries. Changes within the ideological realm of Islam in Central and West Asia – such as the emergence of orthodox schools of the *Quran* and *Hadith* (collection of traditions or sayings of Prophet Muhammad), four schools of Islamic Law and Sufi mystic orders – progressively started impacting India. The Sufis preached love, faith and dedication for one God to the Muslim settlers in India. Their ideas however also influenced the Hindus. Gradually, the Sufis came to organize themselves into twelve orders or *silsilahs*, each led by a *pir* (teacher) based at a *khanqah* (hospice) and followed by *murids* (followers). The *silsilahs* broadly came to be divided in two categories – *Ba-shara* (those following the Islamic law) and *Be-shara* (mostly wandering saints not bound by Islamic law). Of the *Ba-shara* movements, two *silsilahs* became very popular in north India, with Delhi and Ajmer as their prominent centres, during the 13th and 14th centuries – the Chishtis and the Suhrawardis. Irrespective of their *silsilahs* and dispositions, the Sufis helped create a climate of opinion in which people belonging to different sects and religions could live in peace and harmony.

The Chishti order was established by Khwaja Muinuddin Chishti (d. 1235) who came to India around the Second Battle of Tarain (1192). After staying for some time in Lahore and Delhi, he finally settled in Ajmer, which had a sizeable Muslim population, and became very popular. His disciples included Bakhtiyar Kaki who preached mostly in Delhi and was based near Qutb complex and Farid-ud-Din Ganj-i-Shakar who was based in Hansi and Ajodhan in modern Haryana and Punjab respectively. The most famous of the Chishti saints were Shaikh Nizamuddin Auliya and Nasiruddin Chiragh-i-Delhi, both based in Delhi. The Chishtis became popular for musical recitations called *sama* which created a mood of nearness to God.

Why were Sufis considered so important? Why did they play such an important role in the development of buildings and cities? These saints claimed to possess esoteric knowledge which placed them in a special relationship with God. They could therefore act as intercessors on the Day of Judgement. The Sufi saints' grace or *barakat* also had protective and curative properties, and they were believed to possess miraculous powers. The disciples of the Sufi saints were considered protected by God, thanks to their masters' special mystical powers.[9] Many Sufi masters emerged as protectors of cities they inhabited. Nizamuddin Auliya's presence was believed to have protected Delhi against numerous calamities such as the raids of the Mongols. Because of their exalted position in the kingdom of God, the Sufi saints were believed to have an extended spiritual realm. Monuments in and around the Qutb Minar complex, the first UNESCO World Heritage Site described in this book, intersected closely with the spiritual realm of Bakhtiyar Kaki. Many people wanted their bodies to be buried in the vicinity of the Sufi saints. Therefore, the area surrounding the *dargah* of Nizamuddin Auliya (Fig. 6) has perhaps one of the largest concentrations of graves and tombs in all of the Islamic world, and includes the Humayun's tomb complex which forms the second chapter and heritage site explored in the book. One of the finest medieval capital cities, Fatehpur Sikri, the fourth chapter and UNESCO World Heritage Site examined in this book, was in fact built as a tribute to the divine presence of Shaikh Salim Chishti.

The Turkish conquest of north India brought changes in spheres of language and literature as well. While Arabic – regarded as the language of early Islam – continued to be used in a narrow circle of Islamic scholars and philosophers, Persian was fast emerging as the language of literature, administration and diplomacy. It also became the language of the upper classes and their dependents in north India and, after the expansion of Sultanate in the south and the establishment of Muslim kingdoms in the Deccan, the language became prominent in peninsular India. Lahore became a centre of Arabic and later Persian languages and literature. The Persian writings of Amir Khusrau (b. 1252), a *murid* or disciple of Nizamuddin Auliya, and a courtier of several Delhi sultans, are still very well known. He is also credited with creating a new style of Persian called *sabk-i-hindi* ('style of India').

Other areas where the interactions between Central Asian and Indian cultural elements produced highly interesting results are art and architecture. After the initial tensions, the Central Asian art and architectural traditions – brought in by the Turks and enriched by the arrival of the Afghans and Mughals – closely borrowed from the indigenous elements and expertise to produce some of the finest monuments of the time and reach its pinnacle in the iconic Taj Mahal. In fact, all the six chapters about UNESCO World Heritage Sites systematically discuss the developments in what came to be known as Indo-Islamic style of architecture. However, Sohail Hashmi, a conservation activist known for his immersive heritage walks, argues that the usage of the term Indo-Islamic is seriously problematic. In conversations over emails and phone, he suggests the usage of terms like Indo-Turk, Indo-Afghan, Indo-Iranian instead, just like Franco-Roman, Franco-Anglican or Anglo-French. He says it is ahistorical to categorize any architectural style as 'Hindu' or 'Islamic' – there is Hoysala architecture, Chera architecture, Vijayanagara architecture, Jodhpur architecture, Dogra architecture and so on. Then there is Morrocan architecture, Libyan architecture, Ethopian architecture, Abyssinian architecture, Turkish architecture, Uzbek architecture, Iraqi architecture, Iranian architecture, or Afghan architecture. According to Hashmi, it would be simplistic to describe any of the former architectural styles as 'Hindu' or any of the latter as 'Muslim' or 'Islamic'. He explains further that European architecture is referred to by various terms including Roman, Classical, Gothic, Renaissance, Baroque, Spanish, Portuguese, Prussian, Slavic, English, Scottish, Irish or Welsh. It is understood as either a part of a cultural movement or is defined as period/region specific – but never described as 'Christian' architecture. The architecture of the East, on the other hand, is seen mostly in denominational terms. Hashmi argues this is the foundation of the communalization in the history of the region.

Coming back to our discussion, how did the joining of art and architectural styles of the Turks, which represented only a part of the complex and diverse political and cultural world of Islam and Muslims, and Rajputs, which represented a part of the large, diverse indigenous tradition popularly referred to as Hindu, pan out in the Indian context? How did the elements of tension and cultural borrowing manifest in the physical constructions at Lal Kot/Rai Pithora, which became the site of the first Turkish settlement in north India?

LAL KOT TO THE QUTB COMPLEX

Aibek was primarily occupied with territorial expansion and consolidation and ruled largely from Lahore. He, and later his successor, Iltutmish, also had to plan a settlement in north India where the Turks could reside, worship and trade. For this, the site of Lal Kot – stretching from modern-day Lado Sarai to Mehrauli in Delhi – located on the rocky spurs of the Aravalli range, was chosen.

Delhi's first Red Fort, Lal Kot, built by Tomar ruler Anangpal II around 1052 CE is believed to have been further enlarged[10] and fortified by Prithviraj Chauhan and renamed Qila Rai Pithora.[11] The settlement had a circuit of fortifications much of which is difficult to trace now. Walls found to be 5–6 metres thick and 18 metres high at places were interrupted by several gates, only a few of which survive. The Rajput citadel probably had ten gates though some later sources mention thirteen. These gates included those named Badaun, Ranjit, Sohan, Barka, Hauz Rani and Fateh. After the defeat of Prithviraj Chauhan (1192), the Turks occupied Lal Kot or Qila Rai Pithora. They are said to have entered the citadel through the Ranjit gate – near the Fateh Burj or Adham Khan's tomb – which was soon renamed Ghazni gate.

Once in Delhi, the Turks needed a mosque. As per Islamic traditions, a new ruler's name had to be read aloud in the Friday prayers to legitimize his authority. The first mosque of a new area was usually quickly built using the previously used material in part, the spolia.[12] The Turks chose a Rajput citadel containing Hindu and Jain temples as the site for Delhi's first Friday mosque.

Fig. 1 Ruins of the walls of the fortified Rajput citadel Lal Kot which was later taken over by the Turks. Seen in the background is Qutb Minar.

Fig. 2 Remains of the fortification of Alauddin Khalji's new settlement/city Siri.

Fig. 3 Ruins of buildings in the Tughlaqabad Fort.

Fig. 4 Ruins of Muhammad bin Tughlaq's city Jahanpanah, now known as Bijay Mandal.

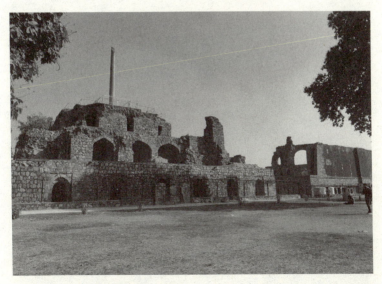

Fig. 5 Remains of a pavilion containing the Ashokan Pillar and a mosque at Firuz Shah Kotla, which once formed a part of Firuz Shah Tughlaq's new settlement Firuzabad.

Fig. 6 The shrine of Nizamuddin Auliya which is surrounded by one of the largest concentrations of graves and tombs in the Islamic world. Photo courtesy Reyan Sinha.

Fig. 7 Lodi-era mosque and gateway at Lodi Gardens, Delhi.

Fig. 8 Qila-i-Kuhna Masjid at Purana Qila in Delhi. Purana Qila formed the site of Humayun's city Dinpanah and Sher Shah's settlement.

Fig. 9 Akbar's multi-storeyed palace pavilion and tomb in Sikandara.

Fig. 10 Ram Bagh, which was built/rebuilt by Nur Jahan as Nur Afshan garden, forms the earliest surviving Mughal riverfront garden in Agra.

Fig. 11 The two-storeyed marble-facing Itmad-ud Daulah's tomb is known for its exquisite pietra dura work and is called the 'Mini Taj'.

Fig. 11 View of Itmad-ud Daulah's tomb from across the Yamuna.

Fig. 12 Chini ka Rauza or the 'Chinese Tomb', named after the mosaic of glazed tiles supposedly brought from China, was dedicated to one of Shah Jahan's senior nobles.

Fig. 12a Interior of Chini ka Rauza.

Fig. 13 Excavated remains of Mahtab Bagh which lies opposite the Taj Mahal on the left bank of Yamuna River.

Fig. 14 *Agra Fort and Yamuna River, as seen from the Taj Mahal.*

Fig. 15 *John Hessing's tomb known as the Red Taj Mahal, Padri Tola, Agra.*

Fig. 16 The principal street of Mughal city Shahjahanbad, leading to Chandni Chowk.

Fig. 17 Central Vista of the 20th-century British imperial city New Delhi.

The temple complex at Lal Kot was destroyed and its spolia was used to build a congregational mosque (Masjid-i Jami or Jami Masjid, now known as Quwwat al-Islam mosque) laying the foundations of what later came to be known as the Qutb complex. A similar mosque, popularly known as *Arhai din ka Jhompra* ('Two-and-a halfday Mosque'), was constructed in Ajmer. The act of destruction of Hindu temples and using their architectural material to build mosques makes such sites hugely contested and controversial in academia and the public domain. They are popularly seen as sites of Hindu–Muslim conflicts and narratives around them are often given a communal colour.

Historians have cautioned us against seeing such acts strictly within frameworks like the 'clash of cultures' or 'clash of religions' in general, or 'Hindu–Muslim conflicts' in particular. They point out that the practice of building new sacred structures in existing sacred places was common across cultures. For instance, the Christians built a Gothic cathedral in the middle of a mosque in Cordoba, Spain.[13] Equally common was the reuse of the old architectural material for newer constructions in the premodern Islamic world. Instances of such reuse of stone, especially where they formed the principal medium of construction, could be seen not only in north India but also in parts of Anatolia, Egypt and Syria. The Great Mosque of Damascus (705–15 CE), for instance, used material from the city's former Christian cathedral to build the mosque.[14] Some scholars say such acts need to be seen within the fragmented political and religious world of India's Middle Ages – when there was considerable disunity and contestation within the groups defined as 'Hindus' and 'Muslims'.[15] We have already discussed the tension and strife between Muslim sects, Islamicized Turks and non-Muslim Turks and among the infant Muslim states in Central Asia between the 9th and 11th centuries. Likewise, there was disunity among the Hindu Rajputs in north India which partly accounted for their defeat at the hands of the Turks. There were regional variations in indigenous 'Hindu' architectural traditions as well. Research from central and peninsular India shows how some Hindu rulers also looted temples of rival Hindu kings, took away their idols as war trophies and publicly displayed them as statements of conquest. Some historians underscore how instances of temple desecration were common in inter-dynastic conflicts among Hindu kings in the early medieval period. Several Hindu dynasties were involved in cases of temple desecration including the Pallavas, Chalukyas, Pandyas, Rashtakutas, Pratiharas, Cholas and Paramaras and Candellas. Hindu kings also engaged in the destruction of temples of their political adversaries.[16]

Delhi's first Friday mosque, Masjid-i Jami soon got an ornately carved stone screen inscribed with Islamic verses. This screen would undergo extensions under the later sultans. A free-standing minar, the Qutb Minar – variously described as a victory tower, a watch tower or a minaret to the Friday mosque – was also constructed. Iltutmish soon built his own tomb near the mosque. But where did the rulers reside? There is little textual evidence about palaces or residential/administrative headquarters around Qutb Delhi. Archaeological excavations at Lal Kot, carried out during 1957–61, revealed evidence of two distinct phases – stonework, identified with the Rajputs and brickwork, attributed to the Turkish sultans. Excavations conducted during 1992–95 further revealed the remains of a palace covered with white plaster, which some scholars have identified as Iltutmish's 'White Palace' (*Qasr-e-Safed*). It was located in the Qutb complex near the mosque, on its north-west side, closer to the Anangtal reservoir.[17]

With the death of Aibek, the Ghurid territory fragmented into four dominions – Ghazni ruled by Yalduz, Sindh under

Qubacha, Delhi governed by Iltumish and Lakhnauti controlled by Khalji sultans. Iltutmish had to overpower the rival claimants and centres of authority. Scholars argue that it is this spat between the rival warlords that made Delhi the imperial capital in the 13th century.[18] It was only after all his principal adversaries were eliminated that the Abbasid Caliph in Baghdad recognized Iltutmish as a sultan, a title Aibek unfortunately could not acquire.

ILTUMISH'S DELHI BECOMES A 'SANCTUARY OF ISLAM' FOR MIGRANTS FROM CENTRAL ASIA

After coming to the throne, Aibek's slave and son-in-law, Iltutmish (r. 1210–36), consolidated Delhi Sultanate's hold over Lahore, Multan and Uchch; Bihar and Bengal; and Gwalior and Bayana. The establishment of Iltumish's military control over north India coincided with significant sociopolitical changes in eastern Iran and Afghanistan. Campaigns of Mongol leader Chengiz Khan or Genghis Khan (1162–1227), in these areas, caused large scale destruction and dislocation of people in the 1220s. By mid-1220s, the Mongols had also made their presence felt in the Indus region and the Sindh. Muslims displaced from central Islamic lands started migrating to eastern Punjab, Gangetic plains and the urban centres of north India. Unlike in the past, these migrants were not Turkish slaves but free *amirs* (military commanders) and learned men like the *ulama* (specialists in religious sciences) and the *ahl-i qalam* or the 'people of the pen'.[19] Faced with the Mongol invasions, the hitherto disparate and nucleated Muslim communities saw in the paramount Delhi Sultanate, *Qubbat al-Islam*, a dome or sanctuary for Islam. Iltumish was quick to extend support and patronage to them. Soon, the sacred capital, *Hazrat-i Dehli* emerged as a sanctuary, a guide and a cohering force for the heterogenous Muslim communities. It had now become the unrivalled centre of the Sultanate.[20] The new sultan's exalted monarchical status was further reinforced by his constructions. New mosques and mausoleums were built and the existing ones – such as the congregational mosque at the Qutb complex in Delhi and *Arhai din ka Jhompra* at Ajmer – were enlarged or transformed. Iltutmish also added three storeys to the capital's iconic symbol of new religiopolitical dispensation, Qutb Minar and built his own mausoleum within the complex. To take care of the problems of water availability in Delhi, he constructed a large rectangular tank called *Hauz-i-Sultani* or *Hauz-i Shamsi* – now known as *Shamsi Talab* – around 3 kilometres to the south of the Qutb complex.

BALBAN'S SULTANATE GETS A NEW HINTERLAND; QUTB DELHI, A NEW SUBURB

The thirty years from 1236 to 1266, following Iltutmish's death, were marked by a succession of weaker sultans – Ruknuddin Firuz Shah (r. 1236); Raziya Sultan (r. 1236–40); Muizuddin Bahram Shah (r. 1240–42); Alauddin Masud Shah (r. 1242–46); and Nasiruddin Mahamud (r. 1246–66) – the first four of them were deposed in less than a decade. This was a period when the sultans reigned but did not rule. This thirty-year period of strife and conflicts was characterized by the decline in the sultan's power, emergence of new alliances and power dynamics and erosion in the geographical reach of the Sultanate.[21] The Mongols had also begun to threaten the eastern frontier along the river Beas. It was in these circumstances that an erstwhile slave of Iltutmish, Ulugh Khan, better known as Ghiyasuddin Balban, took over the reins of the Sultanate.

On becoming the sultan, Balban (r. 1266–87) strengthened the monarchy, and reorganized law and order, justice, army and the espionage system. He suppressed rebellions around Punjab–Sindh in the west and Lakhnauti in the east and repulsed the Mongol attacks. He also systematically decimated the power of the powerful nobles. Delhi once again became the 'Axis of Islam'. Barani, a contemporary chronicler, wrote that the scales of power were however turning in favour of the hitherto 'lowest and basest of the low and baseborn', the Afghans. To counter the frequent raids by the Meos of Mewat, Balban ordered military campaigns against them and got the area around Delhi cleared of forests. Subsequently, he implemented an extended version of this model in the Ganga–Yamuna doab – the forests were cleared; forest dwellers and pastoralists were decimated along with their habitations; and the area was resettled with Afghans, who were given rent-free lands. Henceforth, the doab region played an important role in the agrarian and commercial economy of the Sultanate and gradually developed as its agricultural hinterland.[22]

In this process, while the Sultanate got a new agricultural hinterland, around the Turkish capital grew a new suburb. To solve the issues related to the supply of water, Balban developed a suburb called Ghayaspur at a place where the river Yamuna was closest to the old city, near the Nizamuddin Dargah region of Delhi today. The river turned towards the east from this point. The Delhi around the Qutb complex of today, was now becoming the older part of the city. However, the area continued to remain important for the sultans. Balban's tomb – supposedly the first building in north India to have a true arch – is located in the area at the Mehrauli Archaeological Park.

Balban's grandson and successor Muizzuddin Kaiqubad (r. 1287–90) started building a *qasr* (walled palace) between this settlement and the Yamuna. Scholars say either the site was called Kilokhari or the settlement was located on a village of that name.

The subsequent Khalji rebellion in 1290 not only ended the rule of Balban's incompetent successors but also Turkish monopoly of higher offices in the Sultanate. The Khaljis were non-Turks, of Afghan origins, who had come to India during the time of Ghurid incursions. Some of them had got opportunities for political advancement in Bengal but they had mostly been employed as soldiers by the Delhi sultans to contain the Mongol invasions. The first Khalji ruler, Jalaluddin Khaji (r. 1290–96) tried to develop a new settlement around the 'Kilokhari Palace'. Jalaluddin Khalji was killed by his nephew Alauddin Khalji who became one of the most prominent rulers of Delhi and his reign was marked by crucial new reforms and the expansion of the Sultanate.

SIRI, ALAUDDIN KHALJI'S NEW CITY COMES UP, BUT QUTB DELHI REMAINS IMPORTANT

A locality now dotted by malls, an artisan village, bustling traffic and some nice eateries – can you imagine the modern posh area around the Siri Fort and Shahpur Jat village as the new fortified settlement built by Alauddin Khalji (r. 1296–1316)? Discovered in the late 19th century as a vast area enclosed by mounds, it was Alexander Cunningham, a British archaeologist, who identified this area with Siri, the city/settlement built by Alauddin, often mentioned in the texts of that time. It is said that the city/settlement was built at a site where the sultan had defeated the Mongols. No major structures/buildings have been unearthed from Siri. According to Sohail Hashmi, it could have been more of a garrison town – the sultan wanted to keep his soldiers at one place so that they could be mobilized quickly in case of a Mongol attack.

Alauddin Khalji's reign was a period of ambitious imperial expansion. The Sultanate's control was extended to eastern

Rajasthan, Malwa and Gujarat. For the first time, the Delhi army also penetrated south India as far as Madurai, sacked cities and brought back enormous wealth and numerous elephants. Extension of geographical frontiers were complemented by the consolidation of internal controls including market and price regulations and establishment of direct land revenue relations with the peasantry. The hitherto urban Sultanate acquired a large agrarian base in his time and reached the interiors of north Indian countryside. Alauddin also dealt strongly with the Mongol incursions which had kept shrinking the Sultanate's line of defence towards Delhi from Kabul–Qandhar to Lahore–Multan to the river Beas. He was the first sultan who built a series of fortifications to the north-west of the capital and also fortified Lal Kot by extending its original walls in order to prepare better defences against the Mongols.

Alauddin defeated the Mongols around 1303. It is said that he massacred the inhabitants of the Mongol colony which had come up in Delhi and displayed their heads on the pikes of a tower located outside the city. Others say, he buried their heads in the walls of his new city. The walled enclosures of Siri, around two miles north of the old city of the Qutb complex area, contained the sultan's fabled palace called the 'Hall of a Thousand Pillars' nothing of which remains now. One can only see the ruins of the walls (Fig. 2). Alauddin's attention, however, remained on the Qutb Delhi. Like Iltutmish, he too wanted to stamp his political successes at the site which had become known as the new 'Axis of Islam'. He decided to substantially enlarge the Qutb mosque. Only trivial remains of Alauddin's extensions of the western screen are still visible as also his project, the incomplete Alai Minar, which was originally intended to be double the size of Qutb Minar. The only surviving structure of sultan Alauddin's extension of the

Qutb mosque is the magnificent gateway on the south known as the Alai Darwaza, the 'Exalted Gateway'. The old city around Qutb, which had been more of a fortified Turkish camp, had now grown in population and emerged as a swarming commercial centre. Historian Percival Spear says 'merchants jostled with soldiers in the streets and artists and poets appeared in the court. It was the age of Hazrat Amir Khasrau [Amir Khusrau] the poet and of saint Nizam-ad-din [Nizamuddin Aulia].'[23]

TUGHLAQABAD, GHIYASUDDIN'S CITY AND THE CURSE OF NIZAMUDDIN AULIYA

It seems that the increase in population of Delhi and Siri also led Ghiyasuddin Tughlaq (r. 1320–25), the soldier-founder of a new dynasty, to find another settlement called Tughlaqabad. One can see the ruins of some buildings in the Tughlaqabad Fort (Fig. 3). The new settlement lay around 8 kilometres east of Qutb Minar or Old Delhi, on the southern end of the ridge between modern Badarpur and Faridabad. By blocking the passage of the river Yamuna, a huge artificial lake was created. Across the lake, his successor Muhammad bin Tughlaq constructed the fort of Adilabad linked to Tughlaqabad with a causeway.

It is said that the new city never became fully populated and was abandoned within fifteen years of its construction. Legend attributes this to the curse of the Sufi saint Nizamuddin Auliya. Ghiyasuddin is said to have hindered the construction of a tank – the *baoli* nowadays seen in the Nizamuddin Dargah complex – being built by the Sufi saint. The latter therefore cursed him saying that the new city would be inhabited by none other than the Gujjars, a pastoral community, and jackals. Ghiyasuddin wanted to settle scores with the saint but could not. On his way back to Delhi from Bengal, he was crushed beneath a pavilion erected to welcome him at Afghanpur. Both Muhammad bin Tughlaq, Ghiyasuddin's son who had gone to welcome him, and the saint were suspected of having conspired to kill the sultan.

JAHANPANAH, MUHAMMAD BIN TUGHLAQ'S CITY, AND THE COMING TOGETHER OF SIRI AND QUTB DELHI

Muhammad bin Tughlaq's reign (1325–51) saw the expansion of the Delhi Sultanate in the peninsular India, into Warrangal, Mabar and Kampili, the last Hindu principality in the south. The Deccan however brought with itself a lot of problems as the kingdoms in the region were always restive and the kings and nobles were continuously trying to assume independence. To take care of such disturbances and the threat of a possible Mongol invasion of Delhi, Muhammad bin Tughlaq, in 1327, decided to create a co-capital in Devagiri or the 'Hill of Gods', some 1,500 kilometres away from Delhi in the Deccan and renamed it Daulatabad which means 'City of Prosperity'. The sultan ordered a tenth of Delhi's population to migrate to the south and settle in the Sultanate's new co-capital. A road was built to connect the two cities and rest houses and shaded trees were established along the way. However, many died along the way and many remained deeply resentful for having been uprooted. The sultan also realized that just as it was difficult to rule the south from the north, it was difficult to do the opposite. He therefore shifted his base back to Delhi again in 1334.

Discussions about Muhammad bin Tughlaq's co-capital project and his equally controversial decision to issue token currency, instead of those in actual silver, often overshadow his establishment of a new city within Delhi. Moving away from the cursed Tughlaqabad, the ambitious sultan decided to bring together two important power centres – 'Old Delhi' (Qutb Delhi) of the early sultans which had continued to grow and Alauddin's Siri. He built a large fortification enclosing the entire area between the two cities and called it Jahanpanah which means 'The Refuge of the World'. The walls of Jahanpanah had six gates leading out to the north-west, seven to the south, and three into Siri. Only some remains of the southern wall can be seen now. This enclosure contained a mosque and the royal palace, now known as the Bijay Mandal (Fig. 4). The city of Delhi now stretched from the Qutb to about three miles in the north, consisting of Lal Kot, Jahanpanah and Siri.

The Delhi Sultanate had reached its zenith under Muhammad Tughlaq, but it was proving really difficult to hold together territories incorporated over a century and a half. Cracks had begun to appear in the over-extended state. The last years of the sultan's reign were spent on quelling successive rebellions and he was constantly running from one place to another hardly being able to focus on the affairs of Delhi. Things were very difficult for the new sultan, Firuz Shah Tughlaq (r. 1351–88), a cousin of Muhammad bin Tughlaq, as he tried to reconcile the disintegration of the Sultanate with what had become a regal practice with all ambitious sultans – building of a new city/settlement. And this is how Firuzabad came into being.

A DISINTEGRATING SULTANATE FINDS A NEW SETTLEMENT IN FIRUZABAD NEAR YAMUNA

Not all people know that the heritage site near ITO (so called because of the Income Tax Office) in Delhi, Firuz Shah Kotla – popularly believed to be haunted by djinns – and the nearby stadium, known for some historic day-night cricket matches, once formed a part of Firuz Shah Tughlaq's new palace-fortress and settlement called Firuzabad (Fig. 5). The new sultan inherited a very troubled Sultanate. He tried to restore law and order in north India but let the Deccan and some other areas become independent of the Sultanate. He also undertook measures to placate the nobility, army and the theologians. The principle of heredity was introduced in the appointments to the nobility and army and territorial and revenue assignments or *iqta*. Practices considered un-Islamic were banned and he became known for more austere and conservative measures to hold the Sultanate together.

One area, however, is an exception as Firuz Shah Tughlaq appears to have been determined and passionate about water bodies, buildings and heritage. He built a huge water reservoir in Mahipalpur and also carried out extensive repairs to Suraj Kund and Hauz i Alai, a tank at Hauz Khas in Delhi named after the sultan Alauddin Khalji who commissioned it. Firuz Shah Tughlaq got the tank desilted after which it came to be known as the Royal Tank or Hauz Khas. The sultan was also the father of canal irrigation and brought water from Hansi to Hisar (a town built by him) in the dry channel of the Ghaghar. Sohail Hashmi points out that the sultan began to extend that canal to Delhi to bring water of the Yamuna to the region but could not complete the canal. Firuz Shah Tughlaq repaired the upper two storeys of Qutb Minar which had been damaged due to an earthquake in 1369 and built a stone cupola on the top. He also brought two Ashokan pillars, some 1,500 years old, to Delhi. The Meerut pillar was erected on the ridge near his hunting lodge (*Kushk-i Shikar*), close to the modern Hindu Rao Hospital and the Mutiny Memorial of 1857. The other one, brought from Ambala, was installed in the palace-fortress of a new settlement, Firuzabad – built on the banks of the river Yamuna. Consisting of around eighteen villages, the new settlement (also called new city by some) included the later city of Shahjahanabad, or what is known as Old Delhi now, up to the base of the Ridge, between modern Sabzi Mandi and the Civil Lines.[24] Described as the 'Windsor of Delhi' by Lane Poole, Firuzabad, was the 'New Delhi' of the 14th century.[25] The establishment of Firuzabad also set a new trend in the location of future settlements which were now to adjoin river Yamuna rather than the rocky Aravalli ridge – Sher Shah's Delhi, Salim Garh, Humayun's tomb, Shahjahanabad, and even New Delhi; all are situated within the river's alluvial zone.[26]

Firuzabad did not bring much luck to a disintegrating Sultanate. The final knock perhaps came in the form of the Mongol invasion led by Timur (1336–1405), in 1398. Keen to seize the wealth amassed by the sultans of Delhi over the last 200 years, Timur mercilessly plundered and sacked the towns on the way to Delhi. His depredations are often compared to locust attacks. Timur's invasion gave a death blow to the Sultanate though the last Tughlaq ruler continued to linger on till 1412.

LOOKING FOR NEW RESOURCE FRONTIERS, THE SULTANATE SHIFTS CAPITAL TO AGRA

The Tughlaqs gave way to a new dynasty called the Sayyids in Delhi. In the meantime, the Afghans had become an important political force. They were already in power in eastern India. During the process of the disintegration of the Sultanate, the Afghan chieftains had gained control of Punjab and Malwa and had also bagged important positions in the Bahmani kingdom in the Deccan. In the circumstances that emerged, Bahlol Lodi, the Afghan ruler of Punjab, was called to help the sultan of Delhi against an impending attack by Malwa. Once in Delhi, he decided to stay in the capital and soon displaced the Sayyids and crowned himself the sultan. Bahlol Lodi's reign (1451–89) was marked by frequent confrontations with the Sharqi rulers of Jaunpur, who had declared their independence from the Delhi Sultanate. To gain control over the latter, he invited the Afghans of Roh (region of Pashtunkhwa and Afghanistan) to come to India. This move not only helped him defeat the Sharqis but also changed the complexion of Muslim society in India – the Afghans became numerous and important in both south and north India. Regarded as primus inter pares or 'first among equals', by fellow Afghan nobles, Bahlol Lodi, in accordance with the Afghan tradition, divided his empire among sons and kinsmen at the time of his death. His successor, Sikander Lodi (r. 1489–1517), is regarded as the most important of the Lodi sultans. The new sultan was able to establish law and order, administer justice, make highways safe, take interest in development of agriculture and rent rolls and forbid practices considered un-Islamic.

After defeating the Sharqis of Jaunpur around 1494, Sikander Lodi constructed a Jami mosque at Bagh-i Jud. The Bagh is now known as the Lodi Gardens and the area surrounding the mosque is called Jor Bagh, after the name Bagh-i Jud (Fig. 7). The Lodi Gardens had served as a burial site during the Sayyids and contains the tomb of Muhammad Shah, but during the Lodi period, it probably became the royal necropolis. Two of the three famous Lodi sultans – Bahlol Lodi (as indicated in a paper by historian Simon Digby) and Sikander Lodi – are buried here. The construction of the complex as a dynastic burial site was symbolic of Sikandar Lodi's investment in revitalizing Delhi. His repairs of the two uppermost storeys of the Qutb Minar, struck by lightning, also reflects his intent to revive the city of the sultans.[27] Of course, he wanted to inscribe his name on the capital's 'tower of power'. Later, Sikander Lodi shifted the capital to Agra around 1505 and built a new city for himself. He also founded a new suburb to the north-west of Agra which is named after him, Sikandara. The suburb still contains ruins of some Lodi-era buildings especially an octagonal tomb besides Akbar's tomb built by Jahangir later.

THE MYSTERY BEHIND THE NAME OF AGRA

Despite its huge historical importance, the name 'Agra' does not find mention in any historical source, literary or archaeological, till around the 12th century CE. One however does come across archaeological finds which show that the region was inhabited much earlier. Perhaps it was known by a different name then. There are several theories behind the origin of the word 'Agra' including those connecting the city to Hindu mythology.

Mythological accounts trace the name to Ugrasena, the Yadava dynasty ruler of Mathura who was imprisoned by his tyrant son, Kamsa. Lord Krishna killed his maternal uncle, Kamsa, and restored his maternal grandfather, Ugrasena, to the throne. According to this account, the word Agra stems from 'Ugra' of Ugrasena. The story of Krishna and Kamsa forms one of the most dominant narratives in all popular recollections of the city of Mathura, located around 50 kilometres from Agra. Within this narrative, some even connect the name of Agra to Kamsa's infamous prison house which had numerous heavy bars called *argalas*. If one happens to engage a tourist guide in Mathura, they will most likely be shown a structure popularly known as 'Kamsa's prison house'. Others have attributed the name to Angira – the famous sage of the great epic Mahabharata.

One tradition ascribes Agra's name to a ruler called Agrasena, who is believed to have found the city and made it his capital. He is also regarded as the progenitor of the trading community known as the Agrawals. Some even trace the city's name to a region inhabited by the Agrawals. Still others associate Agra with the word *Agravana* – the advanced post of the Braja-mandala, identified as the

Mathura region, in the ancient times. While most ascriptions to the city's name are mythological, one theory associates the name with an anecdote connected with the life of sultan Sikandar Lodi. A 16th-century chronicler Nimat Ullah Harawi wrote that the sultan was so mesmerized by the beauty of the place that he kept asking his entourage to keep moving forward, *agae*, till he found the desired location for his capital, leading to the name Agra.

However, the first definitive literary reference to the word 'Agra' comes from a poem composed in 1134 by a Persian poet, Masud ibn Saad Salman. He was eulogizing the exploits of a king called Mahmud, the governor of Sindh under Muzaffar Sultan Ibrahim, the ruler of Ghazni. Mahmud Shah attacked the fort of Agra in 1080–81. The poet was accompanying the governor and described[28] the fort as:

> The fort of Agra is built amongst the sand like a hill and the battlements of it are like hillocks. No calamity had ever befallen its fortifications, nor had deceitful time dealt treacherously with it.[29]

Apparently, the poet also quotes Mahmud Shah at one place:

> I was in search of such a large virgin fortress as this which no king of chief has yet taken. Now that my heart has found this fort of Agra, I will bring destruction upon it with my swords and arrows.[30]

Historians say this fort was an earlier version of the modern Agra Fort. Its walls were probably made of baked bricks then and could withstand a regular seige by a disciplined and organized army like that of Mahmud Shah.[31] The fort known as Badalgarh seems to have arisen on the foundations of this old citadel.

Agra has not been specifically mentioned in the histories of the Sultanate. After the conquest of north India by Aibek and Iltutmish, Agra had probably come under Turkish control alongside neighbouring regions like Koil, Bayana and Gwalior. The tenuous control of the sultans of Delhi over the Ganga–Yamuna doab meant that the region kept changing hands. At various points of time, it likely came under the control of the local Rajput dynasties or other Hindu and Jat (an agricultural community) chieftains.[32]

WHY AND HOW AGRA BECAME THE NEW IMPERIAL CAPITAL

Sikander Lodi was probably looking for an alternate site which could provide greater security and stability to his dominions; ensure control over the potentates in the regions around the political centre; bring in more resources from the agricultural sector; and also minimize revenue leakages from commercial sector through better access to trade routes.[33] Delhi failed to provide these conditions to the Lodis adequately.

But why choose Agra over Delhi? Historians differ. Some say Agra could help control the Rajput states in eastern Rajasthan and also regulate trade routes to Malwa and Gujarat. Others say new towns and cities emerged in medieval India primarily because urbanization was one of the key agendas for the Muslim rulers. The answer, however, seems to be more layered. Agra enjoyed several locational advantages, economic and political. The Ganga–Yamuna doab and alluvial soil expanse around Agra was better suited to agriculture than the arid rocky terrain of Delhi. The central location of the doab could also help sustain the dominions of the Sultanate. Finally, the doab region had been one of the most important links in the trade between the eastern and western parts of the subcontinent since ancient times.[34] The advantage that a Delhi-centred power could derive from agricultural production and trade was limited and dependent upon control exercised by the political authority over its ruling class and the immediate hinterland. The Sultanate's control over the Ganga–Yamuna doab had remained very fragile and there were serious problems with collection of land revenue or annual tributes. It worked relatively well with stronger sultans but not so much when weaker rulers occupied the Delhi throne. The moment this authority was compromised, as it happened at regular intervals, Delhi was reduced to a mere regional power. Between 1192 and 1526, Delhi had seven ruling 'dynasties' with more than twenty-five persons assuming the title of sultan and ascending to the throne. In the period between the 13th and mid-16th centuries, incompetent rulers far exceeded both in numbers and duration of their rule. After Firuz Shah Tughlaq, the political authority of the Sultanate had been severely eroded, and a new category of powerful landholders had emerged who started withholding revenue remittances.[35]

Agra was chosen at such a point in time to re-establish centralized political control in the Ganga-Yamuna doab and in the newly acquired territories. The control of regions in the doab like Chandwar, Rapri, Hatkant, Kol, Kalpi, Etawah and Bayana had the added advantage of securing a more regular flow of revenue for the Lodis. The developments in Malwa offered opportunities for uncomplicated reach to the Gujarat coast.[36] Agra also provided a strategic gateway into Rajasthan, Gwalior, Malwa and other regions. It offered a superior connectivity in both controlling wider territories and regulating additional revenue from trade and commercial activities so far untapped from Delhi.[37]

With the shifting of capital to Agra, Delhi was no longer the seat of the Sultanate. It had once again slipped into the ranks of a provincial city, politically. In symbolic terms, however, it continued to remain important. The Lodi-era tombs and mosques can be seen in various parts of Delhi in places such as Green Park, Lodi Gardens, South Extension I & II, Defence Colony and Mehrauli. The 15th century forms an interlude to two important imperial epochs of Delhi: it was an appendix to the Delhi Sultanate and a new preface to the Mughal empire.[38]

THE MUGHALS ARRIVE IN DELHI-AGRA REGION

Towards the later part of Lodi rule, Babur (1485–1530), who later founded the Mughal empire, had begun to knock the Delhi-Agra region. He claimed imperial ancestry from the Mongol 'world conquerer' Changez Khan (1162–1227) and the Turkish 'world conqueror' Timur (1336–1405), also called Timur Lane. The term 'Mughal' is now synonymous with grandeur in almost all forms in the cultural arena but historian Harbans Mukhia cautions, such descriptions would have horrified the dynasty's early rulers in India. He says that the Persian language term, pronounced 'Mughul' in Iran and 'Mughal' in India, came to acquire a generic meaning and broadly signified people of the Central Asian regions, speaking the Mongol languages and dialects. It also referred to other ethnically and linguistically distinctive groups from Central Asia such as the Turkis, Uzbegs, Uighurs, Kirghizes, Kazaks, Kipchaks, Keraits and Naimans – often with as many mixed lineages, shared culture and faiths.[39] In Babur's home in Uzbekistan, the dynasty called themselves Chaghtais – the ones who descended from Chaghta, the son of Changez Khan. In most histories of the dynasty in India right upto the 18th century, they have been described as Chaghtais or Timurids, after Timur. Mukhia agrees with the 18th-century historian Khafi Khan when the latter says: '[I]n reality the word is truly valid only for the tribe of

Turks who had descended from Mughal Khan ... through Chingiz [Changez]Khan, Hulaku, Chaghta and Amir Timur.' The European travellers however were not as familiar with the intricacies of the term and knew and wrote about the dynasty as Mughals, spelt variously as 'Mogoll', 'the Great Mogull', or 'Mughals'. This is how the term gained popular usage.[40]

Why and how did Babur make his journey towards the south and into the Indian subcontinent? By the time Zahir-ud-Din Babur, a fourteen-year-old, ascended the throne of Ferghana valley – the land between the two rivers, Syr Darya and Amu Darya, also called Transoxiana by the Europeans – the complexion of the once-powerful Timurid empire had changed. In addition to successor Timurid principalities fighting amongst themselves, there were other powers in the fray. After capturing Kabul, Badakshan and Qandahar, Babur had been looking towards Hindustan, which mostly meant north India then, to mobilize more resources to maintain his army and kinsmen. During 1505 to 1526, he made five attempts to raid Hindustan and had made deep incursions especially in Punjab.

With the death of Sikandar Lodi in 1517, Ibrahim Lodi had become the sultan. His attempt to create a large, centralized empire met with huge resistance from fiercely freedom-loving fellow Afghans as also from the Rajputs, who had become organized by the 15th and 16th centuries through common descent lines. One of the Afghan chiefs, Daulat Khan Lodi, the governor of Punjab, had become practically independent. Around 1525, Babur received an embassy from Daulat Khan urging him to displace Ibrahim Lodi. Some say, he also received a similar invitation from Rana Sanga to invade Hindustan. The stage was set for the First Battle of Panipat in 1526. Babur's 12,000-strong army met Ibrahim's 100,000 men supported by 1,000 elephants. In the battle, Babur lashed together a large number of carts in the front to act as a defending wall. Between two carts, breastworks were erected on which soldiers could rest their guns and fire – a device used by Ottomans in their famous battle against Shah Ismail of Iran. Babur had also secured the services of two Ottoman master gunners – Ustad Ali and Mustafa. It was Babur's advent with these resources, which made gunpowder usage common in north India. His bowmen also played an important role in the battle. Ibrahim Lodi was killed in the battle and was interned in a tomb at Panipat.

BABUR LAYS THE FOUNDATION OF AGRA AS A RIVERFRONT GARDEN CITY

The First Battle of Panipat brought about some immediate tangible gains for the Mughals. It eliminated the Lodis as a political force in north India and opened the entire area up to Delhi and Agra. Babur asked his son Humayun to immediately take control of the treasures at the Agra fort while he himself camped at Delhi, at about 100 kilometres from the battlefield of Panipat. Once in Delhi, he visited the tombs of Sheikh Nizamuddin Auliya (d. 1324) and Sheikh Bakhtiyar Kaki of Fergana (d. 1236) and also explored the fortress, royal tombs, mosques and gardens of the Delhi sultans. He asked the mosques in Delhi to proclaim his name as the sovereign in the *khutbas*, the congregational noon prayer on Fridays. Soon after, he rushed to Agra. Meanwhile, Humayun was able to lay his hands on a large treasure which, some scholars say, also included the famous 'Koh-i-noor' or 'Mountain of Light' diamond apparently presented to him by the Raja of Gwalior. The latter's family had been confined in the Badalgarh fort, now more commonly known as Agra Fort, by Ibrahim Lodi. The Agra Fort is a UNESCO World Heritage Site and has been explored in a chapter in this book.

Babur reached Agra in May 1526 and soon made it his capital. He is said to have distributed the city's treasures among his people. During the next four years, Babur explored Hindustan. Its animals, plants, buildings and weights and measures find a mention in his autobiography, *Baburnama*.

Babur did not leave behind any grand monuments except mosques in Panipat and Sambhal. He, however, introduced the aesthetics of the Persian–Timurid gardens in Hindustan. His first garden was laid out in 1526 in Agra on a *chahar bagh/char bagh* pattern. *Chahar* in Persian means 'four' and *bagh*, 'garden', so this means a four-fold garden in English or *char bagh* in Urdu. This broadly formed a large architecturally planned, cross-axial four-part garden with raised paved *khiyabans* (walkways), platforms and pools. He got Afghan melons and grapes planted in this garden, situated almost opposite the Taj Mahal, which was to be built much later around the mid-17th century, on the east bank of the Yamuna.[41] Apparently, he also encouraged his companions to lay similar gardens in the whole region. The new emperor assembled his court and commanders in such garden complexes. Babur wrote in his autobiography:

> The people of Hind [local inhabitants] who had never seen grounds planned so symmetrically and thus laid out, called the side of the Jun [River Yamuna] where [our] residences were, Kabul.

From this time onwards, the left bank (in the direction of the flow) of river Yamuna started emerging as a favourite destination for Mughal gardens. This also introduced a new type of urban planning in Hindustan – creation of the riverfront garden as a module of the riverfront city and a *char bagh* with main buildings on a terrace overlooking the river.[42]

DINPANAH, HUMAYUN'S CITY, COMES UP IN DELHI, BUT RUNS INTO PROBLEMS

Before his death, Babur decided to divide his kingdom amongst his sons in accordance with the Mongol–Timurid practice of collective sovereignty. Humayun was to receive Hindustan and the status of *padshah* while Kamran would continue to retain Kabul. Territorial provisions were also made for younger sons, Hindal and Askari. Babur died in 1530 in Agra after directing that his body be returned to Kabul for burial. He remains interned at Bagh-i-Babur in Kabul. Upon his death, Humayun was coronated in the Agra Fort at the age of twenty-two. He constructed a mosque in the village of Kachpura on the left bank of Yamuna in 1530. The structure has recently been restored. However, the emperor had reserved his grand plans for Delhi where he laid the foundations of a new city called Dinpanah ('Refuge of the Faithful') on the banks of the river Yamuna, very close to the Sufi saint Nizamuddin Auliya's *dargah*. Remains of this city could be found in what is now known as the Purana Qila or 'Old Fort' complex (Fig. 8). His city project and reign, however, were constantly interrupted by several rebellions and the rise of the Afghan chieftain Sher Khan in the Bihar–Bengal region and Bahadur Shah in the Malwa–Gujarat area.

After defeating Humayun successively at Chausa (1539) and Kannauj (1540), Sher Khan took control of the Delhi–Agra region under the title of Sher Shah. He founded the Sur dynasty, took Humayun's city project further and built some structures in the Purana Qila area of Delhi. The Agra Fort also came under the control of the Surs. Humayun had to live in exile for around fourteen years in Lahore, Sindh and other areas bordering the Mughal empire. Finally, with the Persian emperor Shah Tahmasp's military support, he regained the throne of Delhi in 1555, from Sher Shah's weak successors and is said to have completed his palace-fortress in Dinpanah. The emperor however did not live long to enjoy the fruits of his victory. In 1556, he fell to his death from the steps of his library, Sher Mandal, in Purana Qila.

AKBAR PREFERS AGRA AS HIS IMPERIAL SEAT, CONSOLIDATES THE EMPIRE

Akbar (r. 1556–1605) was born to Humayun and Hamida Banu Begum while they were in exile. At the time of Humayun's death, Akbar was at Kalanaur in Punjab fighting against the rebel Afghans. In the political uncertainties that followed, the thirteen-year-old emperor had to fight a series of battles to re-conquer the Mughal empire, including a major one against the Afghans. Hemu Vikramaditya, the general and military commander of Adil Shah Suri – Sher Shah's nephew and the last emperor of the Sur dynasty – had rallied Indo-Afghan and Rajput forces and captured Agra and Delhi. Panipat was once again set to decide Delhi's fate. In the Second Battle of Panipat (1556), Akbar's tutor and regent, Bairam Khan, defeated the combined forces led by Hemu to re-establish Mughal control over Delhi and Agra. He became the *wakil* or head of administration and emperor's key advisor, with the title of *Khan-i Khanan*. Some scholars say that the Mughals decamped their court from Delhi to Agra to put pressure on the Afghans, who had moved further down the Gangetic valley into Bihar and Bengal.[43] Broadly and chronologically speaking, Akbar ruled from four imperial seats which acted as capitals during his long rule – Agra (1556–71); Fatehpur Sikri (1571–85); Lahore (1585–98); and Agra again (1601–05). During 1598–1601, he was in the field fighting wars in the Deccan.[44] Apart from re-building the Agra Fort, Akbar established a new capital at Fatehpur Sikri. Both these are UNESCO World Heritage Sites and are explored in two separate chapters in this book.

In his formative years at Agra, the young emperor had to deal with two powerful people and their contending factions within the imperial household – Bairam Khan, his regent, and Adham Khan, the son of his wet nurse and foster-mother, Maham Anga. Bairam Khan had played an influential role during the initial expansion of the empire but had become very arrogant. After subduing him, Akbar married his widow and brought up his son, later known as Abdur Rahim Khan-i Khanan, as his own. The latter's tomb lies close to Humayun's tomb in Delhi. It has recently been restored and opened to the public. In the case of Adham Khan – who had laid claim to the office of the *wazir* (chief minister) and even killed the minister who was in charge – Akbar had him thrown from the parapet of Agra Fort (1561). A grieving Maham Anga died soon afterwards. Akbar had substantial tombs built for her and Adham Khan in Delhi in the Afghan architectural style.

After securing himself from rebellions within the imperial household, Akbar started taking direct control of the empire. Agra had not experienced much development or distinct political patronage since Humayun left for exile around 1540. So, Akbar was to focus on Agra as the capital city in the coming times. But he did not ignore his father's projects in Delhi. Asserting control over Humayun's legacy, the emperor commissioned the construction of a magnificent mausoleum (c. 1562–71) near Dinpanah, the city his father had founded in Delhi. Architecturally, this monument evoked the dynasty's contemporary culture – primarily Islamic Timurid traditions with additional Iranian elements.[45] Known as Humayun's tomb now, this famous architectural complex has been recognized as a UNESCO World Heritage Site and has been explored in a chapter in this book.

Almost simultaneously, Akbar also started rebuilding the Badalgarh Fort in Agra. His architectural style combined central Asian and regional Indian building traditions and was dominantly expressed in red sandstone – which gave a somewhat unifying element – and highlighted with white marble. The old mud-and-brick fort at Agra gave way to a massive red sandstone fort, complex semicircular in shape and with huge bastions. No construction was allowed between the river Yamuna and the fort – a rule which was also followed in the case of Red Fort in Delhi under later Mughal emperor Shah Jahan. Built to serve as official headquarters and residence of the emperor Akbar, Agra Fort and its buildings served the purpose of business as well as comfort and pleasure.

The development of Agra as a riverfront city also resumed alongside and the city grew in its size, wealth and power. Akbar's court historian Abul Fazl tells us: 'abodes were distributed to the grandees' and that 'on either side [of the river] the servants of fortune's threshold [i.e. the court] erected pleasant houses and made charming gardens.'[46] While the left bank was mostly reserved for the imperial structures, the emperor earmarked land on the right bank of Yamuna for residential purposes of the nobility. Soon *havelis* (mansions) started coming up and the area started emerging as the prime location for the political elite. Not much details are available about *havelis* built during Akbar's time. Some contemporary sources however indicate that the *havelis* of important nobles like Khan Alam, Raja Todar Mal, Birbal and Raja Jai Singh were built on the right bank. The building and *katra* (walled enclosure) of Itibar Khan, *Khwaja-sara*, was located in the Hajjam Mandi (Barber's Market) area on the right bank.[47]

Exclusivity of the right bank of the river was maintained. The ruler re-assumed the land and allocated it to some other once a noble had ceased to be in active service of the state. The areas lying further west to the *havelis* was inhabited by other sections of people. For purposes of protection, a wall encircling the city from three sides was constructed. The fourth side was occupied by the Yamuna. Entry into and exit from the city were regulated through several gates and *khidkis* (small gates).[48] The city continued to expand and soon some residential localities started emerging even beyond its boundary wall. The 'Jaipur Map of Agra', the first map of Agra drawn for the Maharaja of Jaipur in 1720s, shows an extensive network of roads that had developed corresponding to the expansion of the city. The north-western part of the city, in particular, appears strewn on the map with a heavy network of roads, suggesting a concentration of population in this part. Residential markings and localities, by and large called *basti*, could be noticed in all parts of the city.[49] A large number of houses in Noori Darwaza, Gokulpura, Nai ki Mandi, Shahdara and the area near Mandi Saeed Khan appear to be more than one-storey high and probably belonged to the economically well-off sections.

Delhi had remained more of a politico-administrative centre for 300 years. However, Agra went beyond that – it developed into a commercial hub producing merchandise for intra-regional trade in north India, that too in less than a century. This became possible, through innovative administrative reforms in the years between 1561–1579/80, which established the supremacy of the ruler and administrative uniformity besides creating a homogenous nobility and an honourable space for local potentates to cooperate with the Mughals rather than confront them. These reforms were singular achievements of Akbar.[50]

After a comprehensive survey of the revenue potential of the empire, Akbar placed all high officials of the empire under a hierarchical order that denoted the size of their contingents and war animals to be maintained by them. This arrangement also organized the military and administration across the empire from his seat of power in Agra and during the subsequent shifts of capital. The magnificent buildings at the imperial seats of power further symbolized this order. Once their ranking in the official order or *mansab* was determined, their emoluments were announced in accordance with the schedule of pay. Finally, a *jagir* – a land assignment of equivalent value was allocated to the officials. To ensure that they did not develop local roots, the *jagirdars* could be transferred from one *jagir* to another within three years' time.[51] The mansabdari–jagirdari system became the basis of incorporation of many local potentates and Rajput and other Hindu chieftains. The Rajput nobles were allowed to retain their territory and given a new *watan jagir*, whose revenue was equal to their salary entitlement according to their rank in the official hierarchy. Akbar entered into matrimonial alliances with Rajputs which facilitated their accommodation in the *mansab* system.

Building upon Sher Shah's administrative reforms, Akbar altered the Delhi Sultanate's old *iqta* system of territorial and revenue assignment to divide the empire into units like *subas*, *sarkars* and *parganas*; parts of this new system and its terms, with modifications during the British raj and in independent India, exist even now. The Mughal empire was divided into twelve *subas* (provinces), which mostly followed natural barriers. Agra formed one of largest of these *subas* and included Agra city and adjoining territories such as Gwalior, Kalpi, Kannauj, Koil, Narnaul and Alwar. Each *suba* was further divided into *sarkars*, varying in sizes and revenue estimates. Finally, the lowest division was called *pargana*.

Using Agra as his imperial seat (1556–71), Akbar launched several military campaigns enabling him to take control of Jodhpur, Chittor, Ranthambor, Kalinjar, Bikaner and Jaisalmer from various Rajput dynasties. He also pushed Mughal control southwards into Gondwana and Khandesh as well as Kangra in the northern Himalayan foothills. His officials also tried to restore Mughal sovereignty over eastern India – Jaunpur, Bihar, Bengal and Orissa – which had agriculturally rich lands; urban centres of artisanal manufacturing; and a strong overseas trade making the Portuguese, Arakanese and other maritime powers very interested in the Bay of Bengal. The influence of all these regions and their traditions travelled back to the Mughal imperial centre in the form of, among many other things, adaptation of the architectural styles which are an integral part of the UNESCO World Heritage Sites of Agra, Fatehpur Sikri and Delhi, explored in various chapters in this book.

While in Agra, Akbar also started patronizing the fine arts, painters, astrologers, calendar makers, calligraphers, chronogram-creators and jewellers. In his personal religious beliefs, he initially patronized the orthodox Sunni traditions. However, he was also exploring a spiritual relationship with the Sufis, living and dead. He gradually started shifting his allegiance from a more orthodox Sunni Naqshbandi order, favoured by his ancestors, to India-based orders, particularly the Chishtis who followed a more incorporative vision of Islam and refrained from overt political engagement. From 1566 onwards, and for the next fourteen years, he started making annual visits to the shrine of Khwaja Muinuddin Chishti in Ajmer which was around 360 kilometres from Agra. In 1570, he made this pilgrimage on foot. His devotion to the Chishti order, particularly Shaikh Salim Chishti, was largely responsible for the shifting of his capital from

Agra to Sikri in 1571. Sikri was located 45 kilometres away and formed a day's marching distance from Agra at that time.

A SUFI SAINT INFLUENCES THE CHOICE OF A NEW CAPITAL, FATEHPUR SIKRI

The shift of the Mughal capital to Fatehpur Sikri seems on the surface to be a sudden decision. However, investigation into the context tells us that there was more than one reason for the building of the new capital. Mughal association with Sikri had begun during the time of Babur. During the Battle of Khanwa (1527) against Rana Sangram Singh of Mewar, Babur had stationed himself on the banks of the lake in Sikri. He is said to have renamed the village as Shukri, indicating 'A Place of Thanksgiving', in recognition of the support he received from the inhabitants during the battle. Babur also started the construction of a garden at Sikri and named it Bagh-i Fath or 'The Garden of Victory'. Some historians say it was probably the name of this garden which later inspired his grandson Akbar to rename the area as Fathpur or Fathabad.[52] Sikri had played an important role in the development of Agra as well. When Akbar ordered the rebuilding of the fort in Agra, the construction material came from the quarries of Sikri. Contemporary sources inform us that around 1,000 cart loads of *sang-i surkh* or red sandstone were brought from Sikri every day. The quarrymen employed by Akbar are said to have constructed a small mosque near the *khanqah* (hospice) of Shaikh Salim Chishti, now known as the Masjid-i Sangtarash or the 'Stone-cutter's mosque'. This mosque is especially noted for its serpentine struts or brackets supporting *chajjas* or stone projections from the top of the building to protect it from the sun and rains – an architectural device also employed in later Mughal buildings.

Shaikh Salim Chishti's influence is known to have played an important role in the building of the new capital in Sikri. Akbar's first meeting with Shaikh Salim Chishti took place in 1568. Akbar wanted a son and requested the saint to pray for him. Later, the emperor was so overwhelmed with the saint's grace that he sent the pregnant Rajput queen Mariam Zamani to Sikri, where she was initially lodged in the Chishti quarters. Akbar ordered the construction a 'lofty palace', identified as Rang Mahal now, for the queen. The next year, a son was born to Akbar and named Salim, who later became known as Jahangir, in honour of the saint. A grateful father now decided to lavish on Sikri the resources of a vast empire.

When Sikri was being built, the emperor erected for his revered saint a white marble mausoleum in the courtyard of the congregational mosque. But Sikri meant a little more than just the presence of the Sufi saint, Salim Chishti. It represented the 'growing need of the emerging empire to have a new capital, a town planned around a visionary, appropriate to the new vision of an empire'.[53]

Sikri as a city was different from Agra; the latter was known for its impregnable palace-fort and a strong political and military establishment. Agra had strong gates and security arrangements in place and many political campaigns were launched from here – it was more about political domination. Sikri was the next stage in the evolution of the empire as it tried to strike deeper socio-cultural roots with focus on integration. The monuments at Sikri also exemplify how the emperor was trying to integrate a population with very diverse socio-religious inclinations, address conflicts within the conservative Islamic clergy and also enhance the spiritual position of the emperor. Scholars say Akbar was exceptionally innovative in designing and building his new court and administrative city – it was an embodiment of his own changing policies and widening religious beliefs. So while some structures within the imperial complex – such as Diwan-i Aam or 'Hall of Public Audience', Diwan-i Khas or 'Hall of Distinguished/Private Audience', harem, *hammam* (bath), *karkhana* (manufacturing centre under state supervision) etc – served the same purpose as their Agra Fort counterparts, others like Ibadat Khana ('House of Worship') served a different purpose.[54]

Sikri bears testimony to Akbar's incorporation of Rajputs in the nobility and marriage alliances with them; his adoption of Hindu and regional architecture; his distancing from the orthodox Sunni traditions and *ulema*; his dabbling with other religious heads including Muslims, Hindus, Jains, Christians, and Zoroastrians in the Ibadat Khana; his veering towards Christianity under the influence of visiting Portuguese Jesuits; his proclamation of the famous *mahzarnama* (1579) which made the emperor the ultimate authority in all matters involving interpretations of the *Quran* and *Hadith*; and the development of a new court culture centring around the 'universal sovereign' – where the service to the emperor paved the way for highest virtue and spiritual-religious merit.[55] The new capital also saw Akbar promulgating the policy of *sulh-i kul*, variously interpreted as 'universal peace', or 'tolerance for all'.

The incorporation of Rajputs manifested prominently in the aesthetics of Fatehpur Sikri: adoption of their ideas of rulership seen in the institution of *jharokha* – a balcony from where the emperor presented himself seated to both the public and private audiences; presence of many Rajput women in the imperial household; and permission to Hindu chieftains to access innermost parts of Akbar's palace, a privilege even denied to the Muslim courtiers.[56]

But Sikri was also about some big conquests for the empire. In 1572–73, Akbar led an expedition to Gujarat. Like its eastern counterpart Bengal, Gujarat was a region of agricultural wealth, hand-made manufacturing and flourishing overseas trade. The Arabian Sea had served as a base for the Portuguese, Ottoman and Indian ships. Upon return, Akbar built the famous Buland Darwaza or 'the Lofty gate' in the congregational mosque complex to commemorate his victory over Gujarat. Sikri now also came to be known as Fatehpur Sikri or the 'City of Victory'.

In 1585, Akbar suddenly left Fatehpur Sikri for Lahore, never to come back to the city again. When he returned, he based himself in Agra. The immediate motive behind this move was the death of his brother Mirza Hakim (d. 1585) who had somehow been able to control the Uzbeg and Safavid invasions. Akbar's positioning at Lahore enabled him to secure the strategic Punjab area and the surrounding regions including Kabul, Lower Sindh, Kashmir and Qandahar and also facilitate commerce. The years 1598–1601 saw Akbar embroiled in warfare in the Deccan primarily against Ahmadnagar and Khandesh. When he returned to Agra again in 1601, he was faced with his son Salim's revolt which threw the empire into instability and factional fights for almost five years. Thanks to the peace brokered by the ladies of the harem, Salim and Akbar reconciled before the latter's death in October 1605.

CAPITAL SHIFTS BACK TO AGRA, JAHANGIR DEVELOPS THE RIVERFRONT CITY

While Akbar was busy supervising the military operations in Deccan, upon the death of his son Murad (1599), his elder son Salim marched to Agra to take control of the city but failed. He then moved 500 kilometres down the river Yamuna to Allahabad, which Akbar had heavily fortified, and established his own court and sovereignty as the emperor-in-waiting. Salim proclaimed himself *padshah*, minted coins bearing that title, and ordered *khutba* to be recited in his name. He also constructed a throne platform inscribed with pretentious verses. This black throne now lies on the riverfront terrace, next to the Diwan-i Khas, in the Agra Fort. Following Akbar's death, Salim ascended the throne at the Agra Fort with the name Jahangir which alludes to him as the 'World Seizer'. On accession, he reportedly ordered a 'chain of justice' to be strung from his throne room to outside of the fort and the promise of the new emperor was that whoever rang the bell would get justice. The new emperor tried his best to confront political challenges of the day. While Bengal remained problematic during much of his reign (1605–27), he was able to establish control over Mewar. Jahangir also sent armies northwards in Kangra, Kashmir and Ladakh. However, Deccan continued to be a thorn in the flesh and the emerging Maratha and Telugu leaders were proving difficult to co-opt in the mansabdari system. Jahangir however fared well vis-à-vis development of fine arts and gardens.

A great connoisseur of paintings himself, Jahangir's court soon developed a painting tradition which became distinguished for naturalism and portraits. He was also a collector of paintings and illustrated manuscripts. Unlike his predecessors, however, Jahangir did not engage prominently in city building or monumental architecture. The emperor did complete and restore or expand the forts and palaces, but he mostly preferred patronizing pleasure gardens and pavilions, hunting lodges, bridges, caravanserais and tombs. Sikandara, known for Akbar's multi-storeyed tomb, was Jahangir's first building enterprise after he became the emperor (Fig. 9). A suburb of Agra founded by sultan Sikandar Lodi, Sikandara was renamed Bihishtabad ('Paradise Town') to honour its new status as the burial place of the great emperor Akbar.[57] In fact, one of the inscriptions in the complex states that the tomb was conceived to be happier than the paradise. Akbar's tomb stands in the centre of a classical *char bagh* whose two principal walkways terminate in one real and three blind gates. It has an imposing gateway with an enormous recessed arch flanked on either side by double-storey arches. The gateway has four towering white marble minarets, one at each corner. Sikandara blends Persian and Indian traditions. It marks a shift from the Timurid-inspired tomb types as it combines the features of the contemporary multi-storeyed palace pavilion and tomb (Fig. 9).[58]

Jahangir was very active in laying gardens in Lahore and Srinagar (including the famous Shalimar Bagh) but it was during his period that the riverfront scheme was fully developed in Agra.[59] Pelsaert, the Dutch trader who visited Agra around 1626, found the city to have streets, houses, bazaars and shops. He records that the gates Akbar had built for security now stood in the middle of the city and the area of the city outside the gates was three times greater in extent.[60] Pelsaert observed: 'the luxuriance of the groves all round makes it resemble a royal park rather than a city.' [61] He lists thirty-three gardens with their names of which a third were created or remodelled during Jahangir's times. Art historian Ebba Koch points out that the earliest surviving Mughal riverfront garden in Agra belongs to Jahangir's time. Currently known as Ram Bagh, it was built/ rebuilt by the emperor's wife Nur Jahan as Nur Afshan garden in 1621 (Fig. 10). Instead of a single solid terrace extending along the entire riverfront – as seen in the Shahjahani gardens – Ram Bagh has terraced parts which contain subterranean rooms and support main pavilions.[62] Among the other gardens of the time, Bagh Dehra, located on the southern point of the city, was usually a halting place before entering the city or used as a camp during hunting in the Rupbas area (now in Bharatpur district). Bagh Parvez, Bagh Wazir Khan and presumably Buland Bagh were also constructed on the left bank of the Yamuna. Of these, Bagh Wazir Khan and Buland Bagh are in a partly preserved state while Ram Bagh attracts quite a few tourists.

The city continued to grow during Jahangir's reign. However, many *havelis* built by the earlier nobles on the right bank of the river do not seem to have survived around the time Pelsaert visited Agra in 1620s. Either, they had possibly changed hands after the death of owners or they were demolished for new constructions. Buildings erected by earlier political elites, were also neglected even by their close relatives after their death.[63] It needs to be pointed out that Mughal nobles, particularly the Muslim ones, had very limited private rights in land and could not bequeath it to their heirs. After the death of the original assignee, any palace or garden would be integrated into the imperial estate. The emperor in turn would keep the building for himself or assign it to someone else. Palaces and gardens therefore went through a *silsila* or chain of owners who could fashion the properties according to their tastes and resources. The tomb was exempted from this regulation and one therefore reads of many powerful Muslim nobles building tomb gardens. The Hindu Rajputs who were assimilated into the administrative system as nobles were better off here; they could usually keep their ancestral lands and build palaces on them.[64] Such regulations regarding private property did not prevent the construction of new *havelis* or gardens.

Ain-i-Akbari, written by Akbar's courtier and historian Abul Fazl, points out that, for five *kos* (one *kos* equals 3.2 kilometres), the river Yamuna flowed along magnificent *havelis* and lush gardens on both sides. Various travellers indicate that the great mansions with magnificent gardens, located along the river, occupied a large part of the city and the contrast between them and the dusty streets and bazaars outside the fort was extreme. And, the city was still growing. Jahangir writes in his memoirs: 'The habitable part of the city extends to both sides of the river. On its west side, which has the greater population, its circumference is seven kos and its breadth is one kos. The circumference of the inhabited part on the other side of the water, the side towards east is 2 ½ kos.'[65] John Jourdain, an employee of English East India Company who visited Agra in early 17th century, and Pelsaert, writing during Jahangir's times, also give similar estimates. According to Jourdain: 'The cittie [city] is 12 cosses [koses] longe [long] the riverside, which is above 16 miles; and at narrowest place it is three miles broade [broad].'[66] Pelsaert records: 'The breadth of the city is by no means so great as the length, because everyone has tried to be close to the river bank, and consequently the water front is occupied by the costly palaces of all the famous lords, which make it appear very gay and magnificent, and extend for the distance of 6 kos or 3 ½ Holland miles.'[67] Abul Fazl's estimate of the expanse of the city comes closer to those given by Jahangir and Pelsaert, which is approximately 61.44 sq. kilometres.[68]

IMPERIAL AGRA DEVELOPS AS THE 17TH-CENTURY COMMERCIAL HUB

The reign of Jahangir and Shah Jahan saw the rise of Portuguese, English and the Dutch East India Company and intercontinental trade. European traders brought in huge quantities of silver and gold from Americas and purchased India-made textiles and other products. Crops from Americas including tobacco, maize, chilli peppers and tomato were also introduced in India during the 17th century. Many Indian traders engaging in such trade lived in and around Agra. By early 17th century, Agra had also become a central commercial market for traders from the subcontinent and outside for procuring goods manufactured in the subcontinent.[69] Many Agra merchants had agents stationed at business centres in the subcontinent for arranging goods and services. Accounts by contemporary European visitors tend to highlight things produced or processed locally or in the neighbouring areas such as indigo dye, textiles (mostly plain dyed and printed), sugar and saltpetre.[70] However, what goes relatively unnoticed is that Agra had become a very important trading point for several other products including building construction material; gold and silver work especially embroidery, laces (kinari), wire making, foil manufacturing and filigree ornaments; woven textiles including velvet, brocade, striped cloth, crafted textiles and Bengal silk; quicksilver and furnishings like carpet; and spices, food grains and ghee (clarified butter).[71] Pelsaert writes (c. 1626):

> All goods must pass this way, as from Gujarat, Tatta; from Kabul, Kandahar, or Multan, to Deccan; from the Deccan or Burhanpur to those places, or to Lahore; from Bengal and the whole East country; there were no practicable alternative routes and the roads carry indescribable quantities of merchandise, especially cotton goods.[72]

A flourishing trade required the constant presence of rich merchants, middlemen and agents, financiers, money changers, insurers, transporters and armed guards. It also necessitated the presence of an extensive network of sarais (rest houses). The state, imperial household, officials and other individuals played an important role in the construction of sarais inside the city as well as along the major trade routes like Agra–Allahabad; Agra–Ajmer;

and Agra–Burhanpur.[73] The residences of the trading class and other sections of the society also developed in a manner similar to the nobility – from north to south, mainly on the right bank. However, these were beyond the houses of the nobility and at a distance from the river. There were different categories of businesspeople living in the city. These included those engaging in banking, finance and moneylending; those who transacted in heavy merchandise from one part of the subcontinent to another and beyond. Many such businesspeople had more wealth than the nobility. French traveller Bernier, who visited Agra in the 1660s, wrote that the in the midst of the *havelis* of the nobility, 'the lofty houses of the Banyanes [Baniyas] or Gentile merchants have the appearance of old castles buried in forests.'[74] Likewise, some travel accounts indicate that the Khatri (a Hindu caste of traders, mostly from Punjab, who dominated trade in north India and Lahore in the 17th century) merchants of Agra were so rich that heaps of coins in their shops looked like heaps of grain. Further, the glitter of jewels illumined the entire market place and there was a huge desire for bullions in the jewellers market.[75] William Hawkins, a representative of English East India Company who visited Agra in 1609 to seek the emperor's consent for the establishment of a factory, mentioned a jeweller named Hira Chand who purchased a diamond worth Rs 100,000 then and presented it to emperor Jahangir. Some locally available commodities such as the Bayana indigo had a tremendous value in the local and international markets and many Asian merchants and European trading companies competed for a larger share of its trade. Some powerful local merchants controlled the production and supply of indigo and saltpetre by forming cartels and dictating prices.[76]

The part of the city which predominantly developed as the residential area of the local business communities was called

Maithan (*mai ka than/sthan*: 'abode of Goddess'). The primary occupants of this locality included Khatris and Brahmin *sarrafs* (money changers) and financiers. With changes in fortunes and diversion of business activities, many such families shifted elsewhere after selling their properties to other trading communities like the Jains. Beautifully carved stone or masonry gateways and dilapidated structures still remind people of the architecture of the 17th and 18th centuries. Maithan also developed as a site for Hindu temples mostly belonging to Shiva and family. This included one credited to Raja Todar Mal, the renowned finance advisor of Akbar as well as those of Batuknath and Gauri Shankar. Temples associated with Shiva/Shaivite cult gradually came up in other localities in the city including Kailash Mahadev (on Delhi-Agra Road), Balkeshwar, Prithvi Nath, Rawali Mahadev and Mankameshwar. Some such temples could also be found in Nai ki Mandi, Loha-gali, and Shahganj in Agra.[77]

Trade also brought Europeans and Christian habitations started coming up near what is now known as the Padritola, then located on the outskirts of the town in the north. Padritola continues to attract tourists on account of a cemetery which houses the 'Red Taj Mahal' (Fig. 15). This locality gradually started expanding and Peter Mundy, a British merchant, reported that even some Khatris started settling there. The European trading companies had either purchased or rented houses to provide accommodation to their employees. Englishmen Steel and Crowther, and later Peter Mundy, stayed in one such accommodation near Pulhattee (*phal-hattee* or fruit and vegetable market) in the central part of the city. No such information is available for Dutch merchants. It's important to remember that many Portuguese missionaries were settling in India during Jahangir's reign; the process had already begun under Akbar. And when the Portuguese naval vessels started capturing merchant and pilgrim ships, including those belonging to the Mughal imperial household, the emperor ordered the closure of Catholic churches in Lahore and Agra.[78]

AGRA BECOMES 'A WONDER OF THE AGE' AND A WORLD CITY UNDER SHAH JAHAN

The later part of Jahangir's reign in Agra marks the ascendancy of Itmad-ud Daulah's family. Originally known as Ghiyas Beg Tehrani, Itmad-ud Daulah was an Iranian immigrant from the Safavid court. He had joined Akbar's service, risen in the administrative ladder and had earned the title of Itmad-ud Daulah or 'Pillar of the State'. The marriage of his widowed daughter, Mehrunissa to Jahangir really opened his imperial fortunes. Within months of marriage, Mehrunissa was conferred the title 'Nur Mahal' or 'Light of the Palace' which soon got elevated to 'Nur Jahan' which means 'Light of the World'. Itmad-ud Daulah rose to become the governor of Punjab and then the *wazir* and *diwan*, two important posts as the head of revenue and finance of the Mughal empire. He became so close to the imperial household that even ladies of the harem were directed not to veil their faces in his presence. The rise of Itmad-ud Daulah and his family – including daughter Nur Jahan and son Asaf Khan along with their Iranian supporters – has led some to label Jahangir's reign as one of a rule by a 'junta'. Historians however clarify that it was only during Jahangir's later years – when his health started failing him – that such factions started coming to fore.

Jahangir finally died in 1627 after his last visit to Kashmir, where he visited every summer. Asaf Khan, one of the most influential Mughal nobles, ousted his own sister Nur Jahan, temporarily installed Dawar Baksh (Jahangir's other son) as the emperor and summoned Prince Khurram from Deccan. Khurram, also known by the title Shah Jahan or 'King of the World', conferred on him by Jahangir, reached Agra in 1628 and was installed on the throne by Asaf Khan who in turn became the chief minister. Shah Jahan's accession was marked by a bloody elimination of potential claimants – a phenomenon that was to become common in future Mughal successions. The thirty-six-year-old new emperor allowed Nur Jahan to retire quietly and the latter focused her attention on completing her father's tomb. Known for its exquisite pietra dura work – fine inlay representing geometrical patterns wine vessels, flowers and cypress and fruit trees – this first complete marble-facing Mughal tomb is also called the 'Mini Taj' (Fig. 11). The two-storeyed Itmad-ud Daulah's tomb, with its characteristic *char bagh* layout, *hasht bihistht* pavilion and mausoleum in the centre, became a template for all Mughal funerary gardens in a riverfront context in Agra till the building of the Taj Mahal (Fig. 11a).

By the time Shah Jahan came to the throne, Agra had already become a big city known for its 'artistic workmanship, literary talent and spiritual worth.' Scholar Abdul Aziz adds: '[It was] as much a centre of the arteries of trade both by land and water as a meeting-point of saints, sages, and scholars from all Asia.'[79] It had become 'a wonder of the age' and 'one of the biggest cities in the world'. Johann Albrecht von Mandelslo, a German traveller who visited Agra in 1638, said it was 'at least twice as big as Isaphan [a major city in Iran known for its Persian architecture].'[80] After becoming the emperor, Shah Jahan changed the name of Agra to Akbarabad, 'the city of Akbar', to honour his grandfather. His historians describe Agra as one of the great cities of the world, surpassing the old Baghdad of the Abbasid caliphs 'in size, beautiful buildings and cosmopolitan population'.

It was a haven for nobles, learned men, artisans and craftsmen.[81] Abu Talib Kalim, Shah Jahan's poet laureate, metaphorically said in his *Padshahnama*:

...

Don't call it Agra — it's a world of peace and safety
In each of its corners is a Cairo and a Damascus
...
Who sees Agra has seen the world.[82]
...

Shah Jahan built many new structures and rebuilt old ones in the city during the first phase of his rule before finally shifting his capital to Delhi in the 1630s. His building activity was the most pronounced and grandiose phase of the empire and has been discussed in the chapters on Agra Fort, Taj Mahal and Red Fort in this book. Here, in this section, we will follow the overall trends of these times to understand how the World Heritage Sites came into being. Shah Jahan began by destroying and renovating many existing buildings at the Agra Fort and constructing three new marble palace courtyards. His reign (1628–58) is known for its grandeur and the emperor's efforts at raising the status of imperial power and splendour in the eyes of the people. This is reflected in imperial projects and court rituals, including the gem-studded golden peacock throne, completed in seven years (1628–35) at the cost of 10 million rupees.[83] The emperor replaced the temporary canopy over assembled courtiers at Agra Fort with a more formal structure of pillared halls, first of wood and then of stone (Diwan-i Aam). His seat or *jharokha* — seen in the forts of Lahore, Agra and later in Shahjahanabad — was made into a raised vaulted loggia, spatially and symbolically separating the emperor from those assembled below. Even the portraits commissioned by the imperial atelier displayed the emperor with a halo. The court scenes, on the other hand, showed courtiers focussed on him seated on the peacock throne, and not interacting with each other. Shah Jahan was different from his predecessors in some other ways as well. He closely identified with the Central Asian Sunni ancestors and Timur, even taking the latter's bearded look. Unlike Babur and Jahangir, who wrote their own memoirs, he commissioned a series of historians to compile his massive official regnal chronicle, the *Padshahnama*.[84]

However, like his predecessors, Shah Jahan had to confront the political problems of the day. He led a military campaign to a restive Orchha; crushed the Portuguese and their Arakanese allies near Hugli in Bengal; and enforced the complete subordination of Ahmadnagar, Bijapur and Golkonda in the Deccan. It was during his Deccan campaign that his favourite wife, Arjumand Banu Begum, better known as Mumtaz Mahal (Itmad-ud-Daulah's granddaughter and Nur Jahan's niece), died in Burhanpur (1631) while giving birth to the couple's fourteenth child. She was first temporarily buried in Burhanpur. Later, the emperor sent her body to Agra where she was finally interned in the famous *Rauza-i-Munauwara* ('Illuminated Tomb') now known as Taj Mahal. Like the Agra Fort, the mausoleum was built on the banks of the river Yamuna (Fig. 14).

During Shah Jahan's period, '[g]ardens with buildings on a riverfront terrace became the more widely used residential form' in Agra.[85] The left bank of Yamuna, however, remained primarily occupied with imperial ones. Among the gardens, one could include Jahanara Bagh – laid by Mumtaz Mahal and gifted to her daughter Jahanara, Mahtab Bagh – on the other side of the Taj Mahal (Fig. 13), Bagh Kasim Khan, Bagh Ajmeri Khan, Bagh

Shah Nawaz Khan, Bagh Wazir Khan, and Bagh Musawi Khan Sadr. Also located on the left bank of Yamuna, very close to Itmad-ud-Daulah's tomb, is the 'Chini ka Rauza' or the 'Chinese Tomb' which was named after the mosaic of glazed tiles supposedly brought from China – a tomb garden dedicated to Allama Afzal Khan, a scholar from Shiraz who was one of Shah Jahan's senior nobles (Figs.12 and 12a). Of these, Jahanara Bagh is in a partly preserved state while Mahtab Bagh, Itmad-ud-Daulah's tomb and Chini ka Rauza figure prominently on tourists' itineraries.

Like the gardens, the city's profile also grew under Shah Jahan's reign. A second city wall, majorly in red sandstone and wider than the earlier one, came up along with large and small sized gates respectively, the darwazas and khidkis. It encircled the city from three sides except the Yamuna. Agra developed linearly along the right bank of the river.[86] French traveller Jean de Thevenot, who visited India in 1666–67, wrote: '...the Town is very long but narrow, and excepting some fair Streets that are in it, all the rest are very narrow and without Symmetry.'[87] The nobility's preference for the right bank continued during Shah Jahan's reign. Further inland were the houses of the bulk of the populace which, in contrast to those of the elites, were several storeys high. Among the buildings that still survive and have some connection with the reigns of Shah Jahan or his son and successor Aurangzeb, one could include the Mubarak Manzil, the tomb of Jafar Khan and the Chattri of Jashwant Singh. Of these, Mubarak Manzil was originally built in 16th century and was first occupied by Akbar's regent Bairam Khan. Subsequently, it changed many hands and was occupied by various Mughal princes including Khusrau, Shah Jahan and Aurangzeb before being renovated by the British in 1817. In its present form, the building is known as Tara Niwas. The Chattri of Maharaja Jaswant Singh, ruler of Jodhpur and a prominent noble of Shah Jahan, is located in the Rajwara area, a name used to describe a stretch containing residences of Rajput nobles. Unlike the *chattris* or small domed pavilions that adorned the roofs of Mughal monuments discussed in the individual chapters of this book, this *chattri* is built on the lines of the memorial structures the Rajput kings erected to honour their dead ancestors. There were many other *havelis* and buildings that once populated an otherwise dense settlement.

With settlements, people and constructions, came bazaars and markets, particularly during the Jahangir–Shah Jahan period, and they developed at different levels. It must be remembered that like the imperial palace-fort, the mansions of princes and nobles in Agra also housed workshops and markets and served as functioned as centres of production and exchange.[88]

There was a large horse market immediately outside the palace-fort where horses from Central Asia could be bought. Bazaars also lined up the sides of major thoroughfares which sold goods like cloth silk, gold, silver work, carpets, indigo etc.[89] French traveller Bernier points out that there were four or five streets running parallel to each other and perpendicular to the river; all terminating in a gate.[90] An interesting feature of some markets in Agra was that they were known after the product or merchandise sold therein. Most of these markets have survived under their original names but their character has changed over a period of time. Concentrated on the right bank of Yamuna, these included Sabun Katra (soap market), Loha Mandi (iron market), Nai ki Mandi/Hajjam Mandi (barber's market), Dal Mandi (pulses market), Heeng ki Mandi (asafoetida market), Neelpara/Chhipitola (indigo maket), Jauhari Bazar (jewellers' market) and Kinari Bazar (lace market).[91] Other market areas included Bazar Dariba, Nadi Bazar, Phal-hattee (fruit/vegetable market), Cheeni Tola (sugar market), Kashmiri Bazar, Gur ki Mandi (jaggery market), Shahdara in trans-Yamuna and Shahganj in the south-west of the fort as well as outside the wall.[92] River Yamuna below Agra was bustling with boats bringing food and goods of various kinds from the doab. The imperial custom houses were located in Sikandara which also had wholesale grain market alongside warehouses and homes of grain merchants.[93]

Tajganj was in fact conceptualized as one of the most important market centres of the city. To organize the market, the area in front of the Taj Mahal was suitably levelled and shops and living quarters were constructed for artisans and merchants. It consisted of six large courts – each surrounded with porticoes containing chambers for the use of merchants. Soon, the area saw the emergence of *sarais*, mandis and some additional dwelling units owned by some nobles and others. Four walled enclosures (*katras*) accessible only through their specific gates still exist here. They carry their original names – Katra Resham (locality of silk weavers), Katra Phulel (locality for perfume sellers), Katra Jogidas and Katra Umar Khan.[94] Enclosed markets/*katras* developed and named after individuals also came up in other parts of the town such as Katra Mir Mughis, Katra Agha Baqar, Katra Wazir Khan and several others.

By the end of 16th century, Agra had become a permanent abode for many. There was also a sizeable floating populace inhabiting the city throughout the year. Ralph Fitch, an English traveller who visited Agra in 1585, said that Agra was bigger than London both in geography and population. By the early decades of the 17th century, Agra had become the largest city of the Mughal empire – it could also match with any other city across continents. According to estimates given by various European travellers and writers, Agra's population was around 500,000 in 1609;

around 660,000 during 1629–43; and around 800,000 during 1659–66.[95] Some historians opine that these figures include large contingents of armed retainers stationed in Agra; unproductively employed people; and those belonging to the menial class.

Agra also became a great cultural centre. Even though the Mughals were proud of their Timurid/Central Asian–Iranian lineage, Agra saw a brilliant assimilation of Indian (sometimes European) elements and the development of what is popularly known as Indo-Islamic culture reflected in the artistic conventions and cultural and intellectual activities such as art and architecture; paintings and illustrated manuscripts; translations of literary works; musical arts and treatises; dance and performing communities; vibrant literary cultures (reinforced with the rise of Braj Bhasa and related poetry and musical compositions around neighbouring Brindavan); and Sufi and Bhakti saints. The cultural values and artistic traditions nurtured in Agra during the 16th and 17th centuries persisted and got transmitted to the Mughal capital Shahjahanabad and other successor states which emerged in the 18th century.[96]

MUGHAL CAPITAL COMES TO SHAHJAHANABAD IN DELHI; AGRA LANGUISHES

Why did Shah Jahan shift the capital to Delhi? Most historians say that it was because of the oppressive heat of Agra. Also, as some say, the city had become too congested for Shah Jahan's extended court and processions. These factors definitely had a role to play but the reasons were deeper. Delhi's geographical location was more strategic for the control of the empire. Further, as the author of the 19th-century biographical work *Maasir al-Umara* said: 'Exalted sultans always had it in mind to cause the world to remember [them] by a permanent monument.' Agra had by then become too small for Shah Jahan's grand and ambitious building plans. Overbuilding and encroachments had led to huge congestion in a city getting progressively eroded by the Yamuna. Even the gates of the palace-fort at Agra had become small for the crowds that would assemble on the court days or festivals and there had been instances of people getting killed or injured. In 1639, Shah Jahan instructed his architects, engineers and astrologers to select a new site in a mild climate somewhere between Agra and Lahore.

The choice of Delhi was facilitated by many factors. It had been the capital and a centre of Muslim rule since the establishment of Delhi Sultanate under Qutbuddin Aibek (who laid the foundations of Qutb Minar). It had remained so until around 1506 when the Afghan ruler Sikandar Lodi (r. 1489–1517) shifted his capital to Agra. Then, after a gap, Shah Jahan's grandfather and the second Mughal emperor, Humayun (r. 1530–40; 1555–56) tried to establish a new capital called Dinpanah ('Refuge of the Faithful') in the modern Purana Qila/Old Fort area of Delhi. Delhi had also remained an importance pilgrimage centre with tombs and graves of Sufi saints and holy men and even the Mughal emperors visited such sites.

Having narrowed on Delhi, Shah Jahan chose a site on the banks of the Yamuna between Firuzabad (the city established by Delhi sultan Firuz Shah Tughlaq) and Salimgarh Fort (built by Afghan ruler Sher Shah Suri's son Salim Shah). This was where the 17th-century Mughal capital Shahjahanabad came into being. The capital was conceived of as *axis mundi*, the centre of the earth where the sacred and the mundane intersected. It is on account of the city being the sacred centre that auspicious times were fixed by Shah Jahan's astrologers for various rituals, ceremonies and celebrations. In the words of Muhammad Salih, an official historian of Shah

Jahan's reign: 'Its four walls ... enclosed the centre of the earth [markaz-i khak].' Salih described it as 'the foundation of the eighth heaven.' Hakim Maharat Khan Isfahani, a geographer writing in the early 18th century, explained thus: '[Shahjahanabad] was always the dar al mulk [seat of empire] of the great sultans and the centre of the circle of Islam [markaz-i dairah Islam].'[97]

Like Agra, Shahjahanabad was located on the banks of the Yamuna. It had an imposing red sandstone walled fort, also called the Red Fort. Like Agra, Delhi's Red Fort – also called Qila-i-Maula ('Exalted Fort') – had strong defences and enclosed the imperial palace complex. During 1651–58, a massive stone wall enclosing the city area of 1,500 acres was constructed around the new capital. This 'Walled City' was punctuated by towers, bastions, gates and entryways. Unlike Agra, commercial streets formed an integral part of the planning of Shahjahanabad's palace-fort. There were two principal commercial streets/avenues at the juncture of which stood the palace-fort. The first ran from Lahori gate of the fort, through the Chandni Chowk (Fig. 16) to Fatehpuri Masjid (also called Fathpuri Masjid/Mosque), built by one of Shah Jahan's wives, Nawab Fathpuri Begum. The second commercial street – stretching from the Akbarabadi/Delhi gate of the fort to Akbarabadi/Delhi gate of the city – became known as the *Faiz Bazar* ('Bazar of Plenty'). There was a third small street known as the *Khas Bazar* ('Special Market') which stretched between the Akbarabadi gate of the fort and the Jama Masjid, the main imperial and congregational mosque. Mosques built by begums and nobles were mostly located on the two principal streets.

Besides these three central markets, there were also shops along the corners and by-lanes of these commercial streets. The central markets invited merchants from other provinces of the Mughal empire as well as from other countries. Traders from

Turkey, Zanzibar, Syria, Yemen, Arabia, Iraq, Khorasan, China, Tibet as well as those from England and Holland brought goods to these markets.[98] In addition to the central markets, there were regional (located within or near the palace-fort and great mansions and patronized by the influential nobles and imperial elites) and neighbourhood markets – dealing with regular day-to-day items like grains, fruits, vegetables, salt, cloth etc.

Shahjahanabad also had gardens. The 1650s were a period of intense garden building activities. However, unlike Agra, the gardens in the new capital were mostly independent of the tombs. These rectangular structures instead contained a central pool with a small open structure called *baradari* (a recreational pavilion with twelve arches, three on each side or a summer house). Four canals connected the central pool to the walls of the gardens. Excluding a few, most gardens lay beyond the city. Prominent among the gardens of Shahjahanabad were Khizrabad (on the banks of Yamuna, 8 kilometres south of the Akbarabadi gate) and Tis Hazari ('Garden of Thirty Thousand', filled with neem trees and located outside of the Kabul gate of the city) laid by Shah Jahan, Raushan Ara (laid by and named after one of Shah Jahan's daughters, around 10 kilometres west of the Lahori gate of the city), Sahibabad (laid by Jahanara Begum, near Chandni Chowk) and Qudsia bagh (built later in 1748 by Nawab Qudsia Begum, wife of the then Mughal emperor Muhammad Shah). The city also had a network of *sarais* at regular intervals for travellers, merchants, scholars and religious specialists. Built by imperial and noble families, the *sarais* contained a pool of water, stables, trees and flowers, and a *katra* for storing travellers' goods.

There are no concrete population figures for Shahjahanabad in the existing sources but Francois Bernier, who lived in the city between 1659–1663, says it was the size of Paris which during the late 17th century was inhabited by 500,000 people. Other estimates indicate that the population of Shahjahanabad in 1650 was around 375,00–400,000 people – out of this, around 250,000 people lived in 1,500 acres within the walled city and another 100,000–150,000 in the 1,800 acres of the nearby suburbs.[99]

With the shift of capital to Delhi – along with the emperor's camp, princes, the nobles, the court officials etc. – Agra went through a period of drastic decline. It remained the 'Abode of Caliphate' as opposed to Delhi which took over and became the Dar-al-Khilafa ('Seat of the Caliphate').[100] The neglect of the city by the ruling elite increased when Shah Jahan was imprisoned by Aurangzeb in Agra Fort (1658). After the former's death in 1666, Agra started losing its sheen and became the site of constant strife between the Mughal governors, the Jats and Marathas.

In 1656, the English East India Company abandoned its factory in Agra and the Dutch apparently followed suit. In the 1680s, according to a report received by the Raja of Jaipur, the Jats pillaged Akbar's tomb at Sikandara and also plundered the villages near the Taj Mahal. By the early 18th century, Agra had declined to a point where a historian of Aurangzeb's reign omitted its name from a list of eight most important cities of the reign.[101] Historians are however divided on the future of Agra after Shah Jahan's departure. Basing themselves on the reports of French travellers Bernier and Tavernier who visited Agra in 1660s – twelve to fifteen years after the departure of the emperor – some argue that Agra continued to remain a viable and bustling city.[102] Those disagreeing with this approach indicate that both the travellers speak of Agra's superiority in terms of buildings rather than people. Agra contained more buildings and could comfortably house the emperor and the court whenever they visited but to say that a pre-modern state could support the continued existence of the two cities does not sound very credible.[103]

Meanwhile Agra Fort and the city also continued to change hands. The Jats kept the Fort under their control from 1761 to 1774. The Marathas took possession of the Fort in 1784 and retained it till 1803 when the British under Lord Lake took control. Agra was incorporated in the North-Western Provinces. After the 1857 Rebellion, the headquarters of Agra government were transferred to Allahabad.

THE 'EMPIRE OF HINDUSTAN' BECOMES THE 'KINGDOM OF DELHI', AND THE BRITISH TAKE OVER

Shah Jahan's later years saw the empire into a war of succession. In September 1657, Shah Jahan suffered a serious intestinal disorder while in Shahjahanabad. He somehow managed to reach Agra. Though the emperor recovered by November 1657, his ill health triggered a war of succession. Shah Jahan tried to diffuse the crisis by declaring his eldest son, Dara Sukoh as his successor while other sons were assigned governorships of different regions. Prince Shuja, who was based in Bengal declared himself emperor and marched to Banaras. Likewise, Murad, who was based in Malwa–Gujarat, declared himself emperor and marched towards Agra with the support of Aurangzeb and his forces from Deccan. Defeating Dara's forces, Aurangzeb reached Agra and imprisoned Shah Jahan. The 'Lord of the World' (Shah Jahan) was to spend the last eight years of his life confined in Agra Fort with his daughter Jahanara Begum being the sole attendant. On his death in 1666 (at the age of seventy-four), Aurangzeb allowed for a small ceremony for his internment next to his beloved wife in the Taj Mahal.

Shah Jahan's imprisonment was a turning point in the history of the Mughal empire. Many members of Mughal family had earlier rebelled against the incumbent emperor including Jahangir and Shah Jahan, but this was the first time, someone had actually deposed and imprisoned the emperor. Aurangzeb had a rushed initial coronation in 1658 near Shalimar Bagh in Delhi and a second full ceremonial installation on the iconic peacock throne in June 1659 when he selected his imperial name – Alamgir ('Seizer of the World') though he remained popular by his other name, Aurangzeb. The new emperor sought support from the orthodox Sunni *ulema* and rid the court culture of the unorthodox and un-Islamic practices. The two life-size stone elephants ornamenting Agra Fort's main gate and those at Delhi gate in the Red Fort in Delhi were demolished and the age-old practice of *jharokha darshan* by the Mughal emperor was stopped. Aurangzeb did not commission much monumental architecture though he built, restored or enlarged many mosques. His delicately ornamented Moti Masjid (Pearl Mosque, 1658–63) within the Red Fort in Delhi was exclusively for the imperial household and court while the Padshahi Mosque (1673–4) adjacent to the Lahore Fort was was the larger one.

In 1679, Aurangzeb left Shahjahanabad never to return to the city or Hindustan again. Until then, he had largely reigned from Shahjahanabad, travelling around relatively rarely; supervising campaigns in Afghanistan, visiting Agra and Allahabad and once resting in Kashmir. Aurangzeb died in 1707 at the age of ninety-one, after five decades of rule. Some historians say that his death marked the end of the empire; others say it marked the beginning of the end. The empire had possibly reached its territorial limits and it was becoming increasingly difficult to hold it together. Popular revolts including those by Jats around Mathura, Sikhs in the Punjab, Marathas in western Deccan as well as those involving rulers of Bijapur and Golkonda and Rajputs of Mewar and Marwar had begun to erode the Mughal empire. Cracks were appearing in the agrarian setup and the jagirdari and mansabdari system and financial imbalances were crumbling the state apparatus. The period also saw the rise of joint-stock trading corporations such as the English, Dutch and French East India Companies who had replaced the Portuguese as the controllers of Indian Ocean trade and the pilgrimage to Mecca. Skirmishes between English and Mughal officials had begun to surface at places like Hugli (1686–90), Bombay (1688–9), Surat (1695–9) and Madras (1702).

The ensuing period was one where the once-powerful Mughal emperor had to rally for support from controlling *mansabdars*, influential courtiers, ascendant military commanders, provincial governors, warlords and dictator regents – the new kingmakers. This was also a period where multiple ageing princes (and sometimes their sons) would declare themselves emperors. Many of these reigned only for a few months barring Muhammad Shah (r. 1719–48) who weakly remained on the Mughal throne for almost three decades.[104]

The Maratha attacks on Delhi (1737) showed the vulnerability of the Mughal rule. Soon there were more. When Nadir Shah left Delhi in March 1739, he carried with himself Shah Jahan's iconic peacock throne, the Koh-i-Noor diamond, bullion, jewels, art treasures, stores and arms all estimated at the cost of 700 million or seventy crore rupees then. Delhi appeared to regain some of its prosperity in the next ten years, but the city was finally destroyed by civil wars, rebellions and invasions during 1751–61. First, the 1753 civil war between the rival ministers Safdarjung (whose tomb now lies near Lodi Gardens) and Imad-ul Mulk who became the *wazir* at the age of seventeen. And then came the invasion of Ahmad Shah Durrani, also called Ahmad Shah Abdali (1757) and the occupation of Delhi by the Marathas (1757–61). Historian

Percival Spear says what Nadir had spared, Ahmad Shah destroyed; what Ahmad Shah overlooked, the Marathas carried away.[105] After Marathas recovered the city, they fought Ahmad Shah's army in what constitutes the Third Battle of Panipat (1760–61) – one of the bloodiest battles in Indian history. Ahmad Shah's army re-entered Shahjahanabad and took more booty before withdrawing to Afghanistan. The battle left the Marathas were too weakened to renew their advance on Delhi for the next ten years. The city had a breathing space. During the next twenty-seven years, Delhi was the centre of a small kingdom held together by the exertions of a series of dictators. The 'Empire of Hindustan' had become the 'Kingdom of Delhi'. The new situation is expressed in a couplet

Sultanat-i-Shah Alam
Az Delhi ta Palam

(From Delhi to Palam
Is the Realm of Shah Alam)[106]

Both Agra and Delhi came under the control of the English East Indian Company when Lord Lake defeated the Marathas. The early decades of the 19th century were one of Delhi Renaissance, centring around the intellectual and cultural activities of the Delhi College (now the Zakir Husain College). But this was not meant to last for long. The year 1857 saw Red Fort and Delhi become the focal point of a massive rebellion which de-staged the colonial administration for some time. The Mughal emperor, Bahadur Shah Zafar was cajoled into taking the leadership of the rebellion. The suppression of the rebellion saw the end of the rule of the Mughals and the East India Company. Queen Victoria (1837–1901) was proclaimed the *Qaisar-i Hind*, the Empress of India. While Calcutta (now Kolkata) remained the seat of the colonial administration, India's new relationship with England was reinforced through three imperial *durbars* (courts) held in Delhi in the years 1877, 1903 and 1911. In the last *durbar*, also known as the Delhi Durbar (1911), the British Government announced the decision to shift the capital from Calcutta to Delhi (Fig. 17), making way for the last imperial city – New Delhi.

1

THE QUTB MINAR AND ITS MONUMENTS

The Kutub Minar...has no parallel in the lands of Islam. It is built of red stone unlike the rest of the edifice, ornamented with sculptures and of great height. The ball on the top is of glistening white marble and its apples are of pure gold...This minaret is one of the wonders of the world for size and the width of its passage is such that three elephants could mount it abreast.[1]

This is how the famous Moroccan traveller Ibn Battuta described Qutb Minar during his visit to Delhi in 1334. A desired picturesque landscape for several aquatints and watercolours produced centuries later by East India Company artists, the Qutb Minar also features in various travel accounts of the medieval and the modern period of Indian history. It still remains one of the top tourist destinations of the country and appears prominently in the Indian government's tourism campaigns. On account of its international popularity, the monument recently featured as the pit stop of the second leg of the second series of the Australian reality game show 'The Amazing Race Australia'.

Located in the southern precincts of Delhi, against the rocky backdrop of arid Aravalli ranges and shrub forests, lies the historic Qutb complex, named after the iconic tower, Qutb Minar. The complex is now surrounded by Mehrauli, a bustling suburb of

> **DID YOU KNOW?**
>
> The Rajput citadel, Lal Kot/Rai Pithora formed one of the key sites where art and architectural traditions of the Turks and Rajputs came face-to-face for the first time in north India. How did this pan out? Did it represent a 'clash of civilizations'? (see pages 77–80) Arches and domes originated with the Sumerians and Romans and later spread to West and Central Asia under the patronage of Muslim kings and Islam. How did the Turkish conquerors of 13th–14th centuries try to replicate their arches and domes in a new land with the help of Hindu stone masons and craftsmen? (see pages 79–80)
>
> What is the mystery surrounding the 1,600-year-old iron pillar located in the Qutb mosque? (see pages 82–83)
>
> Did you know that 'Smith's Folly', a non-descript pavilion now lying abandoned in the outer lawns of the Qutb complex, once surmounted the Qutb Minar, the tallest ashlar masonry minaret in the world? (see page 86)
>
> Would it be correct to surmise that the tomb of the Turks introduced new trends in funerary architecture in India? (see pages 89–90)
>
> Was Delhi's first congregational mosque, now known as Quwwat ul-Islam ('Might of Islam') mosque actually meant to be a 'Sanctuary of Islam'? (see pages 95–97)

Delhi also known for the shrine of Sufi saint Bakhtiyar Kaki and several other tombs and old fortifications of the Delhi Sultanate and Mughal periods. Unlike many other historical sites of the city, the structures within the Qutb complex – mostly tombs, towers, mosques, madrasa and gateways – were not built by any particular dynasty or ruler. They were constructed over time; some constructions do not even have a direct archaeological connection with the primary buildings. The core structures – including the Quwwat al-Islam mosque, the Qutb Minar itself, Iltutmish's tomb, Alai-Darwaza, Alai Minar and Alauddin's tomb-cum-madrasa – belong to the 13th and 14th centuries which was the high point of the Delhi Sultanate.

Among the ancillary structures, the tomb of Imam Zamin was built around early 16th century and some subsidiary buildings like mosques, graves, gates, a garden and a *sarai* (rest house) were built during the late 18th–early 19th centuries. The landscaping of the complex was done by the colonial administration in the early 19th century to make it appealing to the touring British elite.

However, the oldest structure in the complex is the 4th-century CE iron pillar positioned in the courtyard of the Quwwat al-Islam mosque. It speaks of the significant advances India had made in the field of metallurgy and casting in ancient times. The Qutb Minar complex was declared a UNESCO World Heritage Site in 1993.

CIRCUMSTANCES LEADING TO THE CONSTRUCTION OF THE QUTB COMPLEX

Qutb Minar is still visible from most parts of South Delhi though nowadays modern buildings and constructions sometimes obscure the visibility of this iconic historical signpost. In the 13th–14th centuries CE however, the Minar could be seen from a long distance, signifying the presence of a new religio-political dispensation. In its initial years who would have then thought that this monument, located on the margins of a sparsely populated city, would change the future of Dilli, as Delhi was then known, forever?

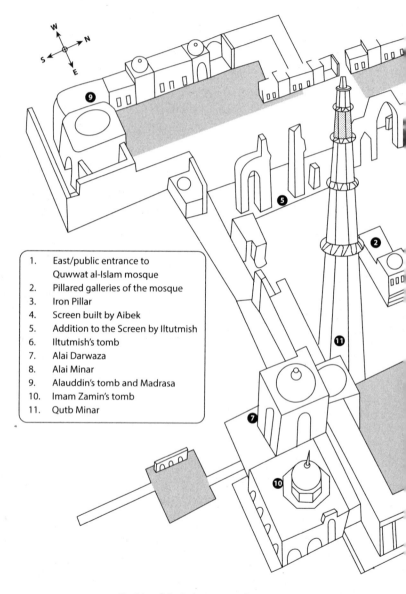

Site Map of the Qutb Minar complex.

The complex's larger historical connections get dwarfed by the height of the Qutb Minar, the tallest ashlar masonry minaret in the world. It is the site of some major historical developments in the subcontinent, including the transition from Rajput polities to Islamic kingdoms, the establishment of the Delhi Sultanate, the development of what is popularly known as Indo-Islamic architecture, and the emergence of Delhi as an imperial city.

North India, between the 10th and the 12th centuries CE, was under the control of lineage- or clan-based Hindu dynasties known as the Rajputs. Two such Rajput dynasties ruled the Delhi–Ajmer region; while the Tomars controlled Delhi, Ajmer was governed by the Chauhans. The village Anangpur in the Badarpur area of Delhi has remains of fortifications built by the Tomars. A well-known reservoir located nearby, Suraj Kund, is also attributed to them. Around 1060 CE, the Tomar ruler Anangpal II shifted his base to the arid Mehrauli region and built a fortified settlement called the Lal Kot (literally, 'Red Fort') and also a deep reservoir known as the Anangtal. The oblong-shaped settlement had a circumference of around 3.6 kilometres and its walls were punctured by semicircular bastions. The citadel was surrounded by a ditch.

The Chauhans of Ajmer are said to have defeated the Tomars around the middle of the 12th century. Historians differ on whether the Chauhans made Delhi their capital or if the settlement remained a frontier town, or if it functioned as a military garrison to the Chauhan stronghold Ajmer, which was about 380 kilometres to the west. It is popularly believed that Prithviraj Chauhan, perhaps the most celebrated of the Chauhan kings, expanded the walls of Delhi's first red fort, Lal Kot, and built a new citadel, Qila Rai Pithora, almost four times the original size. Some scholars however argue that the expansion of Lal Kot took place later under the Turks. In a conversation over email, conservation activist Sohail Hashmi says that what currently come across as the remains of Lal Kot or Qila Rai Pithora are all rubble built with limestone and crushed brick mixture, which was used as the binding material. However, there are parts of the walls of Lal Kot/Qila Rai Pithora in Sanjay Van (a city forest area near Mehrauli and Vasant Kunj) which contain true arches. These are clearly of a post-Prithviraj Chauhan period as the arch could not have been built prior to 1287, the year of its first use in parts of the mausoleum of Delhi sultan Ghiyasuddin Balban (r. 1266–87). In any case, Prithviraj Chauhan was defeated by Muhammad of Ghur (henceforth Ghuri) in the Second Battle of Tarain (1192) following which Ajmer and Delhi were occupied by the Turks. Ghuri soon returned home to Afghanistan leaving the control of Delhi and Ajmer to his favourite slave and army commander, Qutbuddin Aibek.

Aibek decided to make Delhi his seat of power and one of his first tasks was to build a settlement where the Turks could reside, worship and trade. And, he chose the Tomar/Chauhan stronghold Lal Kot/Qila Rai Pithora for that. Soon Delhi's first Friday mosque, which in 19th century became known as the Quwwat al-Islam ('Might of Islam'), came into being. Aibek also laid the foundations of the iconic Qutb Minar which was completed by his successor, Shamsuddin Iltutmish (r. 1211–36, henceforth Iltutmish), and later repaired by rulers like Firuz Shah Tughlaq and Sikander Lodi. The Qutb complex started symbolizing the supremacy of a new religio-political dispensation and most later sultans wanted to leave their imprints at the site. Iltutmish enlarged the congregational mosque and built his own tomb there. Lal Kot/Rai Pithora remained the seat of power till the early 14th century when the new sultan Alauddin Khalji

(r. 1296–1316) shifted his headquarter to a new city/settlement/ military garrison called Siri, about 4.5 kilometres to the north-east. However, Alauddin still chose to leave his architectural imprints at the site which had emerged as the 'Axis of Islam'. He further enlarged the Quwwat al-Islam mosque and added a gateway (Alai Darwaza) to it. He built a madrassa which is believed to contain his tomb. The sultan had also planned a minar (Alai Minar) twice the size of the Qutb Minar, but couldn't live to complete it.

DESIGN AND LAYOUT

As I have already mentioned, the monuments in the Qutb complex were not built by any particular dynasty or king. Further, they were built over different periods of time. The complex was not built according to any specific design or plan, at least not that we know of. The Turks were completely new to the place. What is important to note here is the site they chose – the fortified Tomar/Chauhan stronghold on the rocky spurs of the Aravalli mountain ranges – for their first settlement. And the first structure they built was the congregational mosque (Fig. 1.4). For any deeper historical engagement with the site, it is this Quwwat al-Islam mosque (and not the Qutb Minar) that should form the overarching frame of reference. All other monuments have been planned around this mosque (see the site map).

THE MOSQUE COMPLEX

So why was a mosque so important?

Why was Aibek's foremost task to create a congregational place of worship?

As per Islamic tradition, a new ruler's name had to be read aloud in the Friday prayers to legitimize his authority. Usually, the first mosque of a newly conquered area – as seen in the 8th-century Great Mosque of Cordoba in Spain – was quickly built partially using the previously used material, the spolia.[2] In the Indian context, the Turks destroyed the temple complex of the Rajputs at Lal Kot and used its spolia to build a congregational mosque.

The construction of Delhi's first Friday mosque (and other monuments) however brought to the fore some other contradictions as art traditions brought by the Islamicized Turks came face-to-face with the Hindu and Jaina art forms patronized by the Rajputs of north India. Islam had, right from its very beginnings, exhibited a distrust of the portrayal of the human form; it regarded Allah as the only Creator, the sole artist, the sole *musawwir* or the 'bestower of forms'.[3] Arts in Islam dominantly revolved around representations of the abstract; calligraphy, geometry and arabesque, a design created by interlacing lines, plant stems, flowers or scrolls, rather than humans or natural forms. This was faced with the indigenous Hindu and Jaina temple art forms, patronized in north India by the Rajputs, which celebrated sculptural depictions of deities (Fig. 1.9), mythical characters, humans, animals, flowers and plants. Further, while the craftsmen patronized by the Turks of Central Asia deployed arcuate technique – based on the use of arches and domes – in their constructions, the Indian masons were trained in the indigenous trabeate technique based on the use of posts and lintels between pillars. How did the tensions between two distinct art traditions (popularly associated with elements of two broader religious traditions) pan out in the Indian context, particularly in the case of Delhi's first Friday mosque?

The mosque, as it stands now, has a rectangular courtyard with the pillared galleries on the east, north and south. The *qibla* wall on the west, indicating the direction of Mecca, has completely disintegrated though one can still see remains of the prayer chambers. These chambers are fronted by a free-standing ornately carved stone screen. In front of the screen stands the iconic iron pillar. The construction of Delhi's first Friday or congregational mosque (jami masjid, sometimes also called jama masjid) and its adjacent minaret were celebrated as wonders by 13th- and 14th-century chroniclers and geographers writing in Arabic and Persian as far away as Egypt and Syria.[4]

The Pillared Galleries and the Courtyard

The most controversial part of the mosque is the foundational inscription placed over the eastern gate (Fig. 1.7), which now forms the main public entrance to the mosque. Popularly attributed to Qutbuddin Aibek, the inscription says twenty-seven Hindu and Jaina temples were destroyed to build the structure. Scholars say the absence of mortar or cement – which was introduced by the Turks – in indigenous building techniques facilitated the reuse of the spolia. The pillared galleries and the prayer chambers are also built in the post-and-lintel architectural style used in the construction of temples.

Pillars from Hindu and Jaina temples (Fig. 1.5) carrying motifs such as the bell and chain, *kalasha* or Hindu ritual vessel, *kirti mukha* (Fig. 1.6), a stylized face of a monster, foliage and some sculptures were used to build the galleries or colonnades and the prayer chambers. Images and sculptures, which are considered unacceptable in the Islamic context, were removed/defaced. Upon a closer look, one can still see the remains of defaced divine and human sculptures on some pillars. The colonnades on three sides, excluding the west, have much higher roofs supported on two, sometimes three, pillars stacked over one another. Small entresol apartments reached by narrow staircases were laid at the four corners of the mosque to provide secluded accommodation for the *zanana* (women).

The plinth of the earlier complex was also enlarged to twice its original size to build the platform. The mosque has three entrances in the east, north and south. Its flat trabeate roof has conical/corbelled domes – made from smaller concentric stone rings placed one over the other – at the entrances and in the prayer chambers. There is a special domed pavilion on the north-west corner with a separate entrance carrying carved lions. This probably served as the royal prayer chamber (*muluk khana*) for Aibek.

The Stone Screen

Aibek's imposing stone screen (Fig. 1.10) consists of five arches and, according to an inscription on the south face of the central arch, it was constructed around 1198–99. Later rulers, Iltutmish and Alauddin Khalji, made extensions to it in the north and south side. However, only the additions made by Iltutmish are visible now. Possibly modelled on the *maqsura*, or screen, fronting the Prophet's mosque in Medina, the screen clearly reinforces the Islamic character of the monument. Built of rubble masonry and covered with carved red sandstone, it represents one of the first systematic attempts towards the construction of an arch. The arches, Sohail Hashmi points out, were first used by the Sumerians in their underground water supply systems. The pre-Christian Romans brought them over the ground to build their aqueducts before they began to be used to create vaulted roofs and evolved into the dome. He says that the dome was first used, probably for the Roman Senate and that the Jews were perhaps the first to use it for worship because they were the first congregational religion, followed by the Christians. The Muslims were the last to use the dome for congregational worship. With the spread of Islam, arch-making techniques spread to West and Central Asia. Over a period of time, the true arch – raised by means of wedge-shaped blocks (*voussoirs*) of stone arranged in a radiating half circle with a keystone at the centre – became a standard feature of the architecture patronized by the Muslims of the region.

The Turkish conquerors wanted to replicate the arches and domes in their homelands in the new architectural ventures in north India. However, they hadn't brought with them architects and craftsmen adept in buildings arches and domes. They had to instead rely on local stone masons who, with their experience of constructing temples, came up with a different version of an arch (Fig. 1.11). Known as the corbelled arch, this new structure was built by progressively laying blocks of stone in a row whereby each level projected marginally beyond the row below. This technique was used to build temple entrances. Sohail Hashmi says that the corbel is a much older form of architectural technique in use in different parts of the world. It also forms the link between the trabeate and the true arch in India and had been in use in the country for several centuries before the arrival of the Turko-Afghans and the Iranians. Instances of the use of the corbels could be seen at the temples at Khajuraho, Konark, Mukteshwar, Rameswaram and Bhubaneshwar, to name a few.

Between 1192 and 1287, Hashmi elaborates, we see many examples in the Qutb complex of the corbels being shaped to resemble a true arch. All the arches of the west-facing screen in the congregational mosque are false arches; the main entry of the mosque is also a false arch and so are the arches in the mausoleum of Iltutmish and the arched entry to the Qutb Minar itself. All of these are false arches – corbelled arches being passed off as true arches.

Fig. 1.1 Qutb Minar, as seen from the main entrance.

Fig. 1.2 Balconies separating the storeys of the Qutb Minar.

Fig. 1.3 Calligraphic bands on the Qutb Minar.

Fig. 1.4 Masjid-i-Jami or the Qutb Mosque, now known as Quwwat al-Islam mosque.

Fig. 1.5 Pillars from the Hindu and Jaina temples were reused in the Qutb Mosque.

Fig. 1.6 Kirti Mukha on the pillars reused in the mosque.

Fig. 1.7 Eastern Gate of the Qutb Mosque, now forms the public entrance.

Fig. 1.8 The famous iron pillar in the Qutb mosque.

Fig. 1.9 Statues which once adorned the temples at the Qutb complex.

Fig. 1.10 Screen erected by Qutbuddin Aibek around 1199; the portion added by Iltutmish lies on the right.

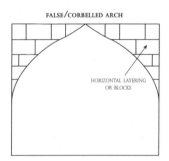 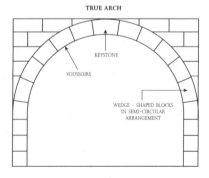

Fig. 1.11 True and False Arch.

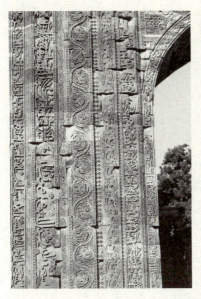

Fig. 1.12 Detail from a screen constructed by Aibek.

Fig. 1.13 Detail from a screen added by Iltutmish to the mosque.

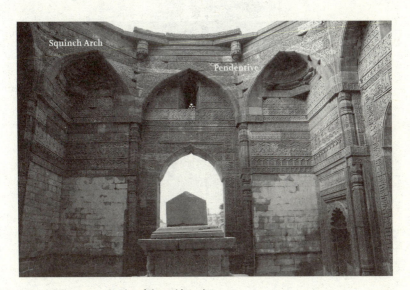

Fig. 1.14 The interior chamber of Iltumish's tomb.

Fig. 1.15 *Alai Darwaza built on principles of architectural symmetry.*

Fig. 1.16 *One of the entrances to the Alai Darwaza.*

Fig. 1.17 The Incomplete Alai Minar.

Fig. 1.18 The madrasa and tomb complex built by Alauddin Khalji.

Fig. 1.19 Smith's Folly.

Fig. 1.20 The Tomb of Imam Zamin.

Aibek's corbelled arched screen contains multiple ornately carved vertical bands (Fig. 1.12). These bands contain carved lotus-like creepers some of which grow from pots; continuous rope/creeper-like patterns with blossoms; and Arabic calligraphy intertwined with continuous naturalistic lotus-like creepers to form the arabesque pattern. Arabic lettering preserved the divine word of the Quran and the holy phrases were duplicated, mirrored and used as ornamentation in architecture in Islam.[5] The calligraphy on Qutbuddin Aibek's screen uses Naksh (one of the earlier scripts, usually small and round) characters. Indigenous influences in the execution of designs associated with Islam however is very noticeable in the Qutb complex. Indian craftsmen made each calligraphic stroke end into a little floral burst.[6] Likewise, kalasha carvings, appearing at the base of the structure, were common Hindu iconographic motifs. The interaction between Turkish (popularly associated with the wider Islamic tradition) and Rajput (popularly associated with the larger indigenous Hindu tradition) art traditions therefore also sowed the seeds of what came to be commonly known as Indo-Islamic architecture. The spandrels on the screen contain a series of circular patterns interspersed with intersecting bands and floral patterns.

On account of the presence of the Victory Sura (Sura al-Fateh) of Quran, often recited before battles; textile patterns; and, shades of colours including beige, red, green and pink on Aibek's screen, some scholars have suggested that it represented a frozen khuja (temporary victory arch) – a stone rendering of block-printed Indian textiles much in international demand on both sides of the Indian Ocean.[7]

The Arabic inscriptions on Aibek's screen, Qutb Minar and other constructions in the complex, mostly deal with the obligations of a good Muslim and the fate of the non-believers, possibly Hindu, Jains and unorthodox Muslim sects. They also indicate that Fazl ibn Abil Maali was the supervisor for Aibek's mosque, the screen and the first storey of Qutb Minar.[8]

The Iron Pillar

In front of the central arch of Aibek's screen stands the iconic iron pillar (Fig. 1.8), which is the oldest artefact in the Qutb complex. The pillar weighs over six tonnes and is around 23.6 feet (7.08 metres) tall, of which 3.6 feet(1.08 metres), is buried below the ground. A Sanskrit inscription – translations of which can be seen on the wall in the northern gallery – records its erection by a mighty king called Chandra, who was a devotee of Hindu God Vishnu, as a *dhvaja stambha* (flag staff) on the 'Hill of Vishnupada'. The inscription also celebrates the king's military prowess. This king has now been identified as Chandragupta II (CE 375–413) of the Gupta dynasty. The pillar also has a fluted bell capital with an *amalaka* (stone disk) so characteristic of the Gupta period. It has a deep hole on the top to possibly support an image of Garuda, the vehicle of Vishnu.

The Pillar has attracted a lot of questions: Why hasn't it rusted in more than 1,600 years despite being made of iron? Who brought it in the Qutb complex, and from where?

Ibn Battuta, the Moroccan traveller, described it as 'an awe inspiring column' made of seven metals. Scientists and metallurgists have, on the basis of chemical examination, explained that it is built of pure malleable iron and has a high phosphorus content that prevents corrosion.

On another level though, the pillar is a curious alloy of myth, legend and history. One that harks back to the very idea of Delhi.

Scholars are divided on who installed the pillar in its current location? Some suggest that it was the Tomar ruler Anangpal who brought the pillar to this site from somewhere in Lal Kot. Interestingly a legend, mentioned in the epic Hindi poem *Prithviraja Raso* composed by the court poet of the Chauhan ruler Prithviraj Chauhan, also connects the pillar to Anangpal. According to the legend, a Brahman told king Anangpal (also known as Bilhan Deo) that the pillar rested on the mythical serpent king Vasuki's hood and was immoveable. Further, his rule would last as long as the pillar stood firm. It is said that, out of curiosity, the king got the pillar dug out only to find its base smeared with Vasuki's blood. Realizing his mistake, he ordered the pillar to be reinstalled. However, even after several attempts, it could not be fixed properly, and the pillar remained loose. The name 'Delhi' is traced to this lore about the *dhilli killi* (*dhilli* meaning 'loose' and *killi*, 'nail'/'pillar') in some popular constructions. The phrase meant that the loosening of the pillar signified the loss of control over Delhi.

On the other hand, some scholars argue that the pillar was brought from outside of Delhi and that it was the Muslim rulers who placed it within the congregational mosque as a statement of conquest. R. Balasubramaniam, who has explored the metallurgy and iconography of the pillar, contends it was originally located at the Udayagiri caves (near Vidisha in Madhya Pradesh) associated with the worship of Lord Vishnu. It was Iltutmish who captured Malwa and brought the pillar to its current location in the mosque.[9] This argument was later endorsed and elaborated upon in the archaeological research done by other scholars as well.[10] Recent research draws our attention to a mid-14th-century text written by Shams-i Siraj Afif according to which Aibek's successor Iltutmish re-erected the iron pillar probably in the late 1220s/early 1230s to perpetuate the memory of his rule.[11]

It was popularly believed that anyone who can join his/her hands around the pillar while standing with their back to it will be granted a wish. Crowds thronging to do this were a common sight until the site administration erected a fence to keep them out.

THE QUTB MINAR

Made of red sandstone and marble, the Qutb Minar (Fig. 1.1) is a 73-metre-tall tapering tower with a diameter measuring 14.32 metres at the base and 2.75 metres at the peak. Inside the tower, a circular staircase with 379 steps leads to the top. Following an accident in 2000 involving the death of several children, the staircase was closed to the public.

The structure was built in multiple stages by different people and, at the time of its construction, it constituted the tallest minaret in the world. The Minar currently consists of five storeys separated by four projecting balconies (Fig. 1.2). The first storey has alternate circular and angular flutings on the facade, the second has only circular flutings, and the third has only angular flutings. The fourth and fifth storeys have no flutings at all. A series of elaborately carved red sandstone *muqarnas* – honeycomb- or stalactite-shaped vaults composed of cells and small arches – support the four balconies and transfer their weight to the body of the Minar. In addition, multiple bands of calligraphy (Fig. 1.3) are carved around the circumference of the structure.

Like the mosque, the Minar also has a contested history. Who built the structure, more specifically, the first storey? How did the structure get its present name? What function did it serve?

The 19th-century Islamic reformist and philosopher Sir Syed Ahmad Khan had attributed the first storey of the Minar to the Rajput king Prithviraj Chauhan. Building on some local legends, he postulated that Prithviraj Chauhan built the structure so that his daughter could view the river Yamuna every day as a part of her daily worship. On the basis of inscriptional evidence; descriptions in contemporary accounts; similarity in structure with 11–12th-century Ghurid minarets in Ghazni; and dissimilarity in design from the Rajput towers – such as the 'pillars of fame' (*kirti stambhas*) or 'pillars of victory' (*jaya stambhas*) – most historians say that the Minar was built by the Turks.

According to the inscriptions on the Minar – which mention the entire history of the builders, repairs and architects – the structure was under construction in 1199 when Aibek had just finished the construction of his stone screen. It can therefore be safely assumed that Aibek erected the first storey. Inscriptions on Aibek's storey are both Arabic (language of ulama and elite in early Islam) and Persian. While the former deal with the Quranic part and are addressed to the non-believers (Hindus and Jains), the latter set of inscriptions relate to the historical part and proclaim the Ghurid co-rulers as the masters 'of the kings of Arabia and Iran, the most just of the Sultans in the world.'[12] Aibek's successor and son-in-law, Iltutmish added the next three storeys around the 1220s. Inscriptions on the minaret belonging to Iltumish's period not just praise the sultan but some also contain Quranic instructions.

Repairs to the Minar

Epigraphic records also indicate that the structure was struck by lightning in Muhammad bin Tughlaq's time (r. 1325–51), but no details about any repairs are available. Lightning struck the Minar again in 1368–69 and knocked off the top (fourth) storey. Firoz Shah Tughlaq (r. 1351–88), who was the sultan then, built two more storeys in red sandstone and marble and also added a small domed pavilion or cupola. The Minar was repaired again in 1503 by Sikandar Lodi when it was struck by lightning.

In 1802–03, the cupola fell off and the whole tower was damaged by an earthquake. This time, Major R. Smith, an army engineer under the rule of the East India Company, was assigned to do the repairs. He was riding high having recently designed St James' Church and the Kashmere gate (both located near the Red Fort).

His repairs, however, came in for a lot of criticism. The facing stones that had fallen were put back without any serious regard for order. The inscriptions therefore became difficult to read. A Gothic-style balustrade (railing) was added to the projecting balconies, but it stood out because it was made of a different shade of stone. Finally, a neo-Gothic style pavilion was put on the top of the Minar above which an additional small dome was placed. The installation of this superstructure was met with enormous resistance both within and outside the colonial administration. So huge was the outcry that Lord Hardinge, the then Governor General, had the superstructure taken down in 1848. Known as Smith's Folly, the pavilion (Fig. 1.19) now lies abandoned in a corner in the outer lawns of the Qutb complex. In the same lawn lies a sun dial installed in 1922 to honour Gordon Sanderson – a former superintendent of the Archaeological Survey of India (ASI) who was killed in the First World War (1914–19).

Name and function

It has not been established with certainty whether the Qutb Minar is named after Qutbuddin Aibek, who commissioned its construction, or Qutbuddin Bakhtiyar Kaki, the famous Chishti Sufi saint whose *dargah* (tomb or shrine) and *khanqah* (hospice) are located close to the site. According to historians, the name Qutub or Cootub Minar became popular only during the British period. The inscriptions on the structure merely refer to it as a minaret (*minareh*).

Contemporary literature, on the other hand, refers to the Minar by two names: 'Qutub Sahab ki Laat' or 'Mazinah of the Juma Masjid'. 'Qutub Sahab ki Laat' connotes the staff of Sufi saint Bakhtiyar Kaki. His staff (*laat*) was believed to pierce the sky and, like the saint himself, connect the heaven with earth and provide stability and shelter to human beings. In popular cosmology, the Sufi was regarded as the *Qutb*, the 'axis around whom the world revolved', and his spiritual domain was known as *Qubbat al-Islam*, the 'Sanctuary of Islam'.[13] No inscription on the Minar mentions the saint's name, though Iltutmish greatly respected him as a spiritual master. The second name, 'Mazinah of the Juma Masjid', is related to the functionality of the mosque. The structure was to serve as a *mazinah*, or minaret, to the congregational mosque from where the *muezzin* (announcer) would call the Muslims for prayer. However, given the height of the Minar, it would have been difficult for anyone to climb it five times a day. Also, prayer calls from the top storey would have not been audible to those on the ground.

Qutb Minar, scholars say, fulfilled more than one purpose. It may have served as a *mazinah* but only from the first storey. Also, it may have served as a watchtower to monitor enemy movements. However, its most probable function would have been that of a victory tower. It would have struck awe in the hearts of local people and also stamped the authority of the ruler on visitors, giving all those who had come from faraway places such as Afghanistan, a psychological boost.[14]

ILTUTMISH AND THE QUTB COMPLEX

The mosque complex was appropriated as a site by those contending for power and political authority in north India during the 12th and 13th centuries, including Iltutmish and other future sultans.¹⁵ Iltutmish came to power in challenging circumstances when there were several claimants to Aibek's political legacy. But, he soon subdued his rivals and extended the frontiers of the new Sultanate to as far as Bengal in the east. An investiture from the Caliph in Baghdad not only legitimized his hold over the Delhi Sultanate but also enhanced his reputation in the Islamic world. His newfound stature as the guardian of Islam was further heightened by his support to orthodox Muslim institutions and the sheltering of many Muslims migrating from Central Asia, in Delhi, in the wake of Mongol invasions in the 1220s. The idea of keeping the Sultanate's diverse multi-ethnic Muslim community united also motivated him to construct and enlarge mosques in north India, particularly Delhi.¹⁶ His interventions in the Qutb complex included additions to the Qutb Minar and the congregational mosque and construction of his own tomb.

Extensions to the mosque

Iltutmish made some significant changes to the congregational mosque built by Aibek, without destroying its earlier structures. He almost doubled the size of the structure by extending its pillared galleries and prayer halls. Wings were added to the north, south and east of the original enclosure in such a way that the minaret – heightened by three storeys – now fell within the extension. The original mosque and its minaret were now both figuratively and literally integrated.¹⁷

The outer entrances on each of the three sides of the mosque were made axial with those of the original mosque. Unlike Aibek, the pillars used in extensions by Iltutmish were not re-used but freshly carved, and do not carry any motifs. They are austere with faceted sides and angular blocks. Secondly, the stone screen of Aibek was extended on both the north and south sides. Iltutmish's additions appear taller, but they use Aibek's corbelled-arch technique. There appears to be a conscious preference here for red sandstone which is associated with royalty in Islam and was also common among Indian ruling class (kshatriyas).[18] Unlike the naturalism of Aibek's screen, the screens added by Iltutmish (Fig. 1.13) become noticeable for the use of high and low relief carving.[19] They are carved with vertical rows of abstract floral pattern interspersed with rows of calligraphy. The additions on the screen made by Iltutmish use advanced forms of Islamic surface decoration. Here, the Arabic lettering shows a sophisticated combination of the squarish Kufic script and intricately and elaborately carved Tughra characters.[20] The highly stylized Tughra script later evolved more systematically as the imperial Turkish calligraphy of the Ottoman Empire.

Iltutmish's tomb

Unlike the Minar, Iltutmish's tomb in the complex has a relatively less contested history. Iltutmish is said to have built it himself around 1235, soon after Sultan Ghari (1231–32) believed to be the tomb of his eldest son, Nasiruddin Mahmud. Sultan Ghari, the first structural tomb in the Delhi region, appears more like a defensive fortress with turrets at the corners. Located north-west of the mosque, Iltutmish's tomb is built on the typical square plan so characteristic of Ghurid brick tombs in Afghanistan. It does not use any spolia and bears a distinctly Islamic character.

The Islamic tomb, scholars point out, introduced a novel form of architecture in India. Hindus, Buddhists and Jains had traditionally cremated their dead. Except for Buddhist stupas, no commemorative funerary monuments had existed in India. By building a tomb, Iltutmish also inaugurated a new trend to be followed by most later Muslim rulers – building their own tombs while still alive and reigning.[21]

The basic design of Iltutmish's tomb consists of a single square chamber roofed by a corbelled dome. To support the circular dome, the square lower part of the inner chamber (Fig. 1.14) was given a somewhat circular shape at the top by means of architectural supports appearing at top corners; squinches (niche/little conical device with a half dome) and pendentives (a triangular bracket which connects the base of a dome with supporting arches). This was the first monument in India to use the squinch arch as an architectural device. The corbelled dome, possibly constructed by means of concentric rings of masonry, collapsed as the indigenous craftsmen were as yet unfamiliar with the technique of constructing a true dome. It is said that Firoz Shah Tughlaq tried to replace the fallen dome, but it still did not survive.

The ashlar masonry of the tomb is covered with carved red sandstone both on the exterior and interior. Its interior has Quranic verses – in both Naksh and the combined Kufic and Tughra characters – carved in red sandstone alongside inscriptional mural decorations. The tomb is regarded as 'one of the most densely inscribed surfaces anywhere in the Islamic world.'[22] The carvings include chapters from the *Quran* that warn the non-believers, underline the goodness of those who follow the message of the God and point towards paradise as the reward for the true believer. The reward of paradise for the believer is a theme repeated in the later Sultanate and Mughal funerary architecture, including the famous Taj Mahal.[23] Marble finds limited introduction in the tomb. It has been used for the construction of the central area of the tomb's three *mihrabs* (niches) on the *qibla* wall and also the cenotaph. The actual burial site – customarily kept at least six feet below the ground – can be accessed through a now-locked underground chamber to the north of the tomb.

The 'foundational inscription' of the Qutb complex which attracts a lot of attention from tourists and historians alike is mired in controversy. Recent research also links Iltutmish to the inscription – on the eastern entrance of the mosque. Some scholars date it to even later. Dated 1191/92, this controversial inscription in Persian is popularly attributed to Aibek. Some ask the question – how could the construction of mosque begin before the capture of Delhi in 1192?[24] Others make some pertinent observations in this regard. First, the inscription is inscribed in Persian and not the usual Arabic; Persian foundation texts only became common during the reign of Iltutmish. Second, the form of inscription suggests it should be dated some decades later. Third, the inscription's general emphasis on removal of idolatry finds an echo in Quranic passages inscribed on those sections of the Qutb Minar that Iltutmish added.[25]

ALAUDDIN KHALJI AND THE QUTB COMPLEX

Following Iltutmish's death in 1236, the Delhi Sultanate was plunged into a long period of turmoil characterized by political instability, power struggles, law and order issues and Mongol invasions. With the exception of a strong sultan like Balban (r. 1266–83) – whose tomb is located in the neighbouring Mehrauli Archaeological Park – no major structures were added to the Qutb area. New monuments were to be added only under the next powerful sultan, Alauddin Khalji (r. 1296–1316), who called himself the 'Second Alexander'. Under him, the Sultanate expanded considerably, including areas as far as Madurai in south India.

Extensions to the mosque

Alauddin also fortified the Lal Kot region to take care of the Mongol threat. The Mongols had made incursions in Delhi in 1300 and 1303. After defeating them, the sultan found a new settlement called Siri which now lies in the area between Hauz Khas and the Asian Games village. Alauddin was also ambitious in his architectural endeavours. Like Iltutmish, his projected extensions at the Qutb were aimed at dwarfing the efforts of his predecessors. He developed a megalomaniac vision for the Qutb complex that would have tripled the area of Iltumish's mosque.[26] The immediate context for Alauddin's ambitious expansion of the mosque was to celebrate his victory against the Mongols in 1303.[27] His interventions in the mosque complex included the Alai Minar; extension of the stone screen built by Iltutmish; and, the magnificent Alai Darwaza (the 'Exalted Gateway'). His death however prevented the full execution of his schemes.

Alai Minar and Alai Darwaza

The unfinished Alai Minar (Fig. 1.17) to the north of Iltutmish's tomb – of which only the rubble core and an interior ramp survives – was planned as a minaret twice as big as the Qutb Minar. Alauddin's extensions to Aibek's stone screen in the north have now largely disappeared but remains can still be seen. What survives, however, is the impressive gateway he built in 1311, the Alai Darwaza (Fig. 1.15). This gate in the south of the congregational mosque was envisaged as one of the four gates to the complex; one gate was planned for the north and two gates for the eastern side of the complex.[28] The gateway consists of a domed chamber (17.2 square metres) with four entrances. The arched entrance to the north – the one opening towards the mosque enclosure – is semicircular while other three are in the shape of a pointed horseshoe (Fig. 1.16). There are extensions to the east and the west of the gateway to combine the Darwaza harmoniously with the enclosure. The dome, which looks rather low from the outside, is interestingly not a separate structure but forms a part of the roofing of a vault. When seen from the inside however, it has an impressive height. The dome has an opening at the top that is capped by another small white marble dome.

The interior and exterior of the gateway are covered with extensively carved red sandstone. The interior has interlocking geometric patterns interspersed with floral or star motifs. The red sandstone exterior is punctuated with narrow white marble panels around the entrances, windows and other rectangular panels. The entrances are decorated with beautifully carved lotus buds on the underside while the red sandstone walls have ornate carvings; *jaalis* (latticed stone screens); verses from the *Quran* and *Hadith* (collection of traditions containing sayings of Prophet Muhammad); and historical inscriptions in Persian. The Quranic inscriptions, on the eastern, western and southern entrances, speak of the need to protect the converts, rewards for the believer and the promise of paradise. The Persian texts, on the other hand, inscribe Alauddin Khalji's religious and political supremacy through expressions like 'the master of the countries of the world, the Solomon-like King', 'the Alexander of the time and age' and even call him the mightiest ruler of Islam. [29] Most scholars reiterate that the Alai Darwaza is the first building in India that employs principles of symmetry and ornamentation popularly associated with architecture in Islam. The basic ornamental or decorative theme of the gateway, seen in the red sandstone-white marble contrasts embellished with geometric patterns in repetition and symmetry, became a model for many later Sultanate and Mughal monuments.

Alauddin's madrasa and tomb

Alauddin Khalji also constructed a *madrasa*, a college/school for Islamic instruction (Fig. 1.18). It is built in dressed grey quartzite around a simple quadrangular court that can be entered on the north side through a triple gateway. The rooms are arranged in two rows: one running from north to south and the other running from east to west. They have true arches and keystones like the Alai Darwaza. In the middle of the east–west wing of rooms lies a large square structure covered originally by a dome (now fallen off) and a projecting portico. This is believed to be the tomb of Alauddin Khalji. One is however unable to trace the cenotaph or the grave marker or any corroboratory inscription.

THE QUTB COMPLEX AFTER ALAUDDIN KHALJI

After Alauddin's period, there were no major constructions in the Qutb complex though the minaret was repaired in 1369 by Firuz Shah Tughlaq and by Sikander Lodi in 1503, when it was struck by lightning. Through their restorations of the minaret, both sultans were underscoring their links with establishment of Muslim political power in north India and Delhi's past. Further, both chose to inscribe their names on Delhi's iconic symbol of power and authority.[30]

The next structure to be built within the complex was the tomb of Imam Zamin (Fig. 1.20) located next to Alai Darwaza. Originally named Imam Muhammad Ali, Imam Zamin was probably an important official in the service of the congregational mosque. He had come from Turkestan during the reign of Sikandar Lodi (r. 1489–1517) and constructed the tomb during his lifetime. This non-imperial burial structure is interesting from the point of view of evolution of tomb architecture. It is a simple square structure with a dome, covered in plaster, rising from an octagonal drum decorated with a double row of *kanguras*, merlons or ornamental bands, and marble panelling above the *chajja*, the sloping projection from the top of the wall to protect the building from the sun and rains. The four walls are perforated with red sandstone screens or *jaalis*, characteristic of the Lodi period. There is a marble *mihrab* to the west, and the entrance towards the south is also done in marble as is the cenotaph and some decorative reliefs in the interior.

The remaining buildings in the complex do not have a direct archaeological connection with the mosque or the Minar. There are remains of a Mughal *sarai* or rest house towards the entrance archway through which visitors now enter the complex. To the north of this *sarai* are the dilapidated remains of a late Mughal garden containing the ruins of some graves in the centre and of a mosque near the western wall. Other than these structures, there are multiple open-air graves, mostly un-named, scattered throughout the complex including some within the mosque's courtyard.

HOW DELHI'S FIRST FRIDAY MOSQUE BECAME THE 'MIGHT OF ISLAM' MOSQUE

Inscriptions on the congregational mosque, now known as the Quwwat al-Islam mosque, simply refer to the structure as an *imarat* (building) or a *masjid* (mosque). Historians point out that the term 'Quwwat al-Islam' or 'Might of Islam' is probably a modern corruption of an older name, '*Qubbat al-Islam*' that meant 'Dome/Sanctuary of Islam' or the 'Axis of Islam'. The name 'Quwwat al-Islam' does not occur in any extant inscription or any chronicle of the Delhi Sultanate.[31] However, we do have references to *Qubbat al-Islam* in contemporary sources. This sobriquet was at first ambiguously used by the contemporary chronicler Minaj-i Siraj Juzjani to describe Iltutmish's Delhi or the spiritual domain of Sufi saint Bakhtiyar Kaki.[32]

Uprooted due to Mongol invasions around 1220s, a large number of Muslims from Afghanistan, eastern Iran, Transoxiana and Central Asian Steppes migrated to north India. Claiming that Iltutmish had brought people from all parts of the Islamic world to Delhi, Juzjani describes the capital of Hindustan in glowing terms as 'the keeper of the Muslim faith', 'the dais of the Muslim community' or 'the Sanctuary of Islam' in the eastern world.[33] Simultaneously, the term *Qubbat al-Islam* was also used to generally describe the spiritual domain of Bakhtiyar Kaki, greatly respected by Iltutmish as his spiritual master. Qutb Minar is mentioned in contemporary accounts as *Qutub Sahib ki Laat* after the saint's staff (*laat*). We have already discussed the related details in the segment on Qutb Minar in this chapter.

When did the mosque become known as the 'Quwwat al-Islam' mosque? It is difficult to find out the exact date/year, but the expression gained currency during the 19th century. Historian David Lelyveld points out that the term 'Quwwat al-Islam' was already in use by the time Mirza Sangin Beg's *Sair ul-manzil* – a comprehensive account of the historical and Quranic inscriptions of Delhi – was published in 1819. The term is also mentioned in Karim Khan Jhajari's Persian manuscript that is a survey of the world and was published in 1845–46.[34] In 1847, the famous Muslim social reformer and educationist, Sir Syed Ahmad Khan published his first major work on Delhi, *Asar-al-Sanadid* (The Remnant Signs of Ancient Heroes). While the first edition of the book was mostly a celebration of Delhi, the second edition, published in 1854–55 with substantial revisions, was strongly influenced by European ideas and methods and grounded in the positivist tradition, where the emphasis is on facts. In the book, he refers to the Qutb mosque by three names – Masjid-i Adina Dehli ya, Masjid-i Jami Dehli ya or Quwwat al-Islam – but does not discuss their origins.³⁵ One of these names, Quwwat al-Islam, stuck and gained currency. After all, it was congruent with the popular constructions of the origin of the mosque; how a military commander built the structure out of the rubbles of Hindu temples and also proclaimed the victory of a new political order of Islam. Syed Ahmad Khan's apparent grounding in positivist/factual history added an element of authenticity to the usage of the term. His 'factual' writings (including his editions of other Persian chronicles) soon became a standard reference for colonial officials, archaeologists and historians. The usage of the term Quwwat al-Islam was also consistent with early colonial administrators' attempt to create a dividing line between the Hindus and Muslims. The controversial legacy of the mosque was also used by the colonial administration to showcase how the rule of the Muslims was a 'violent' period in Indian history and how the British brought about law and order into this chaos.

Many of Syed Ahmad Khan's conclusions were summarized and developed in the reports of the ASI in the 1860s and later in *Epigraphica Indo-Moslemica*, a journal devoted to the study of Arabic and Persian inscriptions. They were also recompiled in J. A. Page's reports on excavations and conservation efforts of ASI in the 1920s. These texts also became the basis of information and interpretation for the guidebooks on Delhi and the Qutb prepared for British tourists around the early 20th century including those by H. C. Fanshawe, Gordon Risley and J. Horowitz.³⁶ Nationalist writings, informed by notions of 'Hindu' India versus 'Muslim' Pakistan in the aftermath of India's Partition in 1947, continued to use the 'Might of Islam' framework to describe the congregational mosque. ASI guidebooks published in the post-independence period also used the term Quwwat ul-Islam and it gradually became the official name of Delhi's first Friday mosque.

QUTB AND THE EMERGING DELHI: KEY INSIGHTS

Delhi transitioned from a provincial town to an imperial capital when the Turks chose, Lal Kot, a Rajput citadel and Delhi's first Red Fort, as the site of the first Muslim settlement in north India. India's interactions with Islam and Muslims did not begin with the advent of the Turks. Long before the Turks, Arab Muslim merchants had played an important part in India's commerce with West Asia, South East Asia and China, between the 8th and 10th centuries. The Arabs had also built mosques in Kerala and colonies of Muslim traders had also come up in some coastal towns of India. However, the Turks started the process of aggressive conquest combining religion and politics.

Qutb Minar was regarded as the 'Axis of Power' or 'Axis of Islam' in north India before the advent of the Mughals and all prominent rulers of the Delhi Sultanate wanted to leave their architectural imprint in the Qutb complex.

The area around Qutb complex was the original 'Old Delhi'. Shahjahanabad and the area around the iconic Chandni Chowk, which are now known as Old Delhi, came into being almost three centuries later.

The decorative theme of Alai Darwaza, Alauddin Khaji's gateway to the Qutb mosque, which combined red sandstone with white marble with geometrical designs in symmetry, inspired many later Sultanate and Mughal monuments. We will discuss this in detail in the chapter on Humayun's tomb.

2
HUMAYUN'S TOMB

So delicately carved, so fair,
The graceful buildings stand,
Such as to us are like the dreams
Of some enchanted land.
He looked upon them as scrolls
Prophetic of our life,
The chronicles where Fate inscribes
Our sorrow, sin and strife ...

This is a part of the poem 'Tomb of Humaioon' by the English poet and novelist Letitia Elizabeth Landon, who based it on an engraving in *Fisher's Drawing Room Scrap-Book* (1833). It clearly depicts the attention the Humayun's tomb complex has continued to gather over centuries. A preferred 'period setting' for pre-wedding photo shoots and picturesque location for Bollywood songs, the monumental heritage complex is now one of the top social destinations of Delhi. The sprawling complex boasts many significant structures of the Mughal era and the spectacular tomb of Humayun stands in its centre. This is indisputably one of the most proportionate and graceful monuments of medieval India. On one side, the complex is surrounded by the teeming Nizamuddin Basti and the Hazrat Nizamuddin railway station and, on the other, by one of the greenest parts of Delhi, comprising the Sunder Nursery,

Delhi Zoo and Indraprastha Millennium Park. The second emperor of the Mughal empire, Humayun, had built the city of Dinpanah which still has its remains nearby. His tomb in the complex was constructed close to the *dargah* or shrine of the Sufi saint Nizamuddin Auliya along the banks of river Yamuna which at that time flowed through this area and has shifted a few kilometres to the east since. Constructed under the aegis of Humayun's son and successor, Akbar, between 1565–72, this is the first garden tomb – a structural form due to assume great significance later – built by the Mughals in the Indian subcontinent. The other monuments in the complex – Isa Khan's tomb and mosque, Bu Halima's garden, Afsarwala mosque and tomb, Arab Sarai, and the Barber's tomb – were built in the 16th century but do not form a part of the original plan of the tomb garden. These structures now form a part of the heritage site buffer zone. Humayun's tomb introduced several architectural innovations in the tradition of tomb and garden landscape in India which saw a culmination in the 17th century iconic mausoleum, the Taj Mahal. It is therefore also described as the 'Precursor of the Taj'.

The tomb was declared a UNESCO World Heritage Site in 1993. A buffer zone was created for the heritage site in 2015. The UNESCO further approved of the heritage site's boundary modification plan in 2016 to include seven more tombs located in the adjoining areas. Humayun's tomb complex has been in news in the recent decades for becoming the first monument to be comprehensively restored with the help of private agencies.

CIRCUMSTANCES LEADING TO THE CONSTRUCTION OF HUMAYUN'S TOMB

Humayun was the son of Babur, a descendant of two notable historical figures – Genghis Khan (1162–1227), the Mongol

DID YOU KNOW?

Humayun was buried four times, the last and final time it was transferred to a crypt in what is now known as the Humayun's tomb in Delhi (see page 103).

Mughal emperors are popularly regarded as the architects of monuments built during their reign. However, Humayun's tomb is one of the few buildings of its time that can be associated with named architects (see pages 106–07).

The walled garden, flowing water and trees bearing fruits and flowers in the tomb complex symbolically recreated the 'Garden of Paradise' as described in the Holy *Quran* (see pages 113–14).

The layout and design of the mausoleum also drew inspiration from Humayun's wooden boat palace (see page 115).

In the late 19th century, the colonial government let out patches of the tomb garden to cultivators for raising municipal funds. Also, after the partition of India in 1947, the tomb complex was used a site for refugee camps for people migrating to/coming from Pakistan. (see pages 122–23).

The 21st-century restoration of the tomb complex, involving private agencies, has provoked sharp debates regarding restoration and conservation of monuments in the Indian subcontinent (see pages 124–26).

---

conqueror and Timur (also Tamerlane, 1336–1405), the Turko-Mongol conqueror and founder of the Timurid empire in Persia and Central Asia. Babur was the king of Fargana, now in Uzbekistan, and had captured Kabul. He defeated Ibrahim Lodi, the Sultan of Delhi, at the First Battle of Panipat in 1526 to lay the foundations of the Mughal empire in India. Babur however preferred to refer to himself as Timurid, a descendant of Timur, and brought with himself Timurid–Persian cultural heritage and ideas of kingship.

Succeeding Babur as the emperor of Hindustan in 1530, Humayun was a person of diverse interests, including astronomy, painting, calligraphy and collecting handwritten and hand-painted books. Soon after ascending the throne at Agra, he laid the foundations of a new city called Dinpanah or 'Refuge of the Faithful', in Delhi in the complex now known as Purana Qila or 'Old Fort'. His city project and reign were, however, constantly interrupted by internal rebellions and the rise of the Afghan chieftain Sher Shah (originally Farid Khan) in the Bihar–Bengal region and Bahadur Shah in the Malwa–Gujarat area. During Humayun's campaign to Bengal, Sher Shah first trapped him in the region and then defeated him successively at Chausa (1539) – on the banks of the river Ganges, from where Humayun barely escaped with the help of an inflated water bag provided by a *bhishti*, a water carrier – and then at Kannauj (1540). Sher Shah then took charge of Agra and Delhi; founded the Sur dynasty; and took Humayun's city project in Delhi further, possibly under the name Shergarh. Humayun and his family had to flee Delhi. They spent a long time wandering in Lahore, Sindh and on the borders of the erstwhile Mughal empire. It was during this fourteen-year exile that Humayun's wife, Hamida Banu Begum, gave birth to Akbar, the future emperor, in 1542 at Amarkot.

Humayun and his family finally found refuge in Persia, now Iran, in 1544 where they received the warm hospitality of the emperor, Shah Tahmasp. During his stay in Persia, Humayun visited Herat, the great Islamic city, and learnt a lot about Persian courts, gardens with flowing water and paintings. When he finally returned to Hindustan, he brought with him two painters who introduced miniature-style techniques at the Mughal court. With the Persian emperor's military support, Humayun also regained the throne of Delhi in 1555 from Sher Shah's weak successors and is said to have completed his palace-fort at Dinpanah. He did not live long enough to enjoy the fruits of his victory. On January 27, 1556, he fell to his death from the staircase of his library at Sher Mandal in Purana Qila (Fig. 2.20). Originally built by Sher Shah as a two-storeyed red sandstone octagonal pleasure pavilion, Sher Mandal had been converted into a library by Humayun. It is said that the Mughal emperor was climbing the stairs of his library when he heard the call to prayer. He seated himself immediately. When he got up, the forty-eight-year-old emperor apparently tripped over his robe and fell to his death from the steep steps.

Humayun's tomb was built several years after his death. He was initially buried in his palace in Purana Qila. Some scholars say that his remains were taken to a temporary tomb in Sirhind, Punjab, to secure them from possible damage by a Hindu king, Hemu. Originally, a general to Afghan ruler Adil Shah Sur, Hemu defeated Tardi Beg Khan, the Mughal governor of Delhi, near Tughlaqabad in 1556 and assumed the throne under the title *Raja Vikramaditya*. Soon after, he was defeated by Akbar at the Second Battle of Panipat in that same year. Following the battle, Humayun was reburied in the Sher Mandal. Finally, in 1565, nine years after his death, the construction of the former emperor's tomb began. The site chosen was on the banks of the river Yamuna, close to the *dargah* of the charismatic Sufi saint Nizamuddin Auliya. The saint's residence, Chilla Nizamuddin Auliya, lies north-east of Humayun's tomb (Fig. 2.15), adjoining the enclosure wall. The tomb was completed in 1572 at the cost of 15 lakh rupees then. By today's calculations, it would translate to more than 1,500 crores in Indian rupees.

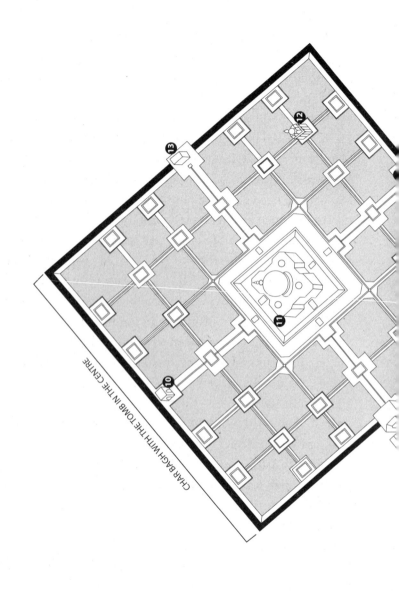

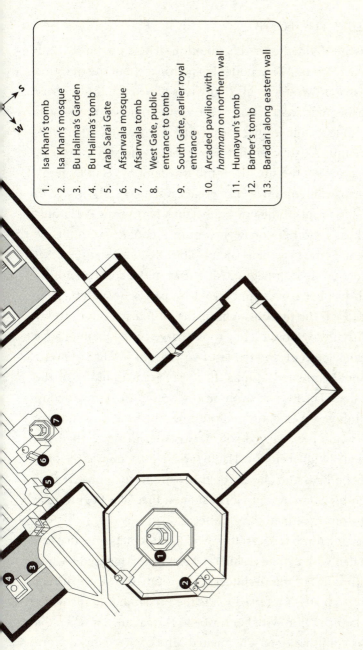

Site map of Humayun's tomb complex.

1. Isa Khan's tomb
2. Isa Khan's mosque
3. Bu Halima's Garden
4. Bu Halima's tomb
5. Arab Sarai Gate
6. Afsarwala mosque
7. Afsarwala tomb
8. West Gate, public entrance to tomb
9. South Gate, earlier royal entrance
10. Arcaded pavilion with *hammam* on northern wall
11. Humayun's tomb
12. Barber's tomb
13. Baradari along eastern wall

WHO BUILT THE TOMB?

Opinions are divided over this question. It was obviously built during the reign of Akbar under his patronage, but the question revolves around which of his two wives played the leading role in overseeing the construction of the tomb. Some say, it was Bega Begum, while the others give the credit to Humayun's other wife, Hamida Banu, Akbar's mother. However, if one were to go by the inscription on the site, the tomb was built by 'Haji Begum'. 'Haji' means someone who has gone on the Haj pilgrimage to Mecca. This means either of Humayun's two wives — Hamida Banu (Akbar's mother) or Bega Begum — could have built the monument. Some historians such as Ebba Koch have argued that the role played by Haji Begum (d. 1582) in the construction of the tomb has been overemphasized by past scholarship. They cite Abu'l Fazl, the principal chronicler of Akbar's reign, to say that Humayun's widow merely took charge of the maintenance of the mausoleum during the last two years of her life.[1] On the other hand, renowned Mughal historian Irfan Habib is of the opinion that Haji Begum's role in overseeing the construction of the tomb gave her status and prestige. She took up residence in Delhi while her beloved son Akbar lived in Agra, then the capital of the Mughal empire. Habib says: 'Humayun was the only husband she had, and she devoted her life to the construction of the tomb.'[2] Some recent works suggest that Haji Begum may have also commissioned the architects.

Humayun's tomb is one of the few buildings of its time that can be associated with named architects. Most historians credit Mirak Mirza Ghiyas as the sole architect of the tomb. It is said that Haji Begum was greatly impressed to see the Persian buildings while on exile in the region with her husband Humayun. So, when the tomb was commissioned, she invited Mirak Mirza Ghiyas from the Persian city of Herat to supervise the construction. On the basis of evidence in contemporary texts, some historians credit both Mirak Mirza Ghiyas and his son Sayyid Muhammad with the architecture of the tomb. Information regarding the architect is provided in two contemporary texts, those by Badauni and Bahauddin Bukhari. Of these, Badauni mentions only Mirak Mirza Ghiyas as the architect. Referring to the other 16th-century text by Bukhari on the other hand, Ebba Koch says that Mirak Mirza Ghiyas and his son Sayyid Muhammad were known architects and poets who had worked for the Timurid court at Herat, for Babur in India, and for the Uzbeg king in Bukhara during Humayun's exile. Once the Mughals came back to power, the son returned to India and was assigned the construction of Humayun's tomb.[3]

REVIVAL OF THE DELHI SULTANATE ARCHITECTURAL STYLE AND HUMAYUN'S TOMB

During his four-year stay (1526–30) in India, Babur laid the foundations of Timurid–Persian scheme of walled-in gardens also known as *chahar bagh* in Persian (*chahar* in Persian means 'four' and *bagh*, 'garden' – four-fold garden) or *char bagh* in Urdu. He built the gardens at Dholpur, Gwalior and Agra. He also built mosques at Sambhal and Panipat. Upon his death, he was temporarily buried in Agra but finally entombed in a beautiful garden on the banks of the Kabul River known as *Bagh-i-Babur* which means, the 'Garden of Babur'. His entombment in Kabul makes clear that the Mughals did not feel quite at home yet in India.[4] Humayun's reign (1530–40; 1555–56), on the other hand, was a turbulent one, a large part of which was spent in exile. His reign is therefore not particularly known for the construction of monuments on any big scale.

The 16th century, however, is known for the revival of the architectural style associated with the early Delhi Sultanate. And,

Humayun's tomb is intimately connected with this revivalist trend. The red sandstone-white marble combination was a favoured architectural scheme ever since it first made an appearance in the Alai Darwaza built by the Delhi sultan Alauddin Khalji in the Qutb Minar complex around 1311. This scheme remained prominent under the Delhi Sultanate until around the construction of Ghiyasuddin Tughlaq's tomb (in the Tuglaqabad Fort) in 1325.[5] This Sultanate style had gone out of fashion in Delhi during the 14th and 15th centuries but had continued uninterrupted in the provincial centres such as Bayana and Kannauj. The early Mughals and Surs looked to Sultanate's architectural heritage for inspiration.[6] Soon the Timurid–Persian style – brought by the Mughals – began to merge with the older Sultanate elements such as red sandstone, inlays of white marble and coloured stones, bud-fringed arches, lotus rosettes, *jaalis* or decorative perforated screens, ribbed domes or domes with lotus and pilasters and indigenous architectural features (popularly seen as a part of the wider Hindu tradition) like *chajja* or sloping stone projections from the top of a building's wall to protect it from the sun and rains, trabeate brackets and *chattris* or umbrella-shaped decorative domed pavilions or kiosks.[7] Manifestations of this revivalist trend could be seen in the Lodi period mosque called Moth ki Masjid, built in c. 1505, in the current neigbourhood of South Extension Part II and in some buildings belonging to or coinciding with the early Mughal and Sur periods such as the mosque of Jamali-Kamali built in c. 1528–29 in the area currently known as the Mehrauli Archaeological Park, the Qila-i-Kuhna Masjid (c. 1534) built in Purana Qila and the tomb of Atgah Khan (c. 1566–67), now in the Nizamuddin Village Area.[8]

Akbar inherited this revived architectural tradition but systematically incorporated other styles. His reign – characterized

Fig. 2.1 Humayun's tomb stands on a high podium.

Fig. 2.2 Architectural features of Humayun's tomb.

Fig. 2.3 *A portion of the char bagh with a pool, also showing an arcaded pavilion on the north wall at the far end.*

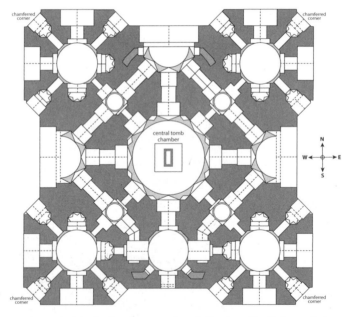

Fig. 2.4 *Hasht Bihistht plan of Humayun's tomb (based on Ebba Koch, Mughal Architecture (revised edition), Delhi, 2014).*

Fig. 2.5 The beautiful ceiling at the entrance of the central tomb chamber.

Fig. 2.6 The white marble cenotaph in the central octagonal tomb chamber.

Fig. 2.7 Tomb stones in one of the smaller octagonal tomb chambers.

Fig. 2.8 Arab Sarai gate.

Fig. 2.9 Arcaded pavilion on the north wall which contained an octagonal tank and a hammam.

Fig. 2.10 The West gate, now the public entrance, seen from inside of the tomb garden.

Fig. 2.11 The South gate, which formed the main entrance during the Mughal era.

Fig. 2.12 Barber's tomb.

Fig. 2.13 *Afsarwala mosque and tomb.*

Fig. 2.14 Isa Khan's tomb is an octagonal one.

Fig. 2.15 Chilla Nizamuddin Auliya, believed to be the popular Sufi saint's residence. Photo courtesy Reyan Sinha.

Fig. 2.16 Neel Gumbad located outside of the eastern wall of Humayun's tomb.

Fig. 2.17 Sabj Burj (Green Dome) now has a blue dome, which was originally green in colour. It's being restored now.

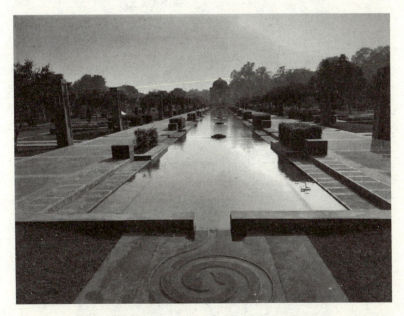

Fig. 2.18 Sundar Nursery, the 16th-century heritage complex, which has been recently restored. Photo courtesy Reyan Sinha.

Fig. 2.19 Dilapidated arched cells of Arab Sarai.

Fig. 2.20 Sher Mandal, Humayun's library in Purana Qila.

by syncretistic incorporation of regions, faiths, cultures – saw the bringing together of architectural elements from Timurid, Iranian, Transoxanian and other regional Indian styles. The clashes in diverse styles were mollified by the unifying effect of the red sandstone as the extensive building material. Red was also the colour reserved for Mughal tents.[9] However, even in the context of intermingling of various styles during Akbar's reign, there was marked preference for the Timurid–Persian kind in particular types of buildings such as mausoleums, *hammams* (baths), pleasure kiosks, caravanserais and smaller mosques. Humayun's tomb also belongs to the genre of buildings inspired primarily by the Timurid–Persian style.

FUNERARY ARCHITECTURE AND HUMAYUN'S TOMB

Humayun's tomb represents the first mausoleum dedicated to a Mughal emperor in India. For that matter, it is one of the first important royal monuments constructed once the Mughals had established their power. Was it meant to reflect the excellence and precision of Timurid–Persian architecture as also the power and glory of the Mughals in India? This tomb is unique in many ways. As art historian Glenn D. Lowry puts it: 'The symbolic qualities of Humayun's tomb reflect [a] bold attempt to create an architecture which grows out of, but is distinct from, earlier Islamic buildings in India and Iran, the two poles of the Mughal world.'[10] He mentions that the tomb's features are so unique that it is impossible to define them in the normal vocabulary of funerary architecture.

Humayun's tomb marks another significant departure in the tomb and funerary architecture in India making them grand and magnificent structures opposed to orthodox Islamic tenets. Tombs have always been a controversial feature in the Islamic tradition.[11]

The *Hadiths* (collection of traditions and sayings of Prophet Muhammad) consider tombs irreligious, heathen and non-Islamic. Praying at tombs is considered polytheism and construction of buildings over tombs is seen as leading to a cult of dead and idolatrous worship. For those in favour of tombs, as long as they were not pompous, structures over burials were seen as a means of providing paradise-like conditions for the dead promised to the faithful in the *Quran*. Such structures gave the protective shade and their heights symbolized proximity to God and paradise. Specific construction plans were symbolic. Thus, four-sided or eight-sided constructions represented the fourth or eighth stages of paradise.[12] The plan of eight paradises first emerged in the palace architecture of north-western Iran under the Turkoman and Timurid rulers of the late 15th century. In the 16th century, this plan was adapted by the Mughals in India.[13]

Domes are always regarded as a symbol of heaven, but large-domed mausoleums were always objectionable in orthodox Islam. Humayun's father and predecessor, Babur, was buried in an orthodox and minimalistic style in an open enclosure in Kabul while Humayun was interned in a large domed mausoleum in Delhi. 'These two extremes set the parameters for the funerary architecture of the Mughals.'[14] Humayun's tomb, 'made a grand imperial statement in Delhi, the old capital of the sultans.'[15] Also from the very beginning, it became a place for a dynastic cult and was regarded as the tomb of a saint. Later emperors paid a pious visit to the mausoleum whenever they came to Delhi and made the ritual circumbulation (*tawaf*).[16]

LAYOUT OF THE TOMB

The main mausoleum – with three Timurid-style arched entrances on each side – is placed on a high quartzite platform (about 6.5 metres high) which contains seventeen arched openings on each side giving access to the burial chamber (Fig. 2.1). The corners of the platform are cut at an angle to meet the corners of the tomb above. A central archway gives access, via steep steps, to the tomb platform. The platform is surrounded by a garden spread over 30 acres. It forms the first of the grand dynastic mausoleums that were to become synonymous with Mughal architecture. It is also here that the monumental scale, so characteristic of Mughal imperial projects, is attained for the first time.[17]

The tomb garden, an expression used to describe the entire complex, is enclosed by 4.6 metres – thick, plastered rubble walls which are 5.8 metres high on the northern, southern and western sides and were built in several stages. On the eastern side was the river Yamuna, which has since moved away from the structure. The centre of the eastern wall has a *baradari* (a recreational pavilion with twelve arches, three on each side) with intricately cusped arches and with a veranda on the eastern front to give a good view of the river. The northern wall has an arcaded pavilion containing an octagonal tank and probably a *hammam* or bath chamber (Fig. 2.9). Behind this pavilion and outside of the enclosure wall is a rubble-built circular well which supplied water to the *hammam* and the channels of the garden. Water was also supplied from a well outside the western wall and from the Yamuna on the eastern side with the help of chutes and channels. The central walkways of the garden terminate at two double-storey gates: a bigger one at the southern wall and the other at the western wall. The West gate is now the public entrance to the tomb garden (Fig. 2.10), while the South gate, once an imperial entrance, remains closed (Fig. 2.11).

Three kinds of stones have been used in the construction of the mausoleum and the walls. The main building is made of pink, red or yellow sandstone with marble panels and a marble-covered dome. The enclosure walls and two gateways have been built from local quartzite with red sandstone and marble inlay. The red sandstone for the main building came from Tantpur near Agra, while the marble came from Makrana in Rajasthan. In those days, construction material and stones were transported either via bullock carts or by boats through the river Yamuna, if they were being brought from Agra.

ARCHITECTURE AND SYMBOLISM

The red-and-white contrast of sandstone and marble, so characteristic of the Delhi Sultanate architectural style, is used very effectively in Humayun's tomb. Plain surface decoration mostly reinforces the tomb's structural form – yellow sandstone spandrels, which are the interspersed triangular area between the rectangular frame around the central arch and its merging upper sides, and white marble panels are used as narrow bands to frame each arch. The building is decorated by lime plaster work and ceramic tiles using geometric and plant patterns as motifs. The decorative six-sided stars – seen in many Islamic buildings as well as in Judaic, Christian and Hindu structures – appear here in the spandrels of the main arches and contain raised marble lotuses in their centre. A *kangura*, which is a merlon or ornamental band, frames the terrace while octagonal pinnaces topped by lotus bloom, also called *guldastas* or flower bunches, project from the outer angular points. The terrace also has pavilions or *chattris* above the imposing entrance and the wings (Fig. 2.2).

Three features of Humayun's tomb deserve special treatment – the paradise tomb garden, the *hasht bihistht* plan, and the true double dome.

The Paradise tomb garden

Gardens always played an important role in the Timurid–Persian scheme of things. Timur's gardens contained encampments decorated with items looted from the nations he captured. His throne was placed over the watercourses, representing the four rivers of life.[18] Gardens were the first architectural expressions of the Mughals when they came to India. They reflected Mughals' love of nature as well as their nomadic life in tents or open pavilions.'[19] Gardens laid by them had strictly planned forms, used uniform architectural elements, fulfilled diverse functions and had strong symbolic connotations. Babur's gardens used the idea of *char bagh* in its widest sense – an architecturally planned garden divided into four quarters by intersecting raised walkways, platforms and pools.[20] By Akbar's time, the idea of tomb garden – a tomb in unison with a garden – had gained ground.

Tomb gardens, including those of Humayun's in Delhi, and later ones like Akbar's in Sikandra, Jahangir's in Lahore, Itmad-ud Daulah's in Agra and Bibi ka Maqbara in Aurangabad, are considered to be the greatest innovations of the Mughals in garden architecture. Symbolically, large square enclosure divided with geometric precision represented the ordered universe. The tomb rose like a cosmic mountain above the four rivers represented by four water channels. Eternal flowers, herbs, fruits, water and birds, such as those found in paradise, added further character to the tomb gardens.[21]

Akbar wanted to set Humayun's tomb within a walled garden with flowing water and trees bearing fruits and flowers. Such a tomb complex would symbolically represent the 'Garden of Paradise' as described in the Holy Quran. The English word 'paradise' in fact comes from the Persian word *pairi daeza* (also called *firdaus*) meaning 'a garden enclosed within a wall.'[22]

The *char bagh* in Humayun's tomb is divided into four parts/ squares by paved walkways (*khiyabans*) and two bisecting central water channels. It has been held that these channels which disappear beneath the mausoleum and reappear on the other side in a straight line, created a visual symbolism of the four rivers – of water, wine, milk and honey – flowing beneath the 'Garden of Paradise' as mentioned in the *Quran* (Fig. 2.3). Each of the four squares of the tomb garden is further divided into smaller squares with walkways, creating thirty-six squares in all. The mausoleum is built on the four squares falling in the centre, one from each of the four quadrants. The walkways are, in turn, underlined by water channels flowing along their centres (See the site map). The points of intersection between the walkways are marked by octagonal or rectangular pools and fountains. They also contain platforms where tents could be pitched for visitors in the past. Fruit/flower-bearing trees like orange, mango, lime, pomegranate, neem, hibiscus and such others were planted in the garden to create paradisiacal symbolism.[23]

The hasht bihistht plan

The crown of the garden is the mausoleum in the centre inspired by the concept of *hasht bihistht*, an allusion to the eight gates of the 'Garden of Paradise'. The eight gates here refer to the eight rooms surrounding the central chamber in the tomb. Ebba Koch underscores that the Mughals derived this concept from their late or post-Timurid tradition. An abbreviated form of the scheme makes its appearance in monuments such as the Sabz Burj and Nila Gumbad (Fig 2.16 and Fig. 2.17) located just outside of the Humayun's tomb; a fuller version in the *khanqah* or hospice of Shaikh Armani in Deh-i Minar, south-west of Herat in late 15th century; and a more complex variety in the *khanqah* of Qasim

Shaikh at Kermin, north-east of Bukhara (1558–59).[24] Unlike the preserved Timurid buildings which employed a strict nine-fold plan more as an exception than a rule, Mughal architecture adopted and further developed the model in a perfect symmetry, and this was faithfully reflected in the elevation.[25] The complete nine-fold plan – as it became current in Mughal architecture – consists of a square or a rectangle, sometimes with corners fortified by towers but more often chamfered or rounded to form an irregular octagon, termed *muthamman baghdadi* by the Mughals. The layout is divided into nine parts by four intersecting construction lines, comprising a chamber at the centre and rectangular open halls in the middle of the sides (Fig. 2.4).[26]

The design of Humayun's tomb appears to have been inspired by the emperor's wooden boat palace, known to us only through its description by Khwandamir (d. 1532), the author of *Humayun Nama*, the biography of Humayun. The floating palace on the Yamuna was made of four two-storey pavilions (*chahar taq*) on boats joined together in such a way that between each of the four (*chahar*), an arch or arched unit (*taq*) was produced. The eight *hasht bihistht* units – Khwandamir uses the synonym *hasht jannat* – formed an octagonal pool between them.[27] Humayun, in his boat palace on the river, simulated a nine-part pavilion, a *hasht bihistht*, leaving the central octagon void rather than covering it with a dome as in actual buildings.[28] A poem at the end of Khwandamir's description, art historian Lisa Golombek informs us, indicates that Humayun was consciously creating such a garden pavilion to indicate paradise: 'And by the union of *char taq*, *hasht bihistht* have appeared there. A reservoir like the *kawthar* (the pool of paradise) has appeared between them.'[29] To complete the picture, Humayun planted several barges with fruit trees, flowering plants and vegetables in this boat palace.[30]

The transformation of Timurid ideas in India marks an important and complex chapter in the history of cultural borrowing. The cemetery in the Islamic tradition was often referred to as *rawda*, a garden – alluding to the paradise garden.[31] Golombek argues that the idea was given its first literal interpretation in Humayun's tomb and the nine-part plan of the pavilion reflected the composition of Heaven itself. Although the plan had acquired a metaphorical meaning in Iran, it became far more explicit in the tombs of Mughal India.[32]

The mausoleum comprises five linked Baghdadi octagons – the one in the centre is taller than the others and contains the main tomb chamber. It is the first example in India of a multi-chambered tomb where the linked chambers are visually independent of each other.[33] The entrance to the central chamber has a beautiful ceiling adorned by coloured plaster designed like the leaves of a palm tree (Fig. 2.5). The central chamber has well-proportioned storeys of arched openings and a notional *mihrab* (niche) on each of the west-facing *jaalis* or latticed screens. The two-storeyed octagonal tomb chamber (Fig. 2.6) is surrounded by smaller octagonal tomb chambers at diagonal points – each housing several tombstones (Fig. 2.7). Humayun's white marble cenotaph lies in the centre of the central chamber and the surrounding floor is decorated in a simple pattern of stars in black and white marble. The four sides of the once-heavily gilded and enamelled chamber are pierced by carved stone *jaalis*, allowing access to light and air. The light coming through the *jaalis* makes interesting patterns on the floor while the breeze kept the chamber cool during the summers. William Finch, an English merchant who visited the tomb in 1611, describes the rich interior furnishing of the central chamber: 'A large room spread with rich carpets, the tomb itself covered with a pure white sheet, a rich *shamiana* [tent] overhead, and in front books on small trestles, besides which stand his [Humayun's] sword, turban and shoes.'[34]

The true double dome

The main chamber is roofed by a double dome which makes its first appearance in the tomb of Sikander Lodi at Lodi Gardens, Delhi. Till around 15th century, most buildings popularly referred to as Indo-Islamic – including the Alai Darwaza in Qutb complex and Ghiyasuddin Tughlaq's tomb in Tughalqabad in Delhi – had half domes that did not curve into a semicircle. Finally, with the Lodi monuments – such as the Bara Gumbad in Lodi Gardens in Delhi – the dome began to assume the shape of a semicircle.[35] The one at Humayun's tomb, however, is the first true double dome. Bulbous in shape, it is mounted on a drum. The double dome has two masonry shells – the outer shell covered by a bulbous marble dome gave it, and the building, an imposing height, while the inner shell kept the ceiling of the central hall in proportion with the interior heights.[36] The lower ceiling of the inner dome also ensured that the sound of the prayers did not get lost. The outer dome is surrounded by rooftop pavilions or *chattris* on the terrace which served as a *madrasa* (college for Islamic instruction) when the tomb was a living monument. Adorned by ornamental brackets, these *chattris* or domed pavilions masked the drum from public view.[37] Blue, green, white and yellow tiles – the kind made in Central Asia – covered the rooftop pavilions as also the walls of the tomb chamber.[38]

The dome is surmounted by a finial as high as a two-storeyed house. The original finial of the tomb was knocked off by a heavy storm in 2014 and was later replaced by an eighteen-foot replica consisting of a sal wood core and eleven copper vessels topped with a brass piece and coated in gold. The restored finial was finally unveiled in 2016.

OTHER MONUMENTS WITHIN THE HUMAYUN TOMB COMPLEX

Constructed during the 16th century, the other monuments now form part of the buffer zone of the World Heritage Site of Humayun's tomb. Each of these structures somewhat reiterates the predominant architectural feature of red-white contrast so characteristic of Humayun's tomb, though the Mughals sometimes used lime plaster mixed with marble dust to mimic the more expensive white marble used at the mausoleum. These monuments also form an integral part of the walk through the tomb complex.

Isa Khan's tomb and mosque

The ticketed walled area leading to a green space has a small enclosure on the right housing Isa Khan's tomb and mosque. Isa Khan was one of Sher Shah's noblemen and had died a few years before Humayun recaptured Delhi. Built in 1547–48, during the reign of Islam Khan, Sher Shah's son, Isa Khan's tomb is octagonal like the tombs of Sher Shah in Sasaram, Bihar, or the Lodis and Sayyids in Delhi (Fig. 2.14). The tomb chamber is surrounded by an arcaded veranda which has battered buttresses or battlements at each corner. The veranda is topped by a stone projection, *chajja* and *kangura* or ornamental bands with pinnacles at angles. The roof contains a squat dome, crowned by a lotus-shaped finial, on a sixteen-sided drum surrounded by eight *chattris*. The mosque located to the west of the tomb has a single prayer chamber divided into three bays. Like the tomb, the mosque is built in grey quartzite faced with red sandstone and the exterior decorated with stucco plaster and glazed tiles.

Bu Halima garden

In the green area, visitors enter the core tomb complex through a garden named after one Bu Halima, a lady of obscure origins. The enclosure walls and gateway of the garden named after her architecturally belong to the 16th century. The garden has a rectangular enclosure with a tomb in its northern half and a gateway with octagonal wings and remains of coloured tiles to the east. The central portion of the eastern gateway contains recessed arches enclosing an arched doorway and a superimposed balcony window supported on four brackets (Fig. 2.8). The garden's enclosure walls have octagonal bastions topped by *chattris* with glazed tilework on the north-east and north-west side. The western wall of this garden was removed in early 20th century to make way for the public entrance to the tomb.[39]

Arab Sarai

The eastern gateway of Bu Halima garden leads to a *sarai* (rest house). It has arched cells, now in a dilapidated condition, and was built around 1560–61 by Haji Begum (Fig. 2.19). According to popular accounts, the structure was built to accommodate 300 Arab reciters of *Quran* she had brought back from her pilgrimage to Mecca. Archaeologist Y. D. Sharma, however, says this structure housed Persian, not Arab, craftsmen and workers engaged in the construction of Humayun's tomb.[40] According to an inscription on the eastern gateway, it was originally an entrance to a *mandi* or market and was built by Mihr Banu, apparently the chief eunuch during the fourth Mughal emperor Jahangir's reign (1605–27). It consisted of arched rooms, now in ruins. The complex now houses the Industrial Training Institute founded soon after India's independence, in 1948. The Institute initially held vocational training classes for people displaced by the partition of the country.[41]

Afsarwala mosque and tomb

Dedicated to some afsar ('officer') – whose identity is not known – both the mosque and tomb are built of local quartzite with red sandstone dressing (Fig. 2.13). The tomb also has marble inlays. One of the marble graves within the octagonal tomb carries the quotations from the Quran and the number 974 (date in the Hijra era corresponding to CE 1566–67) based on which, archaeologists conclude that both buildings may have been built around then. The single prayer chamber of the mosque is divided into three bays and the central bay carries a dome rising over a circular drum and containing a painted circular panel inside. The parapet is furnished with pinnacles. The tomb is octagonal in plan with deeply recessed arches, containing square-headed doorways, on each side and the internal cruciform tomb chamber can be entered through four cardinal directions. The single compartment structure is roofed by a dome rising from an octagonal drum and, as in the case of the mosque, is topped by an inverted lotus and red sandstone finial.

To the south-east of these two buildings, lies another enclosure called Jahangiri Mandi. It was possibly a wholesale market built by Mihr Banu discussed earlier in the segment on Arab Sarai. Towards the western end of this enclosure is a baoli, a water body.[42] Afsarwala mosque and tomb lead to the western gate, the public entrance, of the Humayun's tomb.

Barber's tomb

Located close to the pavilion set on the riverside enclosure is Barber's Tomb. Locally known as 'Nai ka Gumbad', this tomb of red and grey sandstone is a single apartment structure square in plan (Fig. 2.12). It is covered by a double dome rising from a sixteen-sided drum and topped by an inverted lotus finial base. At each corner of the roof terrace, there are chattris containing the remains of original blue, green and yellow tiles. Built around 1590–91, this tomb is probably dedicated to the emperor's favorite barber. The tomb chamber contains two unidentified marble graves inscribed with verses from Quran.

THE TOMB GARDEN AFTER AKBAR

The process of the decline of Humayun's tomb started soon after its construction. With Akbar preferring to rule from Agra, the tomb began to lose its locational importance. The decline of the Mughals in the 17th and 18th centuries further added to the woes of the tomb garden complex, creating severe problems relating to maintenance and upkeep. Scattered evidence from early 18th century points to the tomb complex being inhabited by local people who used the sprawling gardens to grow vegetables near the monument.

The proximity to the Nizamuddin dargah, however, kept alive the sacred importance of the tomb and many later Mughal emperors, princes, princesses and descendants of the royal family were buried within the complex during the 17th to 19th centuries. The mausoleum is said to house the graves of Humayun's wives and Shah Jahan's son and Aurangzeb's brother, Dara Shikoh, besides several later Mughal emperors, including Jahandar Shah, Farrukhsiyar, Rafi ul-Darjat, Rafi ud-Daulat and

Alamgir II. However, in the absence of related inscriptions, it is difficult to identify the individual graves. There are more than 150 graves in Humayun's tomb and in the surrounding garden and the monument is sometimes known as the 'Dormitory of the Mughals' or 'Necropolis of the Mughal dynasty'.

Humayun's tomb came into the limelight during 1857 when the Mughal emperor and the symbolic leader of the rebellion, Bahadur Shah Zafar, sought refuge in the tomb along with his three sons. They were arrested and the three princes were killed by Major William Hodson on the way back to Red Fort while Bahadur Shah Zafar was later tried by British colonial administration and deported to Rangoon, now Yangon, in Myanmar. With the suppression of the rebellion, Delhi came firmly under the control of the British rule. The disintegrating monuments within the tomb garden complex did not receive any attention from the new British rulers till the end of the 19th century. Some changes were, however, made to the complex's landscape to give it an 'English' look. Attempts were made to create English-style lawns around the main tomb. Further, circular beds replaced the four central water pools on the axial pathways and trees were abundantly planted in flower beds.

The descendants of the Mughals apparently remained associated with the tomb garden in some ways even after the 1857 rebellion. Devoid of all royal privileges and entitlements, they mostly survived on alms and were found to be growing vegetables in the tomb garden. The *First Report of the Curator of the Ancient Monuments in India for the year 1881–82* mentions that the main garden with terraced walks and entrance gates had lost much of its original character. It was let out in patches to cultivators for raising municipal funds. The report notes that the cultivators –

until quite recently included descendants of the Kings of Delhi – were growing cabbage and tobacco.[43]

The royal descendants of the Mughals would also entertain foreign tourists visiting Delhi during the latter half of 19th century. They would take such tourists around the tomb garden complex, recount tales of their former glory and have breakfast with them. The southern gate of the tomb has a structure containing a number of rooms. It possibly served as a rest house for tourists and visitors during the late 19th–early 20th-century period.

Lord Curzon, the Viceroy of India between 1899–1905, took great interest in the restoration of the Mughal monuments in Delhi and Agra. He got the original gardens of Humayun's tomb recreated as a part of a restoration project. However, the historic gardens started disintegrating again soon after Lord Curzon left India. He wrote to Lady Curzon: 'The whole place has been allowed to revert. The garden has been let to a native and is now planted with turnips and the whole work of four years is thrown away.'[44]

During the Partition and the communal riots thereafter, Humayun's tomb and Purana Qila became the site for refugee camps. Initially, many Muslim families leaving for Pakistan took shelter in Purana Qila, Humayun's tomb, Nizamuddin Dargah complex, and in the tombs of Chote Khan and Bade Khan in South Extension Part 1. Later, these served as refugee camps for Hindus coming from Pakistan.[45] These camps, which remained in use for almost five years, caused much damage to the principal structure, gardens and water channels. The Archaeological Survey of India (ASI), which later took charge of the site, made repairs to the damages caused by the refugee camps and also undertook small restoration exercises, though not a comprehensive and systematic restoration.

HOW THE TOMB COMPLEX WAS RESTORED IN THE 21ST CENTURY

Humayun's tomb has been in the news in the recent past for renovation and restoration projects, involving for the first time, private firms as well. The first major, privately funded project in the complex was that of the restoration of the garden, accomplished through a partnership between the Archaeological Survey of India (ASI) and the Aga Khan Trust for Culture (AKTC) with the help of the National Culture Fund (NCF). This involved, among other things, restoring the monuments and green spaces; creation of a water circulation system for the walkway channels; planting of trees; and making the fountains functional again. Following the restoration of the garden, a 'public-private partnership agreement' was signed in 2007 to restore the tomb complex. The ASI and the AKTC partnered again, with funding from the Sir Dorabji Tata Trust, and the process was completed in 2013.[46]

How did the restoration of the tomb complex take place? With the idea of restoring the original design of the builders, the craftsmen were asked to remove huge amounts of concrete and cement that had accumulated on the walls, ceilings and floors of many buildings within the garden enclosure on account of 20th-century conservation efforts. The process also involved resetting the sandstone on a large area of the terrace and lifting a good part of the stone plinth buried under 20th-century cement. The stone joints in the dome were also restored to make it watertight.[47]

The craftsmen worked on the surface decoration as well. Lime plaster was applied to the inner surface of the double dome and other tombs on the ground level and design patterns were recreated. Likewise, the tiles on the roof canopies were restored. According to Aga Khan Trust, the underlying idea behind the restoration was to match the standards of Mughal-era craftsmanship while following a craft-based approach to conservation – an approach that could revive these fast-disappearing skills and simultaneously create employment opportunities.[48]

The restoration work provoked sharp debates though not much is currently available by way of systematically published critiques. Some were of the opinion that this is an 'innovative attempt' to restore the important heritage site while others say it amounts to turning the place into 'a caricature of the original tomb'. The AKTC hailed this restoration process as a departure in the history of conservation in India. The restoration was based on the added premise that monuments could be economic assets and their conservation could generate wealth and employment. The process could also act as a catalyst for social change and urban revitalization of the areas including and surrounding the heritage site, such as Sunder Nursery, Batashewala Complex and Nizamuddin Basti. According to the AKTC, the restoration process departed from the 'preserve as found approach' and was executed as 'a model conservation process' in the Indian context – one that combined hi-tech methodology and traditional crafts-based approach.[49]

The Indian History Congress however passed a resolution in its 2015 session, expressing a larger concern over preservation and restoration works being carried out at monuments and archaeological sites by private agencies. In the case of Humayun's tomb, the resolution said: 'Two principles, namely, strict use only of materials that were originally employed in construction and repair, and clear demarcation of the current additions in the name of restoration, have been clearly violated.' Further, '[e]ven colour-schemes appear to have been changed.'[50]

On the other hand, art historian Katharina Weiler underlines 'the need for a critical dialogue with architectural preservation in India as an originally colonial discipline.'[51] According to her, 'the project's aim to revitalize the architectural spirit of Humayun's tomb and original intentions of its builders can be regarded as an innovative attempt. The thoughtful understanding of aspects of authenticity justified a craft-based approach and set a benchmark for the discipline of conservation in the Indian context. Rightly so, inappropriate twentieth-century materials were removed and replaced with traditional materials.'[52] Weiler argues that the 'philosophy behind the conservation of Humayun's Tomb preserved the design and original appearance of the mausoleum rather than conserving its original, authentic material in its deteriorated state.'[53]

While the nature of the restoration process continues to be debated, the tomb has been the site of several interesting developments. In July 2015, UNESCO approved a proposal to include several structures within the complex to the heritage site buffer zone. Further, in 2016, UNESCO added seven more 16th-century garden tombs to the subsequent boundary modification suggested by the AKTC. These include Lakkarwala Burj, Sunder Burj, Sunderwala Mahal, Mirza Muzzafar Hussain's tomb, Chotte Batashewala Mahal, an unknown Mughal tomb and Nila Gumbad. These seven structures had already been included in a conservation project co-funded by the United States Ambassadors Fund for Cultural Preservation (AFCP) following US President Barack Obama's visit to the site in 2010. The year 2017 saw another addition to the profile of Humayun's tomb – India's first sunken museum. Located at the entrance zone of the complex, the museum houses galleries, a library, seminar halls, a crafts centre and a cafeteria. The finial which had fallen off the tomb in 2014 now happens to be the shining star of the museum. And, the recently restored, Sunder Burj and Nursery (Fig. 2.18) is fast becoming Delhi's favourite destination for family outings.

HUMAYUN'S TOMB COMPLEX: KEY INSIGHTS

The 16th century is known for the revival of the architectural style of the Delhi Sultanate, the red sandstone and white marble combination, and Humayun's tomb is intimately connected with this revivalist trend. This style saw its zenith in the Taj Mahal.

Despite opposition to grand and large-domed mausoleums in orthodox Islam, Humayun's tomb was built on a monumental scale. It was therefore also meant to reflect the power and glory of Mughal rule in India.

Humayun's tomb introduced several architectural innovations in the tradition of tomb building in India, including the concept of the paradise tomb garden, *hasht bihistht* plan for the mausoleum and the true double dome. These saw their perfected manifestations in the iconic Taj Mahal in the 17th century.

Although Mughals borrowed from Timurid–Persian cultural heritage, their monuments in India reflect a lot of improvisation. They were more explicit than metaphorical in architectural style and also incorporated regional art traditions.

Sufi saints had an important connection with the monuments and cities during both the Delhi Sultanate and Mughal period, and also influenced their location. The Qutb complex had a connection with the spiritual domain of Bakhtiyar Kaki while the proximity to the *dargah* of Nizamuddin Auliya played a role in the location of Humayun's tomb. Later, Akbar built a new imperial city Fatehpur Sikri, close to the residence of Salim Chishti.

3

THE AGRA FORT

It is a little-known fact that a story around a treasure buried in the strong and mysterious Agra Fort during the 1857 rebellion forms the backdrop to the second Sherlock Holmes novel by Sir Arthur Conan Doyle, *The Sign of Four*. On account of its robust defences, the Agra Fort was always a preferred location for safekeeping of treasures. Following the First Battle of Panipat in 1526, where the Lodis were defeated as rulers of north India, the first Mughal ruler Babur rushed his son Humayun to Agra to take control of the treasures kept inside the fort. During the reign of the third Mughal emperor, Akbar (1556–1605), the Agra Fort became one of the sturdiest fortifications of India and was considered impregnable.

Situated very close to the iconic Taj Mahal, on the right bank of the Yamuna River, the fort is known for its domineering presence over the surrounding riverscape. It remained the seat and symbol of Mughal power before their capital shifted to Delhi around mid-17th century and is the only fort in India that, in some form or other, was inhabited by almost all the early Mughal emperors, from Babur to Aurangzeb. The Agra Fort also marks an important stage in the development of Mughal architecture and the evolution of Mughal palace-forts, polity and ideas of kingship. It was a template for later monuments to follow and this fort's palaces and pavilions heavily inspired the Red Fort in Delhi and buildings in Fatehpur Sikri and Lahore.

> **DID YOU KNOW?**
>
> The Agra Fort underwent at least three major phases of construction: first under the Rajputs and Lodis, second under Mughal emperor Akbar and third under Akbar's grandson and emperor Shah Jahan (see pages 129–30).
>
> Both Akbari Mahal and Jahangiri Mahal were built in the mid-1560s and formed a part of original palace called the Bengali Mahal. The two palaces were separated probably in early 19th century, soon after the British acquired the fort from the Marathas in 1803 (see page 138).
>
> The Hindu practice of rulers showing themselves to their subjects every morning from a window, *jharokha darshan*, became so established under the Mughals that there even emerged a sect of people who would neither eat nor drink without seeing the emperor every morning (see pages 143–44).
>
> Was there a plan to sell the Taj Mahal or did the rumour gain ground on account of the auction of the marble facade and some scattered marble pillars of the *hammam* (bath house) in the Agra Fort by Lord William Bentinck? (see page 148).
>
> By recreating their public audience halls as *Chihil Sutun* or Forty-pillared Halls, were the Mughal emperors claiming the status of ancient kings of Iran, considered exemplary rulers in the Islamic world? (see pages 150–51)
>
> Why are the 'Gates of Somnath', uprooted from the tomb of Mahmud of Ghazni in Afghanistan lying in the Agra Fort? (see pages 154–56)

It is important to remember that the Agra Fort is not a complex built in one era. There were three major phases of construction at the Agra Fort. The first phase of construction is characterized by brick constructions, which took place during the period of Rajputs and Lodis. The second phase was inaugurated by Akbar and his characteristic red sandstone buildings highlighted by white marble. The final phase was seen during the reign of Shah Jahan (1628–58) when many red sandstone buildings were either replaced by white marble or plastered over by white lime to give them a semblance of white marble. The complex took much of its current form during the reign of Shah Jahan. However, the history of the Agra Fort is not just connected with the Mughals – who held sway over the fort between the 16th to early 18th centuries – but also with the Sur Afghans, the Marathas, the Jats, the Durranis and, finally, the British, before the greater part of the complex was handed over to the Indian Army in 1947. Agra Fort was declared a World Heritage Site in 1983.

CIRCUMSTANCES LEADING TO THE CONSTRUCTION OF THE FORT COMPLEX

We have scattered evidence regarding the early history of the fort. However, things become clearer from the time of the Mughals when the fort was rebuilt. A poem written in 1134 CE by Masud ibn Saad Salman, a Persian, mentions that the fort of Agra was captured by Mahmud Shah, the governor of Sindh under Muzaffar Sultan Ibrahim, the ruler of Ghazni. Later, towards the second half of the 15th century, a Rajput king of the name Badal Singh constructed a brick fort at the site and named it Badalgarh. The fort gained prominence when the Afghan sultan of Delhi, Sikandar Lodi (r. 1489–1517) decided to shift his capital from Delhi to Agra. Thereafter, Badalgarh became the residence for the Lodi sultans.

From the Lodis, the fort passed into the hands of the Mughals. After defeating Ibrahim Lodi in the First Battle of Panipat in 1526,

Babur (r. 1526–30), the first Mughal emperor, ordered his son Humayun to rush to Agra and take control of the fort's treasures while he himself camped in Delhi. Soon, Babur reached Agra and made the city his seat of power. He is said to have taken residence in one of the mansions of Ibrahim Lodi located inside the fort. During the next four years, he built some gardens in Agra on the Persian *char bagh* pattern which are four-fold gardens with paved walkways and water bodies. He is also said to have built a *baoli* or stepwell within the fort complex. Babur's son, Humayun (r. 1530–40 and 1555–56) was crowned at the Agra Fort in 1530 but preferred to establish a new city at Delhi called the Dinpanah which denotes 'Refuge of the Faithful'. Following Humayun's successive defeats at Chausa (1539) and Kannauj (1540), the Afghan chieftain, Sher Shah Suri, founder of the Sur dynasty, took control of the Delhi–Agra region. The Surs captured Agra Fort and garrisoned it. An exiled Humayun could recapture his throne only in 1555 with Persian emperor Shah Tahmasp's military support but died soon afterwards. During this time there was almost no new construction at the Agra Fort complex.

With the arrival of Akbar in Agra around 1558, the fortune of the city and the fort underwent a drastic transformation. After staying in Badalgarh for a few years, Akbar decided to rebuild the site as the seat of his government and his court complex for audience to his subjects. The development of the fort under his reign was linked to a larger political, administrative and architectural exercise. Contemporary accounts differ on the time taken to rebuild the fort, but most historians say it took around eight years (1565–73). The construction of forts at Agra and the neighbouring Fatehpur Sikri coincide with the foundation of a slew of fortresses by Akbar across the Mughal empire including Jaunpur (1566), Ajmer (1570), Lahore (before 1580), Attock

Site map of *Agra Fort complex* (based on Ebba Koch, Mughal Architecture, Second edition, Delhi, 2014).

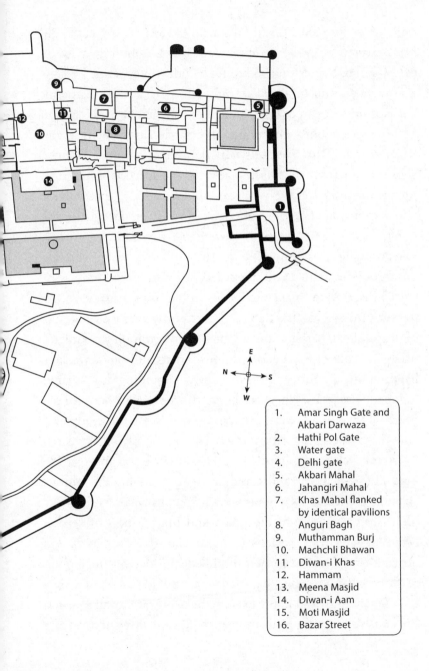

on River Indus (1581), and Allahabad (1583).[1] In Agra, the old brick structures in the complex gave way to buildings with an exterior of red sandstone highlighted with white marble, Akbar's dominant architectural style. Abul Fazl, Akbar's court historian, perhaps provides an exaggerated account when he says that 500 buildings were built within the fort complex in the Bengali and Gujarati styles. However, this remark gives us an important cue about the increase in building activity and imperial interest in Agra as the seat of power. While re-building the fort, the emperor also allocated land on the right bank of the river Yamuna for the nobles' *havelis* or mansions. A new citadel-city came into being. The Portuguese Jesuit missionary Antonio Monserrate, who saw the fort complex in 1580, recorded that besides the emperor's palace there were 'mansions of his nobles, the magazines, the treasury, the arsenal, the stables of the cavalry, the shops and huts of drug-sellers, barbers, and all manner of common workmen.'[2] A large number of imperial servants, artists and other workers lived within the fort complex or the surrounding city. A large number of *karkhanas*, where artists or artificers made goods for the imperial household, were also located within the fort complex.[3]

Akbar's successor, Jahangir (r. 1605–27), regularly visited Agra and even stayed in this fort. However, he was more active in laying gardens in Lahore and Srinagar, including the famous Shalimar Bagh and his reign is known for construction of Akbar's multi-storeyed tomb at Sikandara and the creation of several beautiful riverfront gardens in Agra. The Agra Fort itself was not in focus, it was to be later modified considerably during the reign of Jahangir's son, Shah Jahan. Between 1628 and 1637, Shah Jahan destroyed many existing buildings, renovating some and constructing alongside three mosques and three new marble palace courtyards to suit his architectural taste. Aurangzeb (r. 1658–1707) deposed Shah Jahan, his father, to take control of the fort in 1658 and built two barbicans around the gates and on the riverside to strengthen its defences. When the British captured the fort in 1803, they destroyed many buildings to make way for military structures. The complex now has only around two dozen monuments left, mostly those built by Akbar and Shah Jahan.

DESIGN AND LAYOUT

The fort complex follows an irregular semicircular plan with its chord lying parallel to the river Yamuna. Its eastern side, some 725 metres long, faces the riverbank. Spread over 94 acres (38 hectares) of land, the fort complex is enclosed by a double-battlemented wall of red sandstone punctuated at regular intervals by massive circular bastions (Fig. 3.1). The fort has a circumference of almost 2.5 kilometres; its walls are around 21 metres high; and the complex is surrounded by a broad, deep moat. Most buildings are concentrated in the south-eastern corner of the fort complex in a band-like succession of courtyards along the riverfront. The Yamuna provides a river frontage, a pleasing landscape and fresh air and a constant supply of water.[4] Moving from south to north along the riverfront, there are three courtyards: Anguri Bagh or 'Grape Garden', Machchli Bhawan or 'Fish House' and the Diwan-i Aam or 'Hall of Public Audience'. These three were rebuilt during Shah Jahan's time.

The fort has four gates. Of these, the Delhi gate towards the north and the Amar Singh gate towards the south — now the public entrance to the fort — are the most prominent ones. The other two gates are the Elephant gate or 'Hathi Pol gate' and the Khizri gate, also known as the 'Water gate' because it opens on

Fig. 3.1 *Agra Fort as seen from the public entrance side.*

Fig. 3.2 *The Amar Singh gate.*

Fig. 3.3 The imposing Naubat Khana of the Amar Singh gate.

Fig. 3.4 The ramp leading to the Jahangiri Mahal.

Fig. 3.5 Exterior of the Jahangiri Mahal with Jahangir's bath in the front.

Fig. 3.6 One of the internal rooms in the Jahangiri Mahal.

Fig. 3.7 Central courtyard, Jahangiri Mahal.

Fig. 3.8 Interior of one of the rooms around the central courtyard in the Jahangiri Mahal.

Fig. 3.9 The eastern, river-facing, courtyard of the Jahangiri Mahal.

Fig. 3.10 The white stucco-plastered hall inside the Shahjahani Mahal.

Fig. 3.11 The *Anguri Bagh* complex, as seen from one of the galleries.

Fig. 3.12 The external *dalan* or porch of the *Khas Mahal*, located within the *Anguri Mahal*.

Fig. 3.13 Enclosed internal hall of the Khas Mahal.

Fig. 3.14 Banga-i-Darshan.

Fig. 3.15 From left to right are Jahangiri Mahal, Khas Mahal flanked by bangla pavilions, Muthamman Burj (projecting out) and Diwan-i Khas.

Fig. 3.16 The external dalan in Muthamman Burj.

Fig. 3.17 Shish Mahal with stucco and glass mosaic.

Fig. 3.18 The riverfront terrace in the Machchli Bhawan with the Diwani-i Khas to the right and Hammam to the left.

Fig. 3.19 The marble seat which projects from the southern wing of the Machchli Bhawan courtyard.

Fig. 3.20 Jahangir's black throne on the riverfront terrace in the Machchli Bhawan.

Fig. 3.21 Nagina Masjid is one of the three mosques located within the fort premises.

Fig. 3.22 Arrangement of pillars and arches at the Diwan-i Aam.

Fig. 3.23 Emperor's jharokha or the throne chamber in the Diwan-i Aam.

Fig. 3.24 Moti Masjid flanking one of the arcaded galleries of the Diwan-i Aam.

the eastern riverfront side where the *ghats*, a broad flight of steps leading down to a river, were located.

Historians have pointed out that the regular large-scale residential accommodation was planned only in terms of temporary Mughal camps during Akbar's time. In the Agra Fort, the residential axis was met at an angle by the, now broken, public axis formed by an open bazaar street stretching from the Hathi Pol gate to the Diwan-i Aam courtyard.[5] So this was not entirely symmetrical but the layout of the fort complex was functional to an extent. The overall symmetrical planning of imperial residences became mandatory during Shah Jahan's reign. However, in case of the Agra Fort, Shah Jahan did not alter Akbar's riverfront alignment in his re-building exercise.[6]

The unique design of the fort blended military requirements with aesthetic appeal harmoniously. Before the Strand Road (Yamuna Road) was built in 1837 by the British, the river touched the fort and the *ghats* ornamented with domed pavilions, *chattris* and towers producing a panoramic view. In fact, some covered passages also connected the *ghats* with the harem and the octagonal tower called the Muthamman Burj.[7]

GATES OF THE FORT

Completed around 1568–69, the Delhi gate formed the principal entrance to the fort. It faced the city to which it was connected through a quadrangle. Shah Jahan later reconstructed the area of the entrance when Jami Masjid (also called Jama Masjid), the congregational mosque, was being built outside the fort. It was the first monumental gate of the Mughals and was exquisitely planned. The Delhi gate has the usual strong and towering bastions projecting forward along with battlements and with high merlons on the ramparts.

The Hathi Pol gate formed an inner entrance and originally had a stone elephant with rider on either side of it. Historians say these elephants were probably the replicas of Jaymal and Phatta, the gallant defenders of the Chittorgarh fort annexed by the Mughals.[8] Stone elephants flanking a gate soon became a regular part of Mughal architecture and we see their presence in many later forts. The arched entrance of this gate is flanked on both sides by two-storeyed octagonal towers with battlemented parapets and crowned by a *chhatri* or a small domed pavilion. Built in red sandstone and adorned with white marble, it is profusely decorated and is known for its distinctive *gaja-vyala* brackets which are composite animals with elephant heads. Its ornamented bastions probably served as a *naubatkhana* where ceremonial music was regularly played at fixed times of the day. The *naubatkhana* also announced the movements of the emperor.

The Delhi and Amar Singh gates are architecturally similar: both have a drawbridge, a crooked entrance with dangerous trap points and a steep rise.[9] Amar Singh gate is named after a Rajput chieftain, Rao Amar Singh of Marwar, who assassinated Salabat Khan, an important official of Mughal emperor Shah Jahan in full court in 1644. Amar Singh was killed by Mughal officials present on the scene. Building on the popular belief that Amar Singh had escaped alive by jumping over the ramparts across the moat on a horseback, the British planted a stone torso of a horse on the edge of the moat near the gate originally known as the Akbari gate. They also renamed this entrance as Amar Singh gate (Figs. 3.2 and 3.3) around the mid-19th century.

After ascending the ramp (Fig. 3.4) through the Amar Singh gate, one can see, on the eastern side, two courtyards of Akbar's time: Jahangiri Mahal and Akbari Mahal.

AKBARI MAHAL, JAHANGIRI MAHAL AND SHAHJAHANI MAHAL

Both Akbari Mahal and Jahangiri Mahal were built in the mid-1560s and formed a part of the original Bengali Mahal, which according to the imperial chronicler Abul Fazl, was the newly constructed palace where the emperor seemingly moved in on 11 May 1569. The name 'Bengali Mahal' comes from the use of architectural design borrowed from Bengal as they consist of curved and bent cornices and sloping roofs.[10] Originally, forming parts of a single structure with a homogenous plan, the two palaces were probably separated in early 19th century soon after the British acquired the fort from the Marathas in 1803. Further, the two palaces acquired their respective nomenclatures through guidebooks written in the 19th century. The oldest red-stone palace in the southern part of the fort complex became known as Akbari Mahal and its south-eastern bastion is still known as Bengali Burj. The stone palace in the northern part – where a monolithic granite bowl (7.62 metres in circumference and 1.42 metres in height) built by Akbar's son and successor Jahangir, in 1611, was discovered later – became known as the Jahangiri Mahal.[11] The bowl known as *Hauz-i Jahangiri* or 'Jahangir's bath' now stands in front of the main entrance of Jahangiri Mahal (Fig. 3.5). It was discovered within the fort complex in 1843 and first placed in front of the Diwan-i Aam. Thereafter, it was shifted outside Agra Fort to Company Gardens for a while and finally brought to its current location in 1907.

Jahangiri Mahal and Akbari Mahal form the oldest construction inside the fort along with the six-storeyed *baoli* or step well and the rampart walls. Both Jahangiri Mahal and Akbari Mahal have crooked entrances and enclosing walls to ensure privacy and security. While Akbari Mahal is in a partially preserved state,

Jahangiri Mahal is in reasonably good shape. Akbari Mahal's portico opens in a rectangular courtyard surrounded by large living rooms and a double-storeyed pavilion on the eastern side. Faced with finely carved red sandstone highlighted in white marble – Akbar's characteristic style – the Jahangiri Mahal represents one of the earliest Mughal experimentations in India with complex architectural ideas and is slightly difficult to understand. Absence of any Mughal architectural treatise really handicaps our understanding of the structure and the larger complex. Racy narratives by tourist guides, further complicate the understanding of the architecture and functionality of the structure.

Historians agree that the Jahangiri Mahal represents an amalgamation of various architectural styles and techniques inspired by different geographies and cultures. However, they differ on the exact nature of such influences. Some say it brings together various Transoxanian features – such as the veranda of the east front, facing the river, with its high slender columns (Fig. 3.9) – and the indigenous Gujarat–Malwa–Rajasthan-style courtyard halls. The Mughals picked up the latter, indigenous style, from the early 16th-century architecture of Raja Man Singh of Gwalior who was a nobleman at Akbar's court.[12] Others insist that a complex arrangement of verandas, courtyards, galleries and rooms and halls (Figs. 3.6, 3.7 and 3.8) around a quadrangle reflect the primarily indigenous character of the Mahal. It is argued that the multi-storeyed arrangement of palaces around inner courts reflects the *catuhsala* or four-sided plan of the elevation of the *chowk* or the quadrangle and formed a part of ancient Indian residential architectural tradition.[13] The indigenous component, in such an argument, further manifests in features including the *duchhati* which are double ceilings, one above the other composition with a central, *dalan* (three-sided courtyard); two-storeyed apartments on the sides; a whispering gallery around a hall; and a portal/entrance composition with *jharokha* or balcony windows.[14]

Historians also differ on the architecture of the rooms, halls and ceiling inside the complex. Some feel that most of the rooms are not trabeate — a form of architecture that uses horizontal beams, or lintels, as distinct from the arcuate style, which uses arches and vaults/domes — reflecting the vaulting patterns of the time. These patterns are arches supporting a roof or a ceiling and these get manifested as stucco domes with geometrical patterns and/or arch netting, ribbed domes, lotus domes carved in sandstone, pyramidal vaults with a cut top, coved ceilings which are joined to the wall by concave moulding, etc.[15] Those who contest this stress that the dominant architecture is trabeate, as evidenced by the pillars, beams and lintels, flat ceilings or sometimes *ladao* ceiling consisting of ribs and panels, *chajjas*, sloping projections from the top of the building wall to protect it from the sun and rains, and *chattris*, the domed pavilions.[16] These debates about the nature of the Jahangiri Mahal show the extremely eclectic nature and amalgamation of cultures reached in these monuments.

The striking architectural elements of Jahangiri Mahal include innovative use of Timurid geometric designs, creative adaptations of Indian art forms such as *makara* or crocodile and peacock brackets and various vault designs, and the inclusion of creatures from indigenous art tradition such as the *hamsa* (swan), the parrot and the elephant.[17]

As far as the functionality of the palace is concerned, most scholars hold that it was primarily meant for imperial women and served as Akbar's harem and residence. Historian William G. Klingelhofer's clarification in this context helps us understand the building better. He says that '[a]rchitectural space and design seem to have been a flexible commodity in early Mughal building, adaptable to many and diverse purposes.'[18] It is therefore not really important to understand the exact function of each space or for that matter which rooms were provided for the palace harem, the library, temple and audiences. The palace, he elaborates, served a much broader purpose; it 'was constructed at the conceptual centre of a larger Agra scheme and was intended to serve as the primary architectural embodiment of the imperial seat.'[19]

Between the red sandstone Jahangiri Mahal and the white marble Khas Mahal or the 'Special Palace' lies another structure called Shahjahani Mahal, though there is not enough evidence to back the claim it was built by Shah Jahan. It has a hall, side rooms and an octagonal riverside pavilion. The brick mason and red sandstone construction was plastered in white stucco (Fig. 3.10), to give it a semblance of marble, and painted in colourful floral designs. The so-called Somnath gate, discussed in detail later, is a part of one of the rooms on the western side. The subterranean three-storeyed chambers below Jahangiri Mahal and the area lying to the north contain the *phansighar* or gallows and the *baoli* or step well attributed to Babur.

ANGURI BAGH COMPLEX

Rebuilt on an earlier structure by Shah Jahan, the Anguri Bagh (Fig. 3.11) complex is a three-layered architectural zone set in the harem complex: the upper riverfront terrace is occupied by the Khas Mahal flanked by two identical oblong pavilions; the intermediate layer carries a scalloped, trefoiled tank, an ornamental design resembling a three-lobed clover leaf and the lower zone has, what is known as the 'grape garden', the Anguri Bagh (visitors can still see a grapevine on its lawns).

Khas Mahal

The Khas Mahal is built along the lines of a favourite Mughal pavilion theme: the combination of an enclosed inner hall called *tanabi khana* or *tambi khana* and an outer pillared porch or veranda referred to as the *iwan*.[20] The term *iwan*, as we shall see in the chapter on Fatehpur Sikri, was also used to describe a single vaulted hall with a monumental arched niche set in a rectangular frame, the *pishtaq*. Shah Jahan's court historian Lahauri calls it Aramgah which means the 'emperor's resting chambers'. The spacious inner hall (Fig. 3.13) has beautiful marble screens with glasswork facing the river Yamuna while the remaining white marble surface is beautifully painted in floral and stylized patterns. It also has a number of oblong niches in its wall meant possibly to hold portraits of emperors and princes. The outer porch/veranda (Fig. 3.12) is three-aisles deep and made up of five nine-cusped arches supported on square piers. These multi-cusped arches are popularly known as the Shahjahani arches. It has a sloping stone *chajja*, supported by beautifully carved and moulded brackets, projecting from all sides. The *chajja* protected the building from the sun and rains. Currently, there are two *chattris* or small domed pavilions on the parapet on the riverside but not on the Anguri Bagh side. The marble building is secured on the north and south by thin marble curtains (*sarapada*) to ensure *purdah*, or seclusion for women of imperial household.

Bangla-i-Darshan and Bangla of Jahanara

The Khas Mahal is flanked by two identical rectangular buildings gilded in gold with copper sheets and carrying *bangladar/bangla* roofs (a curved circular roof) and a *chajja*. On the north, is the Bangla-i-Darshan or the 'Imperial Viewing Pavilion' and, on the south lies the Bangla of Jahanara, a pavilion named after Shah Jahan's eldest daughter, Jahanara. Popularly known as Begum sahib, she was declared the chief of the harem in 1631 after the death of Shah Jahan's favorite wife, Mumtaz Mahal, for whom Taj Mahal was built, and Jahanara was also entrusted with the imperial seal which formalized all *farmans* or royal orders.[21] Bangladar was an architectural device originally used in buildings in the Bengal region. After Akbar annexed the Gaur kingdom, many Bengali craftsmen dispersed to other regions, and some naturally sought patronage at the Mughal court.[22] Both these pavilions were originally made in red sandstone but stuccoed with white shell-plaster later to give them the semblance of white marble. There are square rooms towards the sides of the *bangladar* pavilions. The combination of east Indian style of architecture in Mughal monuments forms a unique experience for the visitors here.

The Bangla-i-Darshan (Fig. 3.14), also known as the 'Bangla of Roshanara', after the second daughter of Shah Jahan and Mumtaz Mahal, has pillar brackets and lintel openings. Here, the emperor Shah Jahan made an appearance every morning to his subjects gathered below the fort. The Mughals had borrowed this practice called the *jharokha darshan* from the Hindu kings. 'Jharokha' means a window/balcony and 'darshan', glimpse or view – therefore glimpse from the window/balcony. It is popularly held that *jharokha darshan* originated from a Hindu religious practice of having a glimpse of a god or goddess from a window where s/he appeared every morning for her/his devotees and common people. This practice, which invested royalty with divinity or exalted its status, was picked up by the Hindu kings and, from them, by the Mughals. Akbar was the first Mughal ruler to systematically adopt this practice. He used wood and canvas structures rather than stone and mortar buildings to appear before his subjects every morning, while in the capital.

When he was travelling, *jharokha darshan* would be organized in the imperial tents through dedicated awnings. Gradually, the practice became an integral part of the Mughal kingship and daily court life; it became a medium of transference of divine blessing.[23] The practice became institutionalized and there even emerged a sect called Darshaniyas, during Akbar's time, who believed in the divine powers of the king; and these followers would not eat or drink without seeing the emperor every morning. Later, dedicated windows/balconies were constructed in some buildings in the Agra Fort and in Delhi's Red Fort to institute *jharokha darshan*.

Scholars point out that the Bangla of Jahanara, with its multi-cusped Shahjahani arches, had no specific ceremonial function but indicated her status at the court and provided imperial symmetry to architecture. It formed a part of Jahanara's apartments located towards the end of the southern wing. The three courtyard wings and northern rooms of Jahangiri Mahal were adapted for her and other women. It was here in April 1644 that Jahanara's delicate muslin garment caught fire and she was badly burnt. Shah Jahan was so upset with the incident that he did not attend the court for many days.[24]

Anguri Bagh

The Anguri Bagh happens to be the only garden in the main palace complex. Divided by marble walkways which intersect at the centre in a marble pool, it is laid out in the form of a rectangular *char bagh*. We have discussed the evolution of this concept of the four-fold garden in the chapter on Humayun's tomb and will also explore this for Taj Mahal. Each quarter of the garden has geometrically drawn flower/plant beds. The garden is enclosed by two-storeyed living apartments formed of a modular sequence of open, pillared verandas and small enclosed rooms called *hujras*.

The water devices at Anguri Bagh – tanks, fountains, waterfalls, candle niches and water channels – demonstrate how running and splashing water had become an integral part of the Shahjahani architecture. Akbar, on the other hand, was more fond of *hammams* (bathhouses). Water was supplied to the fort through well laid-out water systems from the Khizri gate and the overhead tanks in the Jahangiri Mahal complex.[25]

MUTHAMMAN BURJ AND SHISH MAHAL

Located between the Anguri Bagh and Machchli Bhawan is a spacious octagonal tower called the Muthamman Burj or octagonal tower ('muthamman', means octagonal) or Shah Burj or imperial tower. This housed the original balcony from where Akbar and Jahangir appeared before the people for *jharokha darshan* every morning. Some paintings show that the emperors used the *jharokha* to also watch elephant fights on the banks of Yamuna.

The battlement of this Burj was also where Jahangir is said to have fastened his famous 'chain of justice' (*zanjir-i-adl*) – a 24.6 metres long and 100-kilogram gold chain with sixty bells – in 1605, to redress the grievances of the people who had been delayed or denied justice. In principle, this implied that the aggrieved could apply directly to the highest judicial authority. William Hawkins, the representative of the British East India Company who visited Agra in 1608 to secure permission from Jahangir to trade from Mughal ports, records seeing the chain, which is also depicted in the contemporary Mughal paintings.

The original tower was rebuilt by Shah Jahan in white marble, profusely inlaid with delicate pietra dura – marble inlaid with precious and semi-precious stones – on both the exterior and interior and roofed with a gilded copper dome. Five sides of the tower project outwards towards the river and are rotated by a *chajja* supported by brackets (Fig. 3.15). Inlaid pillars and a railing/ balustrade with *jaali* or perforated screen decorate this structure which offers a panoramic view of the Taj Mahal at a distance. On the western inner side, the tower leads to a veranda, a hall or *dalan* (Fig. 3.16) with a three-arched opening. The hall has a shallow water basin sunk in the centre with scented fountain. Its walls carry deep ornamental niches along with dados (bas-relief on lower section) inlaid in polychrome or stones with several colours and carved plants. This was the place where the emperor met his highest dignitaries and his sons in secret council and also worked with the court historians Qazwini and Lahauri on editing the official history of his reign.[26] Later, Shah Jahan was confined in this tower by his son Aurangzeb. It was here that Shah Jahan died in 1666 in the company of Jahanara and some other royal ladies in full view of the Taj Mahal, the mausoleum of his beloved wife. His coffin was taken out of the door at the base of the tower and then transported on a boat over the Yamuna to the Taj where he was eventually buried. Later, the building lost some of its original inlaid precious stones during the attacks by Jats of the neighbouring regions during 1761–64.

To the west of the Muthamman Burj is the entrance to a group of basement rooms with waterfalls and pools called the Shish Mahal or the 'Mirror Palace' because the facade has mirror mosaic set in white stucco, a plaster used for covering walls and ceilings for decorative purposes (Fig. 3.17). This glass-art technique was locally known as *ayina bandi* or *ayina kari*. The structure, now closed to the public, has extra thick walls and ceilings to ensure coolness and, a dim interior to allow for the play of light and mirrors. The art of glass mosaic was originally Byzantine and spread with Islam to other parts. The Mughals Indianized the technique by associating it with exquisite relief and incised stucco work, something lacking in the Byzantine style. Further, unlike the saintly figures and florals featuring in Byzantine glass art, the Mughals used Persian motifs and floral and stylized patterns for mural decoration.[27] The reflection of flowing water and light coming from candles on the glass produced a magnificent colourful effect within the Shish Mahal and gave it a romantic appeal.

MACHCHLI BHAWAN COMPLEX

The Machchli Bhawan or 'Fish Palace' complex, lying north of the Anguri Bagh, contains the 'Hall of Private Audience', earlier known as the *ghusl khana*, or bathhouse but later became popular as the Diwan-i Khas, and the *hammam*, both of which are built on the riverside terrace (Fig. 3.18), also called the 'throne terrace'. Below, on the ground floor, lies a quadrangular courtyard surrounded by a double-storeyed structure with arched galleries. It is held that this complex once housed marble tanks and fountains in which gold and silver fish were kept for the amusement of the emperor, hence the name 'Fish Palace'.

Diwan-i Khas

The Diwan-i Khas, occupying the south-eastern corner of the complex, is a large marble pavilion meant for meetings of the private council, exclusive law court, musical performances or inspection of the work of artists employed by Shah Jahan. According to Lahauri, it was built in 1635, around the same time when other buildings of the harem were being completed. Its exterior is protected by a broad *chajja*, a sloping stone projection from the top, supported by brackets. The *chattris*, pinnacles and *kanguras* (merlons or ornamental bands) that once adorned the building are now missing. Like the Khas Mahal, the Diwan-i Khas also has two halls with coved ceilings, both connected with a three-arched opening – the enclosed inner hall or *tanabi khana* and the outer *iwan* or *dalan* or veranda. The outer hall, having double pillars, is beautifully inlaid with floral designs and dados or carvings in the lower part of the wall, similar to that of the Taj Mahal, and multifoiled niches. Lahauri describes the oblong inner hall as being ornamented with paintings and floral designs and adorned in gold.

Hammam

Opposite the Diwan-i Khas, on the northern side of the riverfront terrace, lies the *hammam* rebuilt and refashioned by Shah Jahan. Consisting of various rooms and halls, the structure was decorated among other things by inlay work on the dados or bas relief on the lower section and glass mosaic on the walls and arches. It had provisions for both cold water, the *sard khanah* and warm water, the *garm khanah*. The structure now lies in a ruined state and is closed to the public. Parts of the *hammam* were taken down by Governor General Lord Hastings in 1815 and its pillars were scattered. Some parts of the marble facing of the structure and some marble pillars were later sold at an auction by Lord William Bentinck, Governor General of India from 1828 to 1835, giving rise to the rumour that he also wanted to take down and sell the Taj Mahal.[28] Two of the marble pillars of the *hammam* can still be seen in the Taj Museum.

Throne terrace

The area contains two thrones – one in black stone and the other in white marble – lying between the Diwan-i Khas and the *hammam*. Jahangir's finely carved monolithic black touchstone throne overlooks the Yamuna (Fig. 3.20). Prince Jahangir had rebelled against emperor Akbar and had set up his imperial seat at the Allahabad fort. Later in 1610, once he became the emperor, he brought his black imperial throne from Allahabad and installed it on the terrace of the Diwan-i Khas in the Agra Fort. The crack in the black throne is attributed to the attacks by the Jats of Bharatpur, who later controlled the fort temporarily sometime around 1765. Opposite the black throne and overlooking the ground floor courtyard lies a white marble throne resting on a marble platform. Lahauri says this was occupied by emperor Shah Jahan particularly during summer evenings.

The ground-level courtyard

The courtyard is enclosed by two-storey-high, flat-roofed arcaded wings with Shahjahani columns and multi-cusped arches. Originally the entire structure was covered with shining white lime plaster, traces of which could still be seen in the columns. Behind the arcaded galleries lay the vaulted rooms housing government offices, including the treasury. The open court in the centre was used by the emperor to inspect his hunting animals – hounds, hawks, cheetahs and horses. It also formed the site of animal fights held for the entertainment of the emperor. A marble seat with a baldachin or canopy projects from the centre of the southern wing of the courtyard (Fig. 3.19). It is decorated by baluster columns (a tapering column with a bulb like base and capital formed of leaves) and semicircular arches with a rich, naturalistic acanthus decoration – a flower spike and spiny leaf-like design inspired by European engravings or Corinthian column capitals – first used exclusively in the architecture framing the appearances of emperor Shah Jahan.[29]

DIWAN-I AAM COMPLEX

Located further north of the Machchli Bhawan is a spacious court known as the Diwan-i Aam. Lahauri points out that a cloth tent and, later, a wooden hall served the purposes of the 'Hall of

Public Audience' before the present structure came into being under Shah Jahan.

The main audience hall is a rectangular, pillared building standing on a red sandstone plinth. It has four rows of pillars and pilasters on the north–south axis and ten along the east–west alignment. The hall has double columns on all the three external sides, similar to the Chaunsath Khamba near Hazrat Nizamuddin in Delhi, though this is square in shape. Resting on square bases, these pillars were once carved or stuccoed and the outlines of the bases, shafts, capitals and cusps were gilded. The pillars support engrailed or nine-cusped Shahjahani arches (Fig. 3.22). The emperor's *jharokha*, or throne chamber (Fig. 3.23), projects from the eastern wall of the hall. Its walls, pillars and even the ceiling have stylized floral designs in pietra dura inlay, which is characteristic of Shahjahani architecture. It is held that the naturalistic plant decoration symbolically represented the bloom brought about by the just rule of Shah Jahan.[30] The *jharokha* walls have *china khana* niches – possibly used to keep porcelain vessels – which, according to the contemporary poet Kalim, was China's tribute to the court of Shah Jahan. The hall has a flat roof and its exterior is protected by *chajjas* in turn supported by brackets. While the hall is made of red sandstone, it is plastered in white lime to give the effect of marble. The courtyard of the Diwan-i Aam is surrounded by narrow galleries or verandas with multi-cusped arches. All courtiers and honoured visitors who assembled in the Diwan-i Aam 'would stand deferentially with crossed arms in hierarchically arranged semicircles [separated by railings] centred on his throne, moving outward from highest to lowest'.[31]

On account of its forty-pillar site, the Diwan-i Aam was also known as *Chihil Sutun* or 'Forty-pillared' – the name by which the ruins of Persepolis, in present-day Iran, was referred to earlier.

By recreating the famous audience halls of the ancient kings of Iran, the Mughal emperor claimed the status of exemplary rulers in the Islamic world. However, unlike the original Iranian halls, the Mughal halls followed the plan of a mosque – the closest parallel could be the Pathar Masjid in Srinagar – with a wider aisle in the centre. While in the mosque, the central aisle leads to the *mihrab* or the niche that shows the direction of Mecca, in the case of the Diwan-i Aam, it leads to the emperor's *jharokha*.[32] The idea that Shah Jahan's authority was not only worldly but also spiritual was further reinforced by the presence of a mosque right opposite the audience hall at the centre of the west wing.[33] Some scholars have put forward a somewhat similar concept albeit rooted in Indian thought and philosophy – the forty-pillar site of the Diwan-i Aam was made up of twenty-seven bays which represented the twenty-seven *nakshatras* or constellations. The hall itself denoted the incarnation of the *jagat* (universe) presided by the emperor sitting like the sun.[34] The audience hall of the Agra Fort served as a prototype for development of palaces or buildings at Lahore and the Shahjahanabad fort in Delhi.

MOSQUES

Scholars are divided on whether Akbar built a mosque within the fort premises. Three mosques, built by Shah Jahan, still survive. The Shahjahani mosques are of two main architectural types and both these styles employed had already started becoming distinct earlier during Jahangir's time.[35] To the first category, belong the great city mosques, such as the Jami Masjid of Agra built by Jahanara in 1648. These have prayer halls with *pishtaqs*, which are imposing entrances set in a rectangular frame, surmounted by three or five domes and courtyards surrounded by continuous arcaded galleries with axial gates. To the second category, belong the smaller mosques, mostly with a direct imperial connection. These mosques have an additive system of vaulted bays – they may have flat or concaving coved ceilings, domes or even high *bangla* vaults – and could appear without *pishtaqs* and outer domes. Also, unlike the first category, they do not have minarets – for example, the Moti Masjid ('Pearl Mosque', 1647–53) (Fig. 3.24), the Mina Masjid ('Gem Mosque', completed in 1637, this was Shah Jahan's private mosque) and the Nagina Masjid ('Jewel Mosque') – and were smaller and exquisite for more private use. The Nagina Masjid (Fig. 3.16) is covered by *bangla* vaults and *chajjas* or stone projections which, according to art historian Koch, forms the first instance of such a motif appearing in a Mughal mosque.[36]

Many narratives also mention the existence of a Zanana Mina Bazar, a women's handicraft market, since the time of emperor Akbar. It was a place where royal ladies as well as the wives and daughters of the nobles sold and bought goods like gems, jewellery, embroidered cloths and other luxurious items particularly during the Nauroz, the Persian New Year celebrations. Some historians say this bazaar was held in the Machchli Bhawan complex. It is said that Jahangir met Mehrunissa who later became famous as his queen Nur Jahan, and Shah Jahan, his love Arjumand Banu Begum who later became famous as his queen Mumtaz Mahal, at the Mina Bazar.

AGRA FORT AFTER SHAH JAHAN

During Akbar's reign, the Agra Fort was one of the strongest and most defensible structures of its time. Abul Fazl eulogized the defence potential of the fort saying that even a hair could not pass through the joints on the walls. Even rebellions by his son Jahangir in 1599 and grandson Shah Jahan in 1622 failed to break through its defences. The complex continued to remain Shah Jahan's imperial residence even after he shifted his capital to Delhi in 1638. Shah Jahan's son Aurangzeb tried to capture the fort with the help of military power and guns, but in vain. He finally succeeded in breaking the fort's defences by cutting the water supply through the Khizri gate side. A desperate Shah Jahan wrote:

> ...Only yesterday, I was the master of nine hundred thousand troopers and today I am in need of a pitcher of water...[37]

The emperor Shah Jahan finally surrendered in 1658 and spent the rest of his life confined in the fort. Agra began to lose much of its imperial charm after Shah Jahan's death in 1666, even though Aurangzeb continued to hold court at the fort. In 1666, during Aurangzeb's reign, the Maratha king Shivaji visited Agra and met the Mughal emperor in the Diwan-i Khas. Aurangzeb's death in 1707 weakened both Mughal power and its imperial stronghold and the empire started disintegrating fast. The history of the Agra Fort, for most of the 18th century, remains a story of multiple sieges and pillage, and it changed hands many times, including the occupation of the Jats and the Marathas. The Marathas gained control of the area south of Delhi after defeating the Mughals around the mid-18th century. After the Maratha loss to the Afghan and Rohilla forces led by Ahmad Shah Durrani in the Third Battle of Panipat in 1761, the fort came under the control of the Durranis. The Marathas were however able to regain control in 1785 under the reign of Mahadji Sindhia. John Hessing was a mercenary Dutch officer under General Perron who retook Agra for the Sindhia. He was the commander of the fort from 1799 to 1803 when the Marathas lost the city and the fort again to the British during the Second Anglo-Maratha War of 1803. Colluding with European officers working in the Maratha garrison, Lord

Lake was able to breach the fort from the south-eastern side of the Bengali Burj. Hessing's tomb, also known as the 'Red Taj Mahal' now lies in the Roman Catholic Cemetery in the Padri Tola. With the establishment of the British military garrison at the fort, many Mughal structures were pulled down to construct residential quarters, barracks, stores and so on. The grand courtyard of the Diwan-i Aam, for example, was converted into an arsenal, and many buildings and pavilions were whitewashed and subdivided with mud partitions for the private use of officers. The Uprising of 1857 did not impact Agra so seriously though there were cases of plunder and 'army indiscipline'. The Diwan-i Aam courtyard has a European-style tomb of John Calvin who was the lieutenant-governor of the North-West Provinces at the time of the Uprising and had taken refuge in the Anguri Bagh complex alongside other members of the Christian community.

The fort came under some conservation efforts towards the late 19th century with the involvement of the Public Works Department. Lord Curzon's restoration campaign at the beginning of the 20th century saw many military structures being removed from the premises. Independence, however, brought the military back to the Agra Fort, and a large part of the complex, including the Khizri and Hathi Pol gates, the 'Mina Bazaar' and the Moti Masjid, remains under the control of the Indian Army and is inaccessible to the public. In recent decades, there has been a growing demand from archaeologists, historians, conservationists and heritage enthusiasts that the army should vacate the premises.

HOW 'SOMNATH GATE' LANDED UP IN THE AGRA FORT

The Ghazni gate popularly known as the 'Somnath gate', is now kept in a glass enclosure in the Shahjahani Palace but is not related to the fort or the Mughals in any way. Despite a plaque by the Archaeological Survey of India clearly mentioning the history of the gate to the contrary, some guides still tell you how these gates once belonged to Somnath, a famous Hindu temple in Gujarat.

How and when did these gates turn up in Agra Fort? The answer to this lies in the events surrounding the famous 'Proclamation of the Gates' issued by Lord Ellenborough, the Governor General of India, in 1842.[38] He was appointed to this position amid the First British–Afghan War. In the Proclamation, Lord Ellenborough ordered General Knott, the commander of the British army in Afghanistan, to return to India, and, if he was to return via Ghazni, he was asked to bring back the sandalwood gates installed at the mausoleum of Mahmud of Ghazni. Apparently, Lord Ellenborough had heard that Mahmud of Ghazni, during his plundering campaigns in India around CE 1024–25, had carried away the sandalwood gates from Somnath. Further, these gates had been placed at the tomb of his mausoleum at Ghazni. How and from where he obtained this information is unclear. None of the Turko-Persian sources, which formed the dominant sources of information for Muslim rule in India, mentioned this story. John Wilson, who was later tasked with the investigation of the story of the gates, wrote in late 19th century, that the idea probably originated with some travellers who may have mentioned it to Mountstuart Elphinstone, historian, East India Company civil servant and respected public affairs specialist who had served as the first British envoy to the court of Kabul in the beginning of the 19th century. So, the story, in all probability, was an invention of the folk tradition, a hearsay or a myth.

But Lord Ellenborough's proclamation created an uproar in the House of Commons in England. Questions were raised if he was appeasing the Hindus or catering to national sympathies. Ellenborough's defenders quoted a letter from Ranjit Singh, the ruler of the Punjab, to Shah Shujah, the king of Afghanistan, demanding the return of the Somnath gates from Mahmud's tomb. On subsequent examination, it was clarified, that Ranjit Singh had confused the Somnath temple with the Juggernaut/Jagannatha temple in Puri, Orissa (Odisha).

In any case, the gates were uprooted from Mahmud's tomb at Ghazni and brought to India by General Nott. Lord Ellenborough even made a speech on the occasion which was addressed to the Chiefs and Princes of northern and western India. He proclaimed that he had brought back the sandalwood gates taken away by Mahmud of Ghazni from the Somnath temple. A historical insult, he claimed, had been avenged after 800 years. The incident was projected as one which addressed a long-standing Hindu trauma, reversed the memory of Indian subjugation to Afghanistan in pre-colonial times and also fulfilled Ranjit Singh's demand. In practical terms, it also showed the British in control of Afghanistan despite reverses in the Anglo-Afghan wars.

However, it was soon discovered that the gates – made of deodar wood and carrying Islamic motifs – actually belonged to the tomb of Mahmud of Ghazni, a fact corroborated by the Arabic inscription on the structure. The incident caused a huge embarrassment to the British government and the gates were left abandoned in Agra Fort. And, they have been lying there ever since.

AGRA FORT IN THE HISTORY OF SOUTH ASIA: KEY INSIGHTS

The Agra Fort was one of the strongest and most defensible structures of its times and it remained the seat of power for all early Mughal kings, except Humayun. It was difficult to capture the fort with the help of military power and guns. Mughal prince Aurangzeb succeeded in breaking its defences only by cutting off its water supply (1658).

Despite what the guides tell you about functions of various rooms within the Jahangiri Mahal, it is important to remember that space and design was a flexible commodity in early Mughal building, and they could be adapted to many and diverse purposes.

Red sandstone highlighted with white marble was Mughal emperor Akbar's preferred architectural style and also reflected his keenness to build an inclusive empire. The use of red sandstone as the primary building material also served to unify the different architectural styles and techniques inspired by different geographies and cultures. One can see this very clearly in the chapter on Fatehpur Sikri.

The architectural depiction of a stone elephant with rider on either side of the entrance to Mughal forts is probably inspired by the story of Jaymal and Phatta, the gallant defenders of the Chittorgarh fort annexed by the Mughals.

The art of glass mosaic was originally Byzantine and spread with Islam to other parts. The Mughals Indianized the technique by associating it with exquisite Persian motifs and incised stucco work. This is seen in the structure called Shish Mahal or 'Mirror Palace' in the prominent Mughal forts.

4

FATEHPUR SIKRI

Looking at the buildings of Fatehpur Sikri, in 1854, long after the city had passed its prime as an imperial capital, Robert Minturn, an American tourist, wrote that he felt like 'the king and his court had gone forth to hunt, and would return by evening to their homes.'[1] Most visitors to this abandoned enclosed city get the same feeling even today when they look at the palace complex during their explorations of Fatehpur Sikri. Such is the charm of this once-iconic capital of the Mughals and the mystique surrounding it that it produces at once a sense of magnificence and melancholy. Why were these majestic buildings and this imperial city abandoned within just thirteen to fourteen years of their construction? This question perplexes everyone who visits Fatehpur Sikri.

Located approximately 45 kilometres from Agra, and about 30 kilometres from Bharatpur, the heartland of the Jats, is one of the finest cities of medieval India (Fig. 4.1), Fatehpur Sikri, which is at times also referred to as Fathpur Sikri or just Sikri. Despite its huge historical significance as the capital of the Mughal emperor Akbar during 1571–85, this architectural marvel has always lived in the shadow of its world-famous neighbour, the Taj Mahal and has often been clothed in layers of legend, mystique and folklore. Fatehpur Sikri was a big city with different kinds of structures – palaces, mosques, hospices, mansions, offices and

DID YOU KNOW?

Visitors can access the important monuments of Fatehpur Sikri either through the imperial palace complex (as most tourists do), which centers around Mughal emperor Akbar who found this city, or through the mosque-shrine/masjid-dargah complex, which relates to the charismatic Sufi saint Salim Chishti, whose presence determined the location of the city.

The buildings of Fatehpur Sikri were dominantly influenced by the Gujarati style of architecture, which in turn synthesized pre-Islamic Hindu and Jaina building traditions (see pages 167–68).

Did you know that the planning of Fatehpur Sikri also draws inspiration from a Mughal tent, which was like a mobile mini city? (see pages 168–69).

The city's important buildings are located on a set of three receding plateau levels of a ridge and follow a hierarchical plan (see page 169).

The original ceremonial entrance to imperial complex was not through the Hall of Public Audience as it is now but through the Hathi Pol/ 'Elephant gate' (see page 170). One can access the Hathi Pol while still inside the imperial complex.

Buildings in the imperial complex popularly known as the 'Turkish Sultana's Palace', 'Girl's School', 'Hospital', 'Birbal's Palace', or 'Jodha Bai's kitchen' served altogether different functions (see pages 175–80).

Do you know that the name of Rajput queen Jodha Bai, after whom the principal harem complex is named, does not figure in any contemporary historical sources? (see page 180)

Was it the curse of a dancer and the resultant shortage of water that accounted for the decline of Fatehpur Sikri? (see page 188–89).

bureaucratic establishments, workshops, recreational pavilions, *hammams* (public baths), waterworks, gardens, bazars and markets, fortifications, walls and gateways. Most tourists visiting the site focus primarily on the two different kinds of buildings – the imperial complex, consisting of the royal and other related buildings, and the mosque-shrine complex (also known as the masjid-dargah complex) housing the religious and semi-religious buildings. The entire city was planned around these two complexes. Sikri was declared a UNESCO World Heritage Site in 1986.

Unlike other monuments we have discussed so far, there are some problems in exactly identifying several individual buildings in Sikri. Sometimes, scholars refer to the same building by different names and attributes. The nomenclature and functionality of the structures is largely informed by 'matching' or 'near matching' descriptions of events and anecdotes related to Akbar's life in contemporary accounts – principally, those by Abul Fazl who was Akbar's official historian, the scholar cleric Badauni at Akbar's court and the Portuguese Jesuit missionary Monserrate who stayed at Akbar's court between 1580–82. Archaeological findings and Mughal paintings, primarily Abul Fazl's illustrated *Akbarnama*, also help us reconstruct the history of the individual monuments of Sikri.

Historians also draw attention to other issues complicating our understanding of the site. The names of the structures on plaques put up by the administration are mostly taken from 19th-century tourist guides who were often local residents with no professional training in archaeology or history. A second problem is that the original architectural designs have, in some cases, been demolished or altered in the process of renovation and restoration under colonial rule and afterwards.[2]

CIRCUMSTANCES LEADING TO THE ESTABLISHMENT OF A NEW CAPITAL IN SIKRI

Though the imperial city of Sikri was built during Akbar's time, its history goes back much further. Archaeological findings from the region include Painted Grey Ware (BCE 1200–800) sherds, beads and artefacts belonging to the Kushana and Sunga periods (second c. BCE–second c. CE), besides pre-historic rock shelters. A large number of Jaina sculptures, including one of Shruti Sarasvati, were excavated around Bir Chhabili Tila on the eastern bank of the lake in 1999–2000. Sikri and Bayana came under the control of the Sikarwar Rajputs in the 12th century CE and there is evidence of fortifications built by them. According to one tradition, the word 'Sikri' comes from the Sikarwar Rajputs. The region was subsequently taken over by the Delhi Sultans and remains of mosques and tombs belonging to the Delhi Sultanate period (13th–14th centuries) have been discovered in the city.

The Mughal connection comes with Babur who, as we have discussed earlier, was a descendent of the tribe of the famous Turko-Mongol conquerors – Genghis Khan and Timur (Timur Lane). The first Mughal emperor (r. 1526–30) defeated the Rajput king Rana Sangram Singh of Mewar in 1527 at the Battle of Khanwa, located 16 kilometres from Sikri. According to a legend, he renamed the place 'Shukri' which means 'thanks', to acknowledge the support of the local populace during the battle. Sikri was a non-descript village when the third Mughal emperor Akbar (r. 1556–1605) shifted his seat there in 1571–72.

Most historians argue that Akbar's decision to build an imperial city was largely based on his reverence for the Sufi saint Shaikh Salim Chishti. Akbar had met the saint in Sikri during the winters of 1568–69 while on the way to his annual pilgrimage to Ajmer, the seat of the famous Sufi saint Moinuddin Chishti,

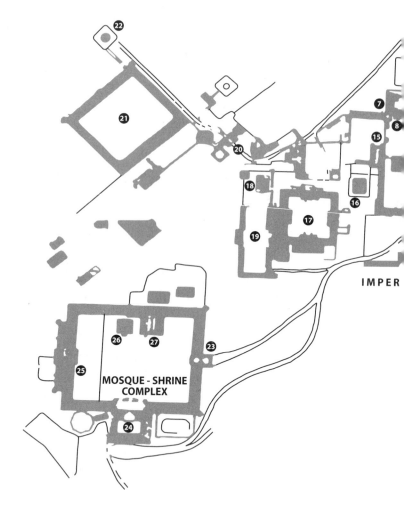

Site map of Fatehpur Sikri.

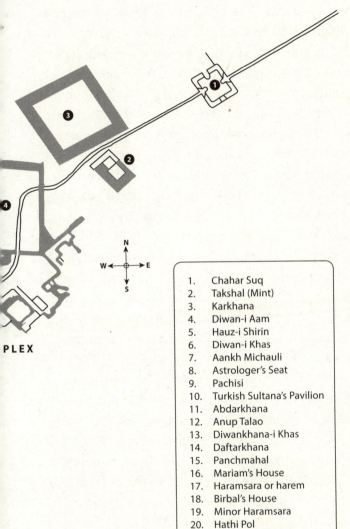

1. Chahar Suq
2. Takshal (Mint)
3. Karkhana
4. Diwan-i Aam
5. Hauz-i Shirin
6. Diwan-i Khas
7. Aankh Michauli
8. Astrologer's Seat
9. Pachisi
10. Turkish Sultana's Pavilion
11. Abdarkhana
12. Anup Talao
13. Diwankhana-i Khas
14. Daftarkhana
15. Panchmahal
16. Mariam's House
17. Haramsara or harem
18. Birbal's House
19. Minor Haramsara
20. Hathi Pol
21. Caravanserai
22. Hiran Minar
23. Badshahi Darwaza
24. Buland Darwaza
25. Jami Masjid
26. Tomb of Salim Chishti
27. Jamaat Khana

and shared his concern about being heirless. The saint predicted that the emperor would be blessed with three sons. And, the prophecy came true. So, when his queen became pregnant, Akbar shifted her to the Chishti quarters in Sikri. Soon, the emperor ordered the construction of a palace, generally identified with the Rang Mahal, near the saint's old *khanqah* or hospice. The palace is now closed to the public. Akbar also commissioned alongside the palace, a new *khanqah* and a mosque. In August 1569, a son was born to Akbar. He was named Salim, after the Sufi saint and later became known as the Mughal emperor Jahangir. In 1571, orders were issued to build the imperial city and nobles, bureaucrats and others were also asked to build their residences. By making Sikri his capital, some scholars have suggested, Akbar was seeking to attach the charisma of the Sufis to his imperial authority.[3] However, Sikri represented much more than that. It also represented the growing needs of an emerging empire to have a new capital – a town planned around a visionary, appropriate for the new vision of an empire.[4]

Why was there a need to go beyond Agra? Broadly speaking, Agra, with its strong fort, represented the political and military component of a new and expanding Mughal empire. Using Agra as his base, Akbar had conquered many Rajput kingdoms in Rajasthan; captured Kangra in the Himalayan region and Gondwana in central India; made forays into the Deccan; and also tried to establish Mughal sovereignty over eastern India. The expansion of the empire had seen incorporation of diverse people, cultures and polities. Akbar's challenge now was to integrate them socially and culturally within the apparatus of the empire. The orthodox Sunni ulema, the religious clerics, would oppose any diversion from established Islamic norms and practices. How should they deal with the differences between and within practitioners of various religions? This was another big question. Creating an exalted status for the sovereign vis-à-vis the courtiers and subjects had also become crucial for the empire. Sikri therefore marked a new phase in the life and career of a maturing emperor and the empire; one which was characterized by more inclusive policies and widening religious beliefs. The architecture, spatial dynamics and cultural milieu of the buildings at Sikri help us appreciate the changes in Akbar's policies.

The emperor was exceptionally innovative in designing and building his new court and administrative city. So, while many structures within the imperial complex served the same purpose as their Agra counterparts, those like Ibadat Khana or the 'House of Worship' served an altogether different purpose.[5] It was in this new space that Akbar started discussions with representatives of different religions, including Muslims, Hindus, Jains, Christians, and Zoroastrians. In the process, he almost veered towards Christianity and in those years the Portuguese Jesuits visiting his court enjoyed a lot of royal patronage and privileges for some time.

Akbar figured a way of dealing with conservative Islamic clerics as well. While at Sikri, he arrogated to himself supreme powers by taking over the role of a *mujtahid*, a jurisprudent or interpreter, of Islamic law. The new capital also saw Akbar promulgating the policy of *sulh-i kul*, variously interpreted as 'universal peace', or 'tolerance for all'.

Sikri also served as the base of some large political conquests. In 1572–73, Akbar led a military campaign to Gujarat. Upon return, he built a monumental gateway called the Buland Darwaza or 'The Lofty gate' to the congregational mosque or Jami Masjid (also called Jama Masjid) complex to commemorate his victory over Gujarat. The city now came to be known as Fathpur or Fatehpur Sikri which means the 'City of Victory'.

Fig. 4.1 *A silhouette of Fatehpur Sikri complex from the Bharatpur side.*

Fig. 4.2 Hiran Minar.

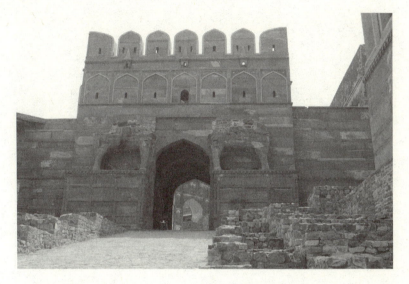

Fig. 4.3 Hathi Pol gate.

Fig. 4.4 Diwan-i Aam showing the imperial pavilion from where Akbar dispensed justice.

Fig. 4.4a Diwan-i Aam pavilion which gave the emperor access to the area within the Daulatkhana.

Fig. 4.5 Diwan-i Khas or Jewel House reinforced the superior power of the emperor.

Fig. 4.5a The richly carved pillar topped by the circular platform inside the Diwan-i Khas has been subject to much debate.

Fig. 4.6 Lockable doors in the thick walls of the Treasury or Aankh Michauli.

Fig. 4.7 *The 'Astrologer's Seat' with its serpentine brackets.*

Fig. 4.8 *Anup Talao complex with Diwankhana-i Khas and Khwabgah, restricted for access, in the background.*

Fig. 4.8a Stone platform in the Diwankhana-i Khas where Akbar would hold discussions.

Fig. 4.8b The view inside the Diwankhana-i Khas.

Fig. 4.9 The exquisitely carved 'Turkish Sultana's Pavilion'(right) as seen from the Anup Talao. The Jewel House is in the background.

Fig. 4.9a The view inside the 'Turkish Sultana's Pavilion'.

Fig. 4.9b Detail of a carving on one of the walls of the 'Turkish Sultana's Pavilion'.

Fig. 4.10 *Abdarkhana* (left) and the four-storeyed Panchmahal in the background.

Fig. 4.11 Storage jar which was meant to store water from the Ganges for the emperor.

Fig. 4.12 Hauz-i Shirin supplied water for cooking. It once collapsed during Akbar's birthday celebrations.

Fig. 4.13 Mariam's House which is also called Sunhara Makan because of its murals and golden paintings.

Fig. 4.14 Entrance to the extremely private Principal Haramsara where Akbar's queens resided.

Fig. 4.14a Courtyard of the Principal Haramsara showing the blue-tiled ribbed roof of one of the residential structures.

Fig. 4.14b The view inside one of the residential structures at the Principal Haramsara.

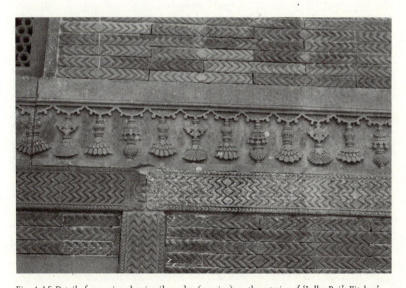

Fig. 4.15 Detail of a carving showing jhumka (ear ring) on the exterior of 'Jodha Bai's Kitchen'.

Fig. 4.16 Birbal's House. with exquisitely carved brackets and chajja.

Fig. 4.17 Masjid-Dargah Complex with Jami Masjid, tomb of Salim Chishti and Jamaatkhana (left to right).

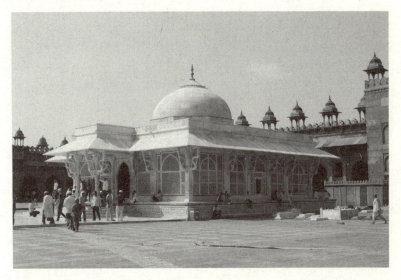

Fig. 4.17a The marble tomb of Salim Chishti with serpentine brackets on the pillars.

Fig. 4.18 The Prayer Hall of the Jami Masjid is profusely decorated with inlaid stone and painted geometrical and floral motifs.

Fig. 4.19 *The jaalis inside Salim Chishti's tomb.*

Fig. 4.20 *Jamatkhana which gradually became a tomb for Salim Chishti's descendants.*

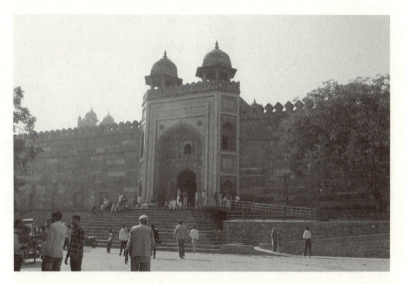

Fig. 4.21 Badshahi Darwaza through which Akbar entered the Masjid-Dargah complex.

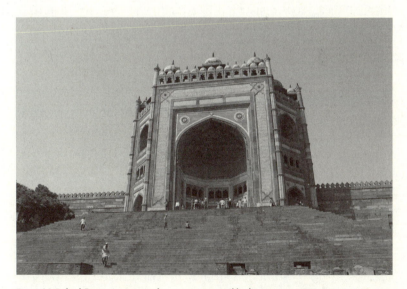

Fig. 4.22 Buland Darwaza constructed to commemorate Akbar's victory over Gujarat.

ARCHITECTURAL DESIGN AND THE INSPIRATION

There is no direct written evidence regarding the architects, supervisors or planners of Sikri. When Akbar decided to build Fatehpur Sikri, he did not have any texts before him which could underline the principles of construction. Neither did the Mughals have any written architectural theory, nor did the prominent Sanskrit architectural treatises like *Shilpa Shastras* or *Vastu Shastras* which were included in Akbar's extensive translation programme.[6] Mughal architectural theories are mostly deduced from the appearance and forms of their buildings.

Mughal emperors mostly influenced the design of their buildings and were popularly regarded as their architects as well. Some also actively supervised the construction of imperial projects. Jahangir (r. 1605–27) insisted on his own design for Akbar's tomb at Sikandara and Shah Jahan (r. 1628–58) had himself represented as his own architect.[7] Mughal miniatures in *Akbarnama* show construction activities in the city including one which depicts Akbar supervising the masons and stone cutters at work.

Most historians agree that the dominant architectural style at Sikri is trabeate, consisting pillars and beams, with some domed pavilions. R. Nath underscores that Sikri represented a systematic incorporation of regional and local influences into the classical imperial art. Local idioms were introduced by anonymous artisans drawn from the areas newly annexed into the Mughal empire, particularly from Malwa–Gujarat–Rajasthan and the Jamuna–Chambal region of Delhi, Agra, Fatehpur, Dholpur and Gwalior. These artisans were proficient in both brick and stone constructions and those from Malwa–Gujarat–Rajasthan were experts in both wood and stone, and could faithfully translate wooden forms into stone.[8]

The dominant influence of the Gujarati style of architecture on the buildings of Sikri is quite evident. Historian S. A. Nadeem Rezavi remarks that Rajput and Gujarati style had already been incorporated in the buildings of pre-Mughal Muslim rulers of those regions in India. In Sikri, the dominant influence appears to be that of Timurid and Gujarati Sultanate architecture.[9] Art historian Ebba Koch even argues that, from a stylistic point of view, Sikri was an architectural response to the absorption of Gujarat into the Mughal empire, the details of which we will discuss in the following paragraphs.[10] The Gujarati Sultanate architecture – which provided a successful model for synthesizing pre-Islamic Hindu and Jaina building traditions – manifests itself in different ways in Sikri.[11]

The primary organizing principle of trabeate constructions on a grid pattern, extendable to halls and galleries, was inspired by Mahmud Begarha's (also known as Mahmud Begada) palaces in Sarkhej near Ahmedabad. Likewise, many imperial buildings in Sikri – containing vaults in the inner central chamber and appearing flat-roofed on the outside – were inspired by the main storey of the Bayana pavilion in Gujarat, where it was used in a residential context. Examples of this style at Sikri include the Emperor's seat at his public court known as Diwan-i Aam; his resting chambers called Khwabgah; and the imperial records office named the Daftarkhana – all three in the imperial complex – alongside Tansen's Baradari, a charming red sandstone pavilion on the ridge near the current *kotwali* or police check post. Another important marker of Gujarati influence is also seen in the architectural vocabulary and décor of palaces like 'Jodha Bai's Palace' in the imperial harem complex. A symmetrically planned courtyard house, it relates to Jahangiri Mahal in the Agra Fort. The dominance of the Gujarati architectural style can be seen in many other structures including the white marble tomb of Salim Chishti (in the mosque-shrine complex) and the Diwan-i Khas (in the imperial complex). All these buildings that show the influence of the Gujarati style have been discussed later in this chapter.

How did the emperor bring these different architectural styles – Timurid, Gujarati, Rajasthani, Gwalior, Malwa and other regional ones – together? Horizontal or vertical surfaces, structural and spanning systems; and patterned pavements at Sikri are all predominantly built in fine-quality red sandstone. Available abundantly in the local quarries, the stone was very malleable and could lend itself to very delicate carving. In the words of Abul Fazl: 'clever workmen chisel it more skillfully than any turner could do with wood.'[12] Red sandstone acted as a sort of unifying agent. It glossed over stylistic clashes resulting from the amalgamation of various forms, besides imparting it the colour of the sovereign. Non-imperial structures were mostly built of rubble held together with lime and gypsum mortar and were covered with lime plaster.

LAYOUT AND PLANNING

Broadly speaking, the layout of Fatehpur Sikri followed two kinds of plan, both overlapping with each other. Horizontally, the colonnaded and flat-roofed structures drew inspiration from a Timurid or Mughal encampment. Vertically, the buildings followed the alignment and contours of a ridge. The Fatehpur Sikri complex is located on a long narrow ridge of the upper Vindhyan mountain ranges and is aligned south-west to north-east.

The Mughal encampment was a mini city on wheels. It was a perfectly ordered arrangement of wood, canvas, cloth houses and tents.[13] In the traditional plan[14] of an encampment, the central area was reserved for the emperor and queens. This was flanked by the area meant for princes which, in turn, was surrounded by the rings of nobles' houses, bureaucratic establishments and workshops. Beyond this, lay the habitations of the common people. The markets were located in a linear pattern on the sides. Within this larger scheme, there was a hierarchical progression from the public to private zones. The buildings in Sikri are similar in form to the tents described in Abul Fazl's *Ain-i-Akbari*, and often use the same fluid vocabulary for pavilions and enclosures.[15]

Important buildings were also aligned with the contours of the ridge and are located on a set of three receding plateau levels. The mosque-shrine complex, consisting of the Buland Darwaza, Jami Masjid, Shaikh Salim Chishti's tomb and some residential quarters, occupies the topmost level of the ridge. The other two levels are occupied by the imperial complex. The King's Palace (Daulatkhana) and the Imperial Harem (Haramsara) occupy the middle level. On the lowest level of the plateau are located the public and semi-public buildings adjoining the imperial structures. These include the bureaucratic establishments, the *karkhanas* or workshops, and office-cum-residences of the bureaucrats. The city was enclosed by a high battlemented stone wall, about 6 kilometres long, on the north, south and east. It was protected by a lake (now dry) on the western side.

Water was supplied to the imperial and mosque complex through water wheels, which lifted the water from the lake, and aqueducts. The civic population and the gardens were located in various zones around the official area at the base of the ridge. They got water either directly from the lake or through wells, step wells or tanks. Most gardens were laid within the city walls, but some were also to be found outside. Also, within these walls existed habitations of merchants, traders, professionals and others. The industrial area, settlements of artisans as well as areas of indigo cultivation, leather works, abattoirs were located close to the city walls or outside of it.

Access to the city was controlled by a series of eight identical gates and, among them, the prominent ones were the Agra and Ajmer gates. These gates restricted movement from public spaces into imperial zones. The palace complex could be accessed from the west, where the lake, Hiran Minar (a circular tower with elephant tusk-like protrusions in stone; also known as 'Elephant Tower') and northern waterworks were located. Some tourist guides say Hiran Minar (Fig. 4.2) was erected as a memorial to Akbar's favourite elephant. Historians think it formed the zero milestone and the tusk-like protrusions on the tower were probably used to hang lamps to guide travellers during the night. The Hathi Pol or 'Elephant gate' (Fig. 4.3) with sculpted elephants is also shown in Mughal miniatures as the ceremonial entrance to the imperial complex.

Modern visitors to the imperial complex take the Agra gate route, pass through buildings known as *kotwali* or police checkpost which was the caravanserai during Akbar's time, then moving on to a building related to a noble but not Akbar's prominent courtier of that name called Tansen's Baradari, and then they walk cross the Dak Bungalow, built later by the British Viceroy, Lord Curzon (1899–1905), to reach the triple-arched gateway – a structure inspired by the design of Tin Darwaza at Ahmedabad in Gujarat – leading into the *Chahar Suq*. Typical of Iran and Central Asia, the *Chahar Suq* was a four-quartered market and its two intersecting roads, crossing each other at right angles, were paved with shops.[16] From the *Chahar Suq*, the visitors enter the palace complex through the north-east of the Diwan-i Aam – a place known for regular public dealings of the emperor. The Diwan-i Aam forms a part of the imperial complex and leads to an astounding set of imperial buildings, most of which are in a well-conserved state.

THE IMPERIAL COMPLEX

Three sets of buildings comprise the imperial complex, all of which are architectural delights – the King's Palace housing the private/residential and public buildings of the emperor, structures associated with the Imperial Harem, and the official or bureaucratic establishments. The King's Palace, generally known as Daulatkhana, or the 'Abode of Fortune', was divided into the Daulatkhana-i Khas or Diwankhana-i Khas which indicates a space with restricted access and contained the Diwan-i Khas or the 'Hall of Private Audience' and the Daulatkhana-i Aam or Diwankhana-i Aam, which means a public space, and housed the Diwan-i Aam, or the 'Hall of General Audience'.

Daulatkhana-i Aam

The Diwan-i Aam was the public court of the emperor. The structure consists of an extensive courtyard enclosed by a colonnade of 114 bays and a projecting raised pavilion in the centre of the west (Figs. 4.4 and 4.4a). This trabeate pavilion adorned with stone screens, vaulted chamber and *chajjas*, or sloping projections from the top of the wall to protect from the sun and rains, formed the emperor's seat. Entry to this court was through the northern gateway opening towards the Hauz-i Shirin or the 'Sweet Tank' and further down to the Hathi Pol. The original plan of the court stands modified now, with the addition of a municipal-style garden and the creation of an opening in the wall of the courtyard for visitors entering from the Agra gate side. The huge stone rings at the foot of the colonnade around the imperial pavilion were possibly used for inspection of animals from the royal stable or exhibiting captured war elephants rather than the common story propagated by the guides that this was a place for publicly trampling those condemned to death.

Daulatkhana-i Khas

The Daulatkhana-i Khas consists of Diwan-i Khas, the two-roomed Diwankhana-i Khas, Khwabgah, Anup Talao, Turkish Sultana's Chamber and some minor structures. The Diwan-i Khas, or the 'Jewel House', is a square-shaped single vaulted chamber, even though it appears like a two-storeyed structure from outside, with openings on all four sides (Fig. 4.5). The interior has a richly carved pillar at the centre supporting a circular platform connected with four diagonal bridges emanating from four cardinal directions (Fig. 4.5a). The circular capital of this pillar, composed of two superimposed tiers of serpentine brackets, is inspired by the surrounding balconies on the minarets of the 15th-century Sidi Bashir mosque in Ahmedabad, Gujarat.[17]

This functionality of the central chamber of the Diwan-i Khas is difficult to establish. Historians and scholars have variously identified the central circular platform as a place from where the emperor inspected the imperial jewels and gems; attended to the ministers seated at the corners (Y D Sharma); or, listened to the arguments from different religions, symbolizing his 'Dominion over the Four Quarters' (Percy Brown). Some, like Giles Tillotson, argue that the central column represented the axis of the world of Hindu cosmology whose occupant, Akbar, wielded supreme power.[18] Still others, like Catherine Asher, have likened Akbar to Lord Vishnu seated on a lotus symbolized by the round column, or to the sun dominating over all regions.[19]

Next to the 'Jewel House' is the so-called Aankh Michauli. literally, 'blind man's buff' – implying, a place where Akbar played this game with the women of the harem. Like the Jewel House, this building also has concealed coffers and lockable doors in the thick walls (Fig. 4.6). Historians have suggested that this was a part of the treasury where gold and silver coins were stored, while the copper coins were kept in the building behind this one which collapsed in 1894. To the south-west of this 'Treasury' containing three large *aiwans* or porticos, stands a kiosk known as the 'Astrologer's Seat' which, scholars say, was modelled on a Cambay-style building in Gujarat (Fig. 4.7). This was possibly the site from where the emperor watched the distribution of copper coins to subordinate officers and the needy.

The large red sandstone courtyard between the Diwan-i Khas and the beautiful pool fronting the Diwankhana-i Khas is known as the *pachisi* — after the cruciform board on which this popular Indian board game was played. Local legend has it that the emperor played the game using slave girls as live pieces.

The Diwankhana-i Khas, containing Akbar's imperial chambers referred to as the Khalwatkada-i Khas and resting place or the Khwabgah (literally, 'Chamber of Dreams'), was a restricted area (Figs. 4.8 and 4.8a). It served as a place for both learned discussions and official business transactions. The Khalwatkada-i Khas sometimes also acted as a private audience chamber, the Diwan-i Khas. Its two-tiered colonnaded porticos perhaps once hosted learned discussions involving 'eloquent philosophers', 'virtuous Sufis' and 'unprejudiced historians' besides official transactions regarding revenues and empire. The chamber has a projecting balcony where the emperor probably received royal guests such as Mirza Sulaiman of Badakshan.[20] There is a large closed room south of the porticos containing a stone platform resting on beautifully carved pillars (Fig. 4.8a). The platform is set against the southern wall, with a window above it. Some historians think this probably was the *jharokha* or window from where the emperor showed himself to his subjects gathered beneath towards the south every day. This practice called *jharokha darshan*, which we also discussed in the chapter on Agra Fort, was instituted by Akbar in Sikri. Others say the window from where the emperor appeared for *jharokha darshan* was in the Khwabgah or the Daftarkhana (Secretariat/Records Office).[21]

The western wall of this structure has a door that leads to the Daftarkhana. Through an insightful reading of the accounts of Badauni – who talks about an Ibadatkhana with four *aiwans* near the new palace – Abul Fazl and Nizamuddin Ahmad, and correlating them with those of Monserrate, Nadeem Rezavi persuasively identifies the Ibadatkhana or the 'House of Worship' with what is now known as the Daftarkhana.[22] This was the place where Akbar's famous religious discussions or disputations were held until around 1580.

Diwankhana-i Khas also has a rectangular room on its east which was once beautifully painted. The lower walls of this room, identified as Akbar's 'private library', have hollows with sliding stone panels possibly used to keep rare books and gifts. This kind of a concealed storage arrangement could also be seen in buildings like the 'Treasury' and Diwan-i Khas. The emperor also had informal chats with distinguished guests in his 'private library'.

Between the exhausting discussions in the Diwankhana-i Khas, a tired emperor would retire to a beautiful chamber on the first floor of the building, called the Khwabgah. This was Akbar's private room or sleeping chamber where he rested and relaxed. The emperor could be joined by the ladies from the harem here whenever he desired. A screened corridor from the west connected the Khwabgah with the Imperial Harem through two structures lying in the intermediate zone – the 'Panchmahal' and the 'Mariam's House' (both discussed later in this chapter). The screened passage continued up to the Hathi Pol, the original entrance to the imperial complex. This offered a secret unhindered passage to the emperor and the royal ladies while moving from one palace to another. Sometimes, while relaxing, Akbar also sought wisdom from the learned ones. He would ask his favourite courtiers such as Raja Birbal or Abul Fazl to read out passages from books or hold informal discussions with them. Badauni narrates the story of a Brahman named Devi who used to be pulled up on a *charpai* (traditional Indian stringed cot) from outside of the building till he reached the level of Khwabgah. Suspended in air, the Brahman would regale the emperor with the myths and legends of Hinduism.

The Diwankhana-i Khas is fronted by tank called Anup Talao which literally means, 'Peerless Pool.' Shaped like a recreational structure, it has a central island linked by four bridges to its sides. It was constructed around 1575–76. Another tank named Kapur Talao, constructed in the palace complex in 1578–79, can now be identified with Sukh Tal located near the Daftarkhana.[23]

To the north-east of Anup Talao is a beautifully carved structure popularly called Turkish Sultana's Pavilion (Fig. 4.9). It needs to be clarified that there was no one called Turkish Sultana in Akbar's court. Further, it would have been impossible to have a *zenana* (female) pavilion/chamber within a predominantly *mardana* (male) area. The pavilion has beautiful carvings (Figs.4.9a and 4.9b) on brackets, pillars, friezes and pilasters, and gives the semblance of intricate woodwork rather than stone masonry. Historians have identified this pavilion, and the columned veranda around it, with the Hujra-i Anup Talao or the 'Chamber of the Anup Talao' – which, as Badauni wrote, was where a religious discussion took place one night in 1571. This room was possibly a pleasure pavilion and may have sometimes been used to receive guests by the emperor.

The Anup Talao is connected through a pillared veranda to a structure known as the Abdarkhana (Fig. 4.10) or the 'Water Store', which is sometimes erroneously called the 'Girl's School' by the tourist guides and local inhabitants, where fruits, water, food and beverages were kept for the emperor. A big water jar now kept in the east of Anup Talao complex, is said to have stored water brought from River Ganges for Akbar (Fig. 4.11). The emperor reportedly only drank water from the Ganga. He however allowed rainwater collected in Hauz-i Shirin or the 'Sweet Tank', (Fig. 4.12) on the ramp near the Hathi Pol, to be used for cooking food for the court in combination with the Ganga water. The kitchen establishment was located near this tank, one of the walls of which is said to have collapsed during a celebration in 1584 and damaged the structures nearby.

Buildings in the intermediate zone

Between the King's Palace and the Imperial Harem, known as the Haramsara, lies the intermediate zone containing three structures: the 'Panchmahal', 'Mariam's House' and the 'Hospital'. The 'Hospital' can even escape the visitors' attention as it is sandwiched between buildings. The so-called Hospital looks like a pitched-roof building with carved and reclining stone roof on the outside and profusely decorated roof panels inside. Connected to the Daulatkhana via the 'Treasury', it possibly served as a 'haramsara guesthouse' or a nursery school for young princes where the Jesuits also taught. The wall separating the Haramsara from this intermediate area was unfortunately removed during renovations carried out in the 19th century.[24]

The 'Panchmahal', also called 'Chaharsuffa' – a structure with four platforms or floors – is a four-storeyed, entirely columnar structure of diminishing sizes surmounted by a domed kiosk(Fig. 4.10). This monument is a very picturesque one and appears prominently in all tourism campaigns related to Fatehpur Sikri. 'Panchmahal' is screened on all floors except the ground. Interestingly, none of the columns on the first floor are alike, as some are circular while others are octagonal and they are ornamented with the typical Hindu bell and chain motifs, like the ones we discussed earlier in the chapter on the Qutb Minar complex. Connected with a screened passage with both the Khwabgah and principal Haramsara, this building may have served a recreational purpose for the imperial family and offered a good panoramic view of the surroundings.

Mariam's House is not named after a Portuguese queen called Marie as the guides would have us believe (Fig. 4.13). The structure is also called Sunhara Makan which means the 'Golden House' or the 'Painted House', after the beautiful murals and gold-coloured paintings that once decorated it. Some scholars think this belonged to the queen mother, Hamida Banu Begum, also called Mariam Makani ('Equal in Rank to Mary').[25] However, after a careful analysis of the available information, the most recent study by Nadeem Rezavi clearly indicates that it was Akbar's private dining chamber. Mariam's House was privately connected to the Abdarkhana, where food and beverages were laid out, through a private door. Separated from the private quarters of women's apartments and located outside the public Daulatkhana area, where affairs of the state were conducted, this may have been a special dining hall where the emperor both dined alone and could sometimes be joined by the women of the harem.[26] It was literally and figuratively located at the intersection of the public and the private and, together with the Abdarkhana, occupied a central location in the imperial palace complex. Sunhara Makan's central hall had portraits of women and angels and the building was profusely painted with court and hunting scenes, elephant fights, polo games, and so on. Reflecting European, Persian and indigenous influences, the paintings conveyed the imperial nature of the room and conveyed messages of power and heroism that were complemented by emperor's dining spectacle.[27] The emperor dined alone in a structure where no men were allowed to enter. Contemporary sources indicate that he had more than forty courses served in huge dishes and his sealed food passed through various stages, and accompanied by several attendants, before reaching the dining table.

Haramsara complex

The core structures that form the Haramsara complex include the principal Haramsara (or Shabistan-i-Iqbal) popularly known for 'Jodha Bai's Palace', and 'Birbal's House'. The former was the private zenana area where Akbar's wives lived including Akbar's first Rajput queen and the mother of his first child, Salim or Jahangir, also called Mariam Zamani ('Mary of the Age'). It is said that the emperor had several wives from among Muslims and Hindus, and some say he had a Christian wife as well, resulting mostly from political alliances. It is said that he allowed them to follow their religion and faith within the harem complex. We do not have concrete information regarding the exact number of wives Akbar had but names of three principal queens are known – Ruqayya Sultan Begum, who was the daughter of Mirza Hindal, Salima Sultan Begum, who was the widow of Bairam Khan, his former regent, and Mariam Zamani, the mother of Jahangir.[28]

The harem had emerged as an important institution of the Mughal state and the senior queen was not only the mistress of the imperial household but also the guardian of the two imperial seals which were required to be stamped on the *farmans* or royal orders, to formalize them.[29] Life in the harem was mostly communal and was designed to provide both private and shared space to the women living there.[30] The dominance of Rajput/'Hindu' architecture of the principal Haramsara makes it clear that Akbar's Rajput queen stayed here along with other inmates.

A single gate with a staggered entrance leads to the principal Haramsara, a double-storeyed structure once guarded by eunuchs. Its privacy is only partially disturbed by the *jharokhas* or windows on the first floor (Fig. 4.14). The ground floor of the principal Haramsara consists of unconnected chambers and porticos on all four sides and a large square courtyard in the middle (Fig. 4.14a). The bases, columns and capitals in the central rooms have carvings inspired by Rajput traditions (Fig. 4.14b). The upper floor contains chambers in the centre of each side and at the corners. The monotony of the red sandstone is broken by the azure blue tiles (originally found in Multan) on the ribbed roof of the upper rooms on the northern and southern pavilions. A structure called Hawa Mahal or the 'Wind Palace', is attached to the northern wall of the principal Haramsara. It was connected with a screened viaduct, containing arabesque designs, to the Hathi Pol.

Outside of the principal Haramsara, lies a lean-to-roof structure popularly known as 'Jodha Bai's kitchen'. Like the 'Turkish Sultana's Palace', this building also has beautiful floral and geometric carvings. The guides make it a point to show to the women tourists the *jhumka* (earring) designs carved on its walls

(Fig. 4.15). Historians suggest this building probably served as the office for the Haramsara or imperial clerks.

It is important here to clarify the popular misconceptions surrounding Jodha Bai (also referred to as Jodh Bai), the so-called Rajput queen of Akbar. She exists prominently in guides' narratives, fiction and Bollywood films, but her existence is negated by historians. Prominent Mughal historian Irfan Habib argues that Jodha Bai is not a historical character. It's true, he says, that Akbar married the eldest daughter of the Amber ruler Raja Bharmal, but her name is not mentioned anywhere, and she was certainly not Jahangir's mother. 'The myth can be attributed to some guide who may have taken British officers around Fatehpur Sikri arbitrarily referring to various palaces as Todar Mal's, Birbal's or Jodha Bai's.'[31] Historian Shireen Moosvi, who has published extensively on Akbar, also clarifies that there is no mention of Jodha Bai in *Akbarnama* or other Mughal documents of the period.[32]

Like Jodha Bai's palace, 'Birbal's House' is also erroneously named. Scholars have pointed out that it was impossible for Raja Birbal, one of the famous Hindu courtiers of Akbar, to have occupied the building – no male, not even a prince, was allowed to enter the female quarters. The corbels, exquisitely carved brackets, together with the *chajja* of this palace exhibit typical Hindu influences, while the pilasters have geometrical patterns common in architecture associated with Muslims and Islam (Fig. 4.16). Birbal's house was one of the earliest palaces to be constructed at Sikri (around 1571) and has a relatively independent character. It might have been used to house someone holding high esteem at Akbar's court – probably the queen mother, Hamida Banu Begum, or the other senior queens like Ruqayya Sultan Begum or Salima Sultan Begum. The other ladies-in-waiting were presumably housed in the so-called Mina Bazar, which could have been the minor Haramsara. The Nagina Masjid, meant for the women of the Haramsara and the beautiful small garden to the north also formed a part of the Haramsara complex.

Where did the princes stay? On the basis of its vicinity to the Daulatkhana and the royal waterworks in the southern section, historians have identified the Hakim's House with the princes' quarters.[33]

A number of departments including those dealing with the kitchen, mint, tents and carpets, translations, paintings, arsenal, and such others were located within and around the Daulatkhana complex. The complex was surrounded by rings of bureaucratic establishments, houses of the nobles, office-residences of bureaucrats and habitations of common people. Among the famous nobles' houses, we may include the ones popularly known as Abul Fazl Faizi House, Hakim's House, Khan-i-Khanan's House and Tansen's Baradari.

THE MOSQUE-SHRINE COMPLEX

The other major concentration of buildings lies in the mosque-shrine complex (Fig. 4.17) which is alluded to as the 'private property part' by the guides to the visitors, made famous because of its association with the Sufi saint Shaikh Salim Chishti. Belonging to one of the most influential Sufi sects in India, the Chishtis, he was a descendant of a famous Sufi saint, Fariduddin Ganj-i Shakar and had stayed in Mecca for some time before settling down in Sikri. It is said that the local quarrymen working on the ridge for the stone required to build the Agra Fort had constructed a red sandstone mosque in Sikri for the saint around 1565. This came to be known as the Stone Cutters' Mosque. Akbar later built the Jami Masjid on the highest point of the ridge.

Jami Masjid

Completed in 1571–72, Jami Masjid was conceived as one of the largest mosques of its times and ascribed to the saint. Legend has it that Akbar himself occasionally cleaned the floor of the mosque and called the ritual prayer, *azan*. The mosque also played an important role in Akbar's political ascendancy. It was here, in 1579, that Akbar read the *khutba*, the recitation during Friday prayers, to proclaim his sovereignty and also issued the public edict, *mahzarnama*, making him the ultimate authority in all matters involving interpretations of the *Quran* and *Hadith* (collection of traditions containing sayings of Prophet Muhammad), above Muslim religious scholars and jurists.

The mosque follows the traditional style of a central courtyard, with colonnades on three sides. There is a small pool in the centre for ritual ablution. On the west side is the prayer hall or sanctuary. Divided into seven bays, the prayer hall is an arcade of pointed arches (Fig. 4.18). The central dome is dwarfed by the central *pishtaq*, an imposing entrance or a monumental arched niche enclosed by a rectangular frame, while the lateral domes get somewhat blurred behind a row of *chattris* or small domed pavilions or kiosks.

Tomb of Salim Chishti

Towards the end of his life, Salim Chishti moved from his house near the Stone Cutter's Mosque to a new *khanqah* or hospice near the Jami Masjid. The present tomb was built over the saint's *zawiya*, the meditation chamber, around 1580–81. The tomb underwent several additions over a period of time. Known as 'an architectural cameo', the tomb is particularly known for its ornate serpentine brackets, *chajjas* and the parapet (Fig. 4.17a). The tomb style – an inner domed chamber surrounded by concentric ambulatory verandas often closed on the outside by latticed marble or sandstone screens, the *jaalis* (Fig. 4.19) – was inspired by the 16th-century tomb of Shah Alam (1531–32) in Ahmedabad. This style was also repeated, on a grander scale, in the Mughal tomb of Shaikh Muhammad Ghauth in Gwalior in 1563.[34] Most pilgrims visiting the tomb tie holy threads on the *jaalis* in the hope that the saint will fulfil their wishes. Visitors also frequently encounter local artists singing qawwali (spiritual music sung by Sufis) or holy chants in front of the tomb.

Jamaat Khana

Adjoining the saint's tomb is the Jamaat Khana, also called the 'Tomb of Islam Khan'. This is a red sandstone structure encircled by perforated stone screens. Jamaat Khanas were originally Chishti *khanqahs* consisting of a single hall with a thatched roof.[35] The structure's large dome is surrounded by thirty-six small-domed kiosks (Fig. 4.20). Originally meant to be a common religious place for Shaikh Salim Chishti's distinguished disciples, it later became a tomb for his descendants. The semi-colonnaded hall at the back of Jamaat Khana once formed the place where the *sama* – music and songs performed by the Sufis to reach mystical ecstasy – was held.

Buland Darwaza

The mosque-shrine courtyard is crowned by the famous Buland Darwaza, seen by some historians as a grand assertion of imperial power. Measuring 40 metres in height (add to that another 12 metres by way of stairs), it is an imposing structure with a huge-arched *iwan*, a single vaulted hall, around an imposing human-scaled entrance, the *pishtaq*. Such an *iwan* is seen regularly in Timurid and Mughal buildings and is repeated in the Badshahi

Darwaza, near the current car park, and the Masjid's prayer hall entrance.[36] The Badshahi Darwaza on the east of the complex was the royal entrance (Fig. 4.21).

The Buland Darwaza, which is 53.63 metres high and 35 metres wide and approached by forty-two steps, forms one of the highest gateways in the world and an astounding example of Mughal architecture(Fig. 4.22). On one side of the stairs, towards the south-east, lies a ruined courtyard which some scholars have identified as the mosque's Langar Khana or public kitchen meant for the poor. On the other flank, to the south-west side of the stairs, there is an arcaded water reservoir. Local boys jumping into the waters from the walls of the mosque to impress the tourists used to be a very common sight till sometime back.

The Buland Darwaza is made of red and buff sandstone and decorated by carving and inlaying of white and black marble. The imposing entrance, the *pishtaq* stands in the middle of the three projecting sides of an octagon centering upon the apex of a dome in the entrance hall. The central arch is flanked on either side a by three-tiered facade. The structure is surmounted by a perforated parapet or an ornamental band called *kanguras*, behind which lay domed pavilions. The central arch is set in a rectangle framed by bands of Quranic verses and topped by a row of domed pavilions between two *guldastas* which are pinnacles topped by flower bunches. This kind of a *pishtaq* appears later in the Great gate at the Taj Mahal. Like Humayun's tomb, the spandrels – the interspersed triangular area between the rectangular frame around and merging upper sides of the central arch – are set in white marble. A Persian inscription on eastern side of the central arch records Akbar's conquest of the Deccan in 1601 CE.

Another inscription on the gate, providing evidence of the eclectic nature of Akbar's worldview, documents the influence of

Jesuits and Christianity. It repeats Jesus' advice to his followers to not consider the material world as a permanent home:

> Isa [Jesus], son of Mary said: 'The world is a Bridge, pass over it, but build no houses upon it. He who hopes for a day, may hope for eternity; but the World endures but an hour. Spend it in prayer for the rest is unseen.'

SIKRI AFTER AKBAR

Under Akbar, this village became the cultural, commercial and administrative centre of the empire. It is estimated that around 1580 CE, the total population of this city was just short of a quarter million. Ralph Fitch, the English traveller who visited the city around 1585, wrote: 'Agra and Fatehpore [Fatehpur Sikri] are two very great cities, either of them much greater than London and very populous.' This picture is somewhat countered by another version which talks about the 'sudden decline' of the city – a narrative emphasized primarily by the tourist guides but even some travellers and historians. William Finch, an English merchant who travelled to Fatehpur Sikri in 1610, wrote that it had declined as a capital city soon after the death of Akbar. It had turned into a 'waste desert' and was 'very dangerous to pass through in the night.' That the city was 'abandoned' or 'deserted' soon after Akbar left is a picture now firmly ingrained in popular imagination.

In July 1585, Akbar's half-brother Mirza Hakim died in Kabul. Expecting troubles from rivals in the north-west region, including the Shah of Persia and the Uzbek ruler of Badakshan, the emperor shifted the imperial seat to Lahore and ruled from there for the next thirteen years. Akbar's presence (1586–98) in Lahore helped in establishing Mughal control over the strategic Punjab and surrounding regions including Kabul, Lower Sindh,

Kashmir and Qandahar. It also brought the advantages of a flourishing commerce to the empire. When the emperor left Lahore in 1598, he came back to Agra instead of Fatehpur Sikri. Why did the emperor abandon the new capital within just thirteen to fourteen years of its construction? The answer may be more complex as there are many reasons for this shift. Perhaps, Akbar never intended to make Fatehpur Sikri a permanent imperial capital. It was comparatively better situated for Akbar's imperial designs in Rajasthan, Gujarat and the Gangetic plains. Agra, on the other hand, had continued to remain a flourishing economic and trade site and its fort was comparatively more impregnable. After the Lahore sojourn, Agra was also better situated to deal with the political unrest in the Deccan. Some historians have offered a more spiritual-religious explanation for the shift of the imperial seat. They say Akbar's reverence for Sufi saints was a factor behind the choice of Fatehpur Sikri as an imperial capital and the later change in Akbar's religious temperament was the reason for the city's decline. By 1585, the emperor's connection with Sufism had become considerably diluted and he also stopped going on pilgrimages to Ajmer.[37]

Other scholars however shift the terms of the debate by arguing that Fatehpur Sikri's 'decline' has to be seen in relative terms – decline in the status of the city from an imperial capital to an ordinary town. It however continued to remain an important mercantile centre flourishing in carpet-making and indigo-manufacturing.[38] Peter Mundy, the English trader who visited the city in 1633, still described it as a flourishing city though the palace buildings had been ruined. It also survived as a pilgrimage centre for the disciples of Salim Chishti. Many pilgrims, with desire for an offspring, continued to visit the saint's shrine to seek his blessings.

Evidences show that the city retained its imperial connection at least until the reign of Shah Jahan, the fifth Mughal Emperor. Akbar himself visited the town briefly in 1601 to pay a visit to Mariam Makani, the queen-mother who continued to live there even after the former's migration. Both Jahangir and Shah Jahan took refuge in Sikri when Agra was hit by the plague. Jahangir stayed in Sikri for three-and-a-half months in 1619 and the twenty-eighth solar birthday of the prince Khurram (later Shah Jahan) was celebrated here. The emperor also visited the residences of his nobles, Itmad-ud Daulah whose tomb in Agra is known as the 'Baby Taj Mahal' and Asaf Khan in Sikri during his stay. He also ordered Akbar's *chaugan* or polo ground, near the lake and adjacent to the Hiran Minar, to be enclosed and converted into a reserve for antelopes.[39]

Jahangir's son and successor, Shah Jahan, in fact made several visits to Sikri, including setting up a camp in the region when he rebelled against his father and laid seige to Agra. Shah Jahan made multiple visits to Sikri — in 1628 when he ascended the throne and had a weighing-in ceremony, 1635, 1637, 1643 and then in 1644 when the plague broke out in Agra. He also had his own palace constructed outside Akbar's and stayed there during his last two visits in 1653 and 1654.[40]

Sikri also continued to supply red sandstone for Shah Jahan's ambitious architectural projects including the Taj Mahal. After Shah Jahan, the city became less visible though there are stories about the coronation of a later Mughal emperor Muhammad Shah Rangila in Sikri in 1719–20. Some historians say it was Rangila who got the *pachisi* board created in the Daulatkhana complex. In the late 18th century, Jats and Marathas held control over the city. By the 1840s–50s, some imperial buildings were being used by colonial officials and, after the suppression of the revolt of

1857 – in which locals led by the descendants of Salim Chishti participated – some buildings were used as reception areas and eateries for the visiting *sahibs* and *memsahibs*. The city came under conservation efforts of the British during late 19th and early 20th centuries when many imperial buildings were freed from the clutches of official administration and the villagers.

WAS SHORTAGE OF WATER THE REASON FOR DECLINE OF SIKRI?

There are several theories regarding the decline of Fatehpur Sikri, the most important being that the city declined because of the shortage of water. Most guides taking visitors around the monument complex underline the scarcity of water as a factor in the abandonment of the city.

According to a popular local legend, the waterbodies in the region dried up because of the curse of a dancer named Zarina. The dancer was falsely implicated in a case involving the theft of Jodha Bai's golden bangles. Theories upholding the role of water shortages in the decline of the city have been systematically countered by historians working on the site. The availability of water was never a problem at Sikri. Babur's decision to set up a camp here during his battle against Rana Sangram Singh in 1527 was related to the fact that Sikri happened to be 'a well-watered ground'. Akbar later dammed the water body and converted it into a lake. Historian Nadeem Rezavi argues that the city had enough water; besides the lake, there were at least thirteen stepwells and eight tanks, apart from several others spread across the city.[41]

The presence of waterbodies – lakes, public baths or *hammams*, *baolis* (step wells), tanks, garden channels and waterworks – indicate how availability of water was integral to the planning of the city. They served a variety of utilitarian, aesthetic and recreational purposes. Water was brought from the lake and supplied to the official/semi-official areas through a network of storage tanks and aqueducts. Fatehpur Sikri probably constitutes the largest surviving concentration of *hammams* in Mughal India. The Hakim's Baoli, one of the largest step wells located close to the southern waterworks, still supplies water to the town.[42] Other waterbodies are also being discovered. A recent excavation conducted by ASI revealed a square water tank with a fountain in the centre at the Todarmal Baradari. Water was, therefore, not the reason for the decline.

In fact it was political expediency which led to the move of the imperial capital, as we have discussed – political instability in the north-west of the Mughal empire following the death of Akbar's half-brother, Mirza Hakim in 1585. And once the emperor came back from Lahore in 1598, he shifted to Agra because it offered a more strategic setting for countering political unrest in the Deccan region. The years between 1598–1601 saw Akbar hugely embroiled in a war against Ahmadnagar and Khandesh besides battling against his own son Salim, who was trying to take control over Agra. The son, whom the father had sought through divine intercession, had attempted to upstage the father.

FATEHPUR SIKRI, AN IMPERIAL CAPITAL: KEY INSIGHTS

Fatehpur Sikri represents the first systematic attempt on the part of the Mughals to establish a completely new city (Agra had a past). Architectural features of its buildings were adopted, in a refined form, in later monuments or city projects.

The lives of early Mughal capitals predominantly revolved around the presence of the emperor. If Akbar shifted his base for a long duration, the capital changed accordingly. He ruled from at least four imperial seats/capitals – Agra (1556–71), Fatehpur Sikri (1571–85), Lahore (1585–98) and Agra again (1601–05). Between 1598–1601, he was in the field fighting wars in the Deccan.

Agra Fort and its mighty bastions symbolized the strength and expansion of the Mughal empire under Akbar. The buildings at Fatehpur Sikri, on the other hand, reflect his attempts at integrating diverse people, religions, cultures, and polities. They tell the story of the maturing of the emperor and the empire.

The two monument complexes at Fatehpur Sikri – the imperial and the masjid-dargah – also represent the co-existence of two different power centres, one spiritual and the other political. Also, how politics patronized but also derived legitimacy from religion and spiritualism.

The imperial complex brought together the private and public world of the Mughals. It housed not just the private and residential palaces but also the offices of the emperor alongside other bureaucratic establishments and workshops.

Fatehpur Sikri did not decline suddenly after Akbar's departure to Lahore. It continued to survive as an ordinary town and was known for its carpet-making and indigo-manufacturing or for the pilgrimage to Salim Chishti's tomb.

5

THE TAJ MAHAL

Former American President Bill Clinton once said: 'There are two kinds of people in the world. Those who have seen the Taj Mahal and love it and those who have not seen the Taj and love it.' What is so attractive about the mausoleum that most visitors fall in love with it at the first sight? What made British officer W. H. Sleeman's wife, who visited the Taj Mahal in 1836, remark: 'I do not know how to criticize such a building but I can tell what I feel. I would die tomorrow to have such another [mausoleum] over me.' Why do people from across the world crave to see and pose with the Taj Mahal at least once in their lifetime? The reasons include the monument's various superlative attributes such as beauty, grace, aura, mysticism, perfection, architectural brilliance, otherworldliness, immateriality, eternal fame and much more. The mausoleum, whose marble colour is known to change by the hour, day and season, subsumes within its architectural depths layers of meanings and symbolisms. And an informed visitor will always be able to experience the monument differently.

The iconic Taj Mahal is located on the banks of river Yamuna in Agra, close to the Agra Fort. It was built by the fifth Mughal emperor, Shah Jahan, during 1628–1658, in memory of his favourite wife, Arjumand Banu Begum, better known in history as Mumtaz Mahal. Described variously as 'a monument of conjugal love', 'a testimony to the power and glory of Shah Jahan', 'a symbol for excellence', 'a teardrop on the cheek of time', the Taj Mahal not only forms one of the most iconic and emblematic representations of India but is also considered the greatest architectural achievement in the world of Indo-Islamic architecture. The monument has been appropriated by the Mughals, the Europeans, the colonial British power, the nationalist Indian state and now the modern-day politicians for a variety of political and ideological purposes. However, the monument continues to remain an architectural masterpiece and was declared a UNESCO World Heritage Site in 1983. Taj Mahal has been in news in the recent years on account of progressive discoloration of its marble and appearance of brown and green spots on its surface. According to experts, it is under grave environmental threat because of severe air pollution.

CIRCUMSTANCES LEADING TO THE CONSTRUCTION OF THE TAJ MAHAL

Mumtaz Mahal died in Burhanpur in June 1631 soon after giving birth to the couple's fourteenth child, Gauharara Begum. She was accompanying Shah Jahan on a military campaign directed against one of his nobles, Khan Jahan Lodi, who had rebelled and joined hands with the rival Deccan sultanates. She was first buried in a garden in Zainabad on the opposite bank of river Tapti in Burhanpur. Subsequently, the plan for a monumental funerary garden palace for the queen was inspired by a verse of Shah Jahan's goldsmith and poet, Bibadal Khan – 'May the abode of Mumtaz Mahal be paradise'.[1] The search for an appropriate piece of land for her tomb began soon after her burial. A carefully identified place on the right bank of the river Yamuna – a point where the river takes a sharp turn and flows eastwards – was chosen as

DID YOU KNOW?

Mumtaz Mahal, in whose memory the Taj Mahal was built, was buried three times, the third and final time in a crypt inside the mausoleum (see pages 192–94).

The idea behind the Taj Mahal was to create an earthly replica of the house of Mumtaz Mahal in the Gardens of Paradise and it was conceptualized as a masterpiece for ages to come (see page 207).

The *mihman khana* did not have any specific function; it was built more as a mirror image or *jawab* (answer) to the mosque to reinforce the principle of bilateral symmetry (see page 207).

The bazaars and caravanserais formed an integral part of the planning of the mausoleum and represented its material world as opposed to the mausoleum complex which reflected the spiritual domain (see page 201).

The Taj Mahal was built over a network of foundation wells dug to stabilize the sand on the bank of the Yamuna (see pages 205–06).

Do you know that several important corporate brands, hotels, musical concerts and albums derive their name and inspiration from the Taj Mahal? (see pages 217–18)

Was there ever a plan to construct a rivalling Black Taj Mahal? (see pages 220–21)

the site of the proposed tomb. This land belonged to the Rajput Raja of Amber, Jai Singh, grandson of Raja Man Singh, one of emperor Akbar's prominent nobles. The former was willing to donate the property, but Shah Jahan insisted on giving him four havelis in Akbarabad (Agra) in exchange. Mumtaz Mahal's body was taken out from Zainabad garden and sent to Agra with a team led by Shah Shuja, the emperor's second son despite strictures in Islam over delays in burial and transportation of corpses over long distances.² On reaching the city in January 1632, she was buried for the second time on a piece of land which now lies to the south-east corner of the mosque on the riverfront terrace. A small domed building was also constructed. Later, her body was taken out for the third and final time and enshrined in a crypt inside the mausoleum that became known as the Taj Mahal.

CONSTRUCTION OF THE MAUSOLEUM COMPLEX

There is scattered evidence on the process of construction of the tomb complex of the Taj. Its construction possibly started in January 1632. By May 1633, when Mumtaz's second *urs* or death anniversary, which metaphorically means 'marriage' of the soul with God after a person's passing, was being held, the white marble platform housing the tomb chambers had been completed. Peter Mundy, the English merchant and traveller who visited Agra during 1632–33, says that work on the tomb complex including the bazaars and caravanserais of Taj Ganj had begun. By the time of Mumtaz's twelfth *urs* in 1643, the mausoleum and subsidiary structures had been completed. By 1647–48, the Great gate (*darwaza-i rauza*) had been completed.³

Who were the architects? There is no definitive evidence regarding the architects of the tomb. Chroniclers of Shah Jahan's reign credit the emperor with the design of the complex. The emperor is often represented as the chief architect who had daily meetings with his team. Most historians suggest that Shah Jahan himself designed the concept plan, which was executed to the last detail by a collective of architects including Ustad Ahmad Lahauri, who is credited with laying the foundations of the Red Fort in Delhi later; Mir Abdul Karim, mentioned as the supervisor of the construction process; and, Makramat Khan, also mentioned as the supervisor, who later supervised the construction of the Red Fort in Delhi. However, Amanat Khan is the only person whose signature appears at several places in the Taj complex as the calligrapher of the Quranic inscriptions.

The architects worked with the best artisans and craftsmen drawn from across the country. Lahauri, Shah Jahan's court historian, informs us that skilled men drafted from all parts of the imperial territories including the *sangtarash* (stone cutters), *parchinkar* (inlayers), and those who did carving in *munabbatkar* (relief) worked alongside the labourers. French merchant and traveller Jean-Baptiste Tavernier who visited Agra in 1640–41 and again in 1665 wrote that 20,000 men worked unceasingly on the complex for twenty-two years while Spanish priest Sebastian Manrique, who briefly visited Agra in 1641, claimed 1,000 men were employed every day for work. The cost of construction of the entire complex then came to around 50 lakh rupees against earlier estimates of 40 lakhs.[4]

The buildings at the Taj are made of burnt bricks which are called *lakhuri* covered with *sang-i-surkh* (red sandstone) and *sang-i-marmar* (marble) slabs held together with iron clamps and dowels. The red sandstone came from Fatehpur Sikri, some 40 kilometres from Agra and Rupbas, 45 kilometres south-west of Agra, while white marble, which are translucent with grey or black streaks, were brought from Makrana quarries in Rajasthan, on bullock carts. Polished plaster of *chuna*, particularly a calciferous stone from Gujarat known as *sang-i Patiali* ('stone from Patiali') or *sang-i mahtabi* ('moonlight stone') were used for surface finish to give the appearance and shine of marble.

The red sandstone and white marble combination – so characteristic of the imperial architectural projects of the Delhi Sultanate – had gone out of fashion in Delhi during the 14th

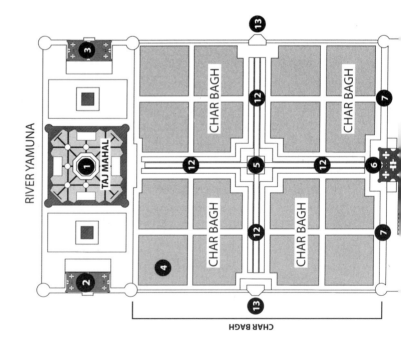

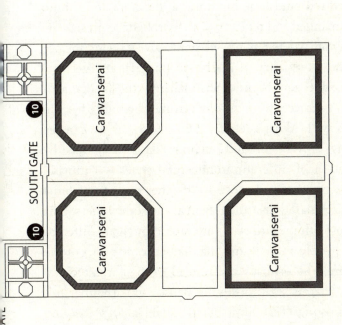

Site map of the Taj Mahal complex (based on J. A. Hodgson's plan, 1928).

1. Main Mausoleum
2. Mosque
3. Mihman Khana, guesthouse
4. Place where Mumtaz Mahal was first buried
5. Central Pool
6. The Great Gate
7. Double-arcade gallery for distributing alms
8. Jilaukhana or Forecourt
9. Khawasspuras, meant for the attendants of the mausoleum
10. Sahehi Burj, unnamed tombs
11. Bazar Street
12. Water Channels with walkways
13. Naubatkhana, or the drum house

and 15th centuries. It made a comeback in the 16th century and Humayun's tomb in Delhi and the Jami Masjid at Fatehpur Sikri are two excellent examples of this style. Red sandstone also had significance in the Persian origins of the Mughal empire, where red was the exclusive colour of the imperial tents. Prominent art historian Ebba Koch points out that the hierarchical use of red sandstone and white marble can be traced to *Vishnudharmottara Purana*, an eighth-century Hindu religious text which recommended white stone buildings for Brahmins and red stone buildings for Kshatriyas. By using this colour combination, the Mughals were trying to identify themselves with the leading classes of Indian society and also articulating their imperial status.[5] Shah Jahan's reign saw a further shift in this trend – privileging of marble over red sandstone structures so characteristic of Akbar's period. Several red sandstone buildings at the Agra and Lahore forts were dismantled and replaced with marble structures. Some existing ones were painted in lime plaster to give it the semblance of marble. The ascendancy of marble in imperial architectural projects reached its zenith under Shah Jahan in the Taj Mahal.

Shah Jahan's projects were different from his grandfather's in other ways as well. Akbar's reign (1556–1605), as we can see in the buildings at Agra Fort and Fatehpur Sikri, was marked by an amalgamation of different architectural styles – Timurid–Persian, Trans-oxanian and those from other regions of India such as Malwa, Gujarat, Rajasthan, Bengal and some others. This was congruent with the emperor's attempt to integrate different geographies, people and cultures that had become a part of the Mughal empire. The primacy of Timurid–Persian architectural style, under Akbar, is seen mostly in mausoleums (Humayun's tomb) and mosques (Fatehpur Sikri). Shah Jahan's absolute and centralized rule, on the other hand, saw the ascendancy of

Timurid–Persian or Iranian cultural elements in most imperial projects. Systematic efforts were also made towards raising the status of imperial power in the eyes of the people. The impression of these two factors could be seen among other things, in marble buildings in Agra Fort, the famous gem-studded golden peacock throne, the forty-pillared 'Halls of Public Audience', the finding of a new imperial city, Shahjahanabad in Delhi, raised vaulted seat of the emperor in the 'Halls of Public Audience' in the forts of Agra, Shahjahanabad and Lahore, and the imperial paintings displaying the emperor with a halo. Taj Mahal displays the influence of both the Timurid–Persian elements and imperial splendour in a classic architectural form.

DESIGN, LAYOUT AND ARCHITECTURE

What makes the architecture of Taj Mahal so striking? Its beauty, strong symbolism, futuristic vision, balance between the spiritual and the material, and, above all, a graceful and aesthetic presence – all these attributes are combined with great attention to detail. The sophistication and perfection of architectural principles and practices, we shall see in the ensuing discussion, gets reflected, among other things, in bilateral symmetry and uniformity of shapes; surface ornamentation; selective use of naturalism; and hierarchical grading of materials, forms and colours. Of these, hierarchical grading, for instance, manifests in the difference in designs between the ground, lower and upper parts of the mausoleum (Fig. 5.1), as also between its exterior surface and walls of the internal burial chambers. Another example of hierarchical grading can be seen in the differential use of construction material for different parts of the complex. The mausoleum, for instance, is built in white marble while the subsidiary structures in red sandstone with white marble

Fig. 5.1 Heirarchical arrangement of designs with geometrical motifs at the bottom and floral motifs at the upper levels.

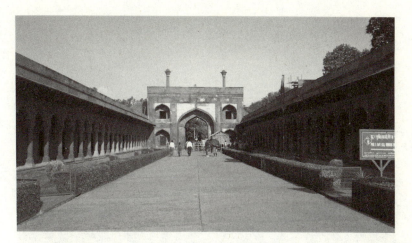

Fig. 5.2 The West gate.

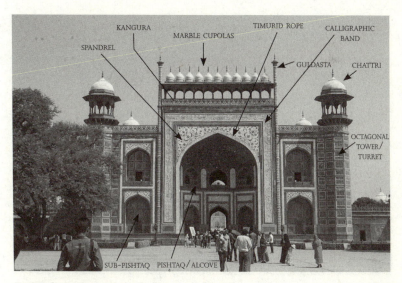

Fig. 5.3 The Great gate with the jilaukhana in the front.

Fig. 5.4 Double-arcaded gallery flanking the Great gate where alms were distributed among the poor.

Fig. 5.5 The Taj Mahal looks smaller from the main gate but looms large when one comes near.

Fig. 5.6 The char bagh with the waterways and the Great gate, as seen from the tomb.

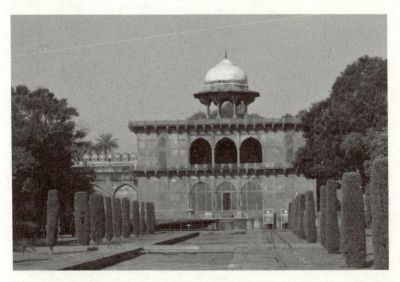

Fig. 5.7 The naubatkhana at the west end of east-west walkway.

Fig. 5.8 The riverfront terrace on which the Taj stands, as seen from the opposite bank of Yamuna.

Fig. 5.9 Taj Mahal flanked by mihman khana (left) and the mosque (right), as seen from Mahtab Bagh.

Fig. 5.10 The Mosque, as seen from the Tomb.

Fig. 5.10a Mihrab, minbar and patterns for prayer mats inside the mosque.

Fig. 5.11 Mihman khana, as seen from the Tomb.

Fig. 5.12 Dados with plant blossoms found in the mosque and mihman khana. These also appear in the Taj Mahal in marble.

Fig. 5.13 Detail of an incised painting made in sgraffito technique. Such paintings adorn the walls of the mosque and mihman khana.

Fig. 5.14 Octagonal pavilions which frame the corners of the tomb complex, seen here is the one on the riverside.

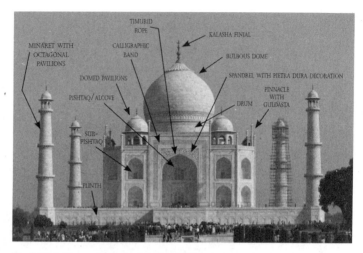

Fig. 5.15 Architectural features of the Taj Mahal.

Fig. 5.16 Free standing, detached minaret at the Taj Mahal. Minarets are attached to the four corners of the podium.

Fig. 5.17 *Attached minarets at the entrance gateway of Akbar's tomb at Sikandara.*

Fig. 5.18 *Pietra dura (Parchinkari) designs bordering flowering plants on the Taj.*

Fig. 5.19 *An excavated portion of Mahtab Bagh.*

Fig. 5.20 Reflection of the Taj in the Yamuna River, around sunset. Photo courtesy Aakash Chakrabarty.

highlights. In terms of core architectural elements, the Taj Mahal is also known for its strong symbolism and futuristic vision.

The idea was to create an earthly replica of the house of Mumtaz Mahal in the Gardens of Paradise. However, the structure was also meant to reflect the power and glory of the Mughals, in particular, Shah Jahan. The objective was to construct 'a masterpiece for ages to come' increasing the 'amazement of all humanity' if one were to put it in the words of Shah Jahan's historian Qazwini.[6] It was built with posterity in mind and the viewers were a part of its concept.[7] There were also provisions for the future upkeep of the monument.

No ground plan of the Taj complex prepared by the Mughals is known to us. On the basis of drawings prepared later, the complex seems to have been planned in a rectangular shape and is aligned from north to south (see site map).

Broadly speaking, the complex consists of two major units: the riverfront terrace and the *char bagh* enclosed with a high boundary wall (except on the riverside), having broad octagonal pavilions at each corner (Fig 5.14); and the two subsidiary open courtyards surrounded by an arcade, the forecourt or *jilaukhana* which literally means, 'in front of the house', and the Taj Ganj.

As one moves from the river to the city side (north to south), first comes the rectangular riverfront terrace containing the mausoleum flanked by an identical-looking mosque and *mihman khana* or 'guest house'; then appears the square *char bagh* or the four-fold garden; third, the rectangular forecourt lined by two residential courtyards, the *khawasspuras*, and two unnamed tombs popularly known as the Saheli Burj; and, finally, to the extreme south of the complex and spilling into the city, lies the squarish Taj Ganj containing two cross-axial bazaar streets and four caravanserai courts at the four corners.

The Taj complex can be approached from three gates – the East gate or 'Fatehabadi Darwaza'; the West gate or 'Fatehpuri Darwaza'; and the South gate, on the Taj Ganj side and difficult to access – all of which open into the forecourt. Of these, the first two gates are identical and are commonly used by the visitors (Fig. 5.2). Flanked by two later buildings, Fatehpuri Masjid and an unknown tomb, both these gates are lined with bazaar streets leading to the forecourt. Income generated from the goods sold in these bazaars and from the rental of accommodation to travellers and animals in the caravanserais accounted for two-thirds of the *waqf* (endowment) of rupees 300,000 created by the emperor for the upkeep of the Taj. The remaining one-third came from annual revenues of thirty villages earmarked for this purpose in Agra. The bazaars and caravanserais represented the material world of the monument which were designed from the very outset to attract tourists. In 1691, Shah Jahan's successor Aurangzeb ordered governors of every province (twenty-one provinces in total) to send Rs 2,000 as a standard practice to the Taj Mahal's caretaker.[8]

Jilaukhana or the Forecourt

The *jilaukhana* or forecourt was a new structural intervention. Shah Jahan was very particular about court etiquettes and mannerism and ceremonial behaviour and wanted these to also get reflected in his architectural projects. Agra Fort – where he rebuilt many structures – did not have a forecourt. The forecourt made its first appearance in Jahangir's tomb built by the emperor in Lahore. It was executed in a more developed form – with proper streets, bazaars and residential buildings – in the Taj. The *jilaukhana* consisted of a rectangular courtyard lined by two identical residential courtyards in the north, the *khawasspuras*, meant for the attendants of the mausoleum as well as two identical tombs (possibly of two lesser wives of Shah Jahan) in the south. It is in the forecourt that the visitors would step down from their horses and elephants and assemble in style before entering the tomb complex.

The Great Gate

To the north of the *jilaukhana* lies the Great gate, the *darwaza-i rauza* ('gate of the mausoleum'). Symbolically, it represents the entrance to the Islamic paradise. Built in the tradition of detached Islamic gateways, found in the front of mosques and tombs, this structure prepares the visitors for what lies ahead of them – the 'Gardens of Paradise' and the mausoleum. The imposing structure of the Great gate is built in red sandstone with white marble inlay outlining its each structural element (Fig. 5.3). It has a large *pishtaq* or a monumental arched niche in the centre, set in a rectangular frame, and is flanked on either side by two tiers of niches, also called alcoves or sub-*pishtaqs*. Alcoves or *pishtaqs* are also popularly understood as deep sunken arches. The central arch is highlighted by a triple rope moulding or frame, a Timurid architectural element; arabesques or interlacing floral patterns, inlaid in white marble with semi-precious stones in the spandrels or the interspersed triangular area between the rectangular frame and the upper sides of the arch; and bands of calligraphed Quranic verses outlining the rectangular frame. These features are also replicated in the main mausoleum and the flanking mosque and guesthouse or *mihman khana*. The corners of the Great gate contain octagonal towers or turrets surmounted by octagonal *chattris* or domed pavilions or kiosks, also seen in the mosque and *mihman khana*. The *pishtaq* is topped by a row of eleven small white marble cupolas or small domed pavilions supported by four arches, set between freestanding pinnacles topped by flower bunches called *guldastas* – a feature which emphasizes the loftiness of the entrance and is also seen in Buland Darwaza within the Jami Masjid complex in Fatehpur Sikri. The selection of Quranic verse inscribed on it describes the structure as an 'entry into paradise' and highlights its sacredness.

> ...But O thou soul at peace,
> Return thou unto thy Lord, well-pleased and well-pleasing unto Him
> Enter thou among my servants,
> An enter thou my paradise [9]

The northern side of the Great gate is flanked by two galleries with double arcades or gallery – like structures containing a range of arches supported on pillars (Fig. 5.4). Giving the semblance of a pillared hall within a pillared hall, these galleries are decorated with stately architectural elements like multi-cusped arches, faceted columns and carved floral bases – indicating the importance of this imperial gesture under Shah Jahan. Here the poor received alms, three times a week, during the rainy season. This practice formed a part of the charities endowed by the emperor for the redemption of the soul of Mumtaz Mahal. The other occasion of giving of alms being the commemoration of her death anniversary.[10]

The Paradise Garden

The Great gate gives a stunning first full view of the Taj set in the garden complex. Someone long ago said, beauty is in the eye of the beholder. If anything, the proverb centralizes the act of 'seeing'. What if, then, you could control that very act of seeing? The Taj is a perfect example of how the this act can be manipulated. Perhaps this is why it continues to intrigue visitors to this day. From the gate, the mausoleum looks small and distant (Fig. 5.5). As one approaches the Taj, it begins to expand and look bigger and many architectural features become noticeable. This was the element of optical control embedded in the design and approach to the monument.

The 'paradise-like garden', as the contemporary chroniclers called it, was an ideal setting for the ethereal beauty of the house of Mumtaz Mahal. We have already discussed how the Mughals sought to create an architectural imagery of the Quranic paradise on earth through a walled garden, with flowing water and flower- and fruit-bearing trees. In some ways, the walled garden at the Taj reiterates this sophisticated imagery but it also goes beyond. The garden at the Taj presents a slightly different, a more improvised version of the char bagh in relation to the tomb. The four-fold garden is divided into a system of paved walkways or khiyabans, water channels, parterres or systemic arrangements of flower beds and stone-bordered, star-shaped flower beds (Fig. 5.6). Each quadrant is further divided into four by sub-walkways. In the centre of the garden is a raised marble water pool containing five fountains. Symbolically, it represented the celestial Kausar, the Prophet's river in paradise.

There is an important improvisation of the positioning of the tomb in the char bagh at the Taj complex. In the classical pattern, the mausoleum is placed at the centre of the char bagh, as seen in the tombs of Humayun in Delhi, Akbar in Sikandara, Itmad-ud Daulah in Agra and Jahangir in Lahore. In the Taj complex, the mausoleum was placed at the end of the four-fold garden, on the riverfront terrace. This gave a sense of depth to the mausoleum when seen from the gateway. Some scholars think that the location of the mausoleum at the end/head of char bagh had an underlying political symbolism. They argue that this was done to fit in a cosmological diagram where the Taj represented the 'Throne of God'. The mausoleum was meant to exemplify the perfection and authority of Mughal leadership. The 'Garden of Paradise' formed a setting for the location of the 'Throne of God' on the Day of the Judgement.[11]

Coming back to other features of the garden complex, there are two identical pavilions, now called *naubatkhana*, or the 'drum house', at the end of east-west walkway. These pavilions are also known as *baradari*, a recreational pavilion or Jal Mahal (Water Palace). The pavilion located at the western-garden wall now houses the museum (Fig. 5.7).

Nothing definite is known about the original plants in the Taj garden. Going by the reports published later, it possibly included trees like cypress, cotton, medlar, etc; flowering plants such as roses, marigold and poppies; rare aromatic herbs; and fruit-bearing trees such as mangoes, oranges, grapes, pomegranates, bananas, lime and such others. The garden was irrigated by water brought from the Yamuna through aqueducts and distributed through earthenware pipes. One of the most unusual features of the Taj garden is the even distribution of water with equal pressure from the lotus-bud-shaped fountains. This was done by inserting copper pots in the water course between the underground water pipes and the fountains.[12]

The Riverfront Terrace

The riverfront terrace – appreciated well only from the opposite bank of the river – was one of the first structures to be built by Shah Jahan's architects. For building this solid block of brick-and-mortar platform (Fig. 5.8), the sand on the riverbank had to be stabilized first. Art historian Ebba Koch draws attention to poet Kalim's lyrical verse which offers a unique account of this technical feat – of foundation wells encased in wood and filled with rubble, mortar and iron.[13] The terrace, also described as *chabutra* in contemporary accounts, was built on this network of foundation wells.

> ...They make a well (chah) to manage the work, from wood,
> and set it firmly into the sand
> Then they take out the sand from inside it, until solid earth
> comes from its depth.
> In this well stone and iron are buried until they reach
> the level of the surface ...[14]

Kalim's account is also supported by findings of the excavations around the foundations of the Taj carried out in the 1950s.

Viewed from the side of river Yamuna, the terrace had two doors (now blocked) below the two corner towers which could be accessed through a wide flight of stairs, or *ghats*, when approached by a boat. This is how Shah Jahan entered the tomb complex through the Yamuna River. The centre of the terrace once had a series of open arches through which light reached the now inaccessible and mysterious *tahkhana* or underground chamber – a cool gallery lined by a series of rooms along the riverfront. The terrace is covered in red sandstone – its rear or river facade has arches carved with *jaalis* or perforated screens, floral and tree motifs with inlays of white marble while the front and the top side are adorned with geometrical motifs in red sandstone of varying shades and white marble.

Viewed from the Great gate side, the monuments on the terrace were built on the principle of strict bilateral symmetry with emphasis on the features of the central axis – the elevated tomb and its four minarets flanked by a mosque to the west and a *mihman khana* (guest house) to the east.

The Mosque and the Mihman Khana

Built in red sandstone, both the mosque and *mihman khana* serve as mirror images of each other and reinforce the principle of bilateral symmetry (Fig. 5.9). Of these, the mosque had a clear religious function while the *mihman khana* was built more as a *jawab* (answer) to the former and housed visitors to the site. In the late 18th and 19th century, however, many British officials and Indian princes used it to host banquet parties.

The facade of both these two identical structures look like a replica of the Great gate with some differences – the row of eleven marbled cupolas over the *pishtaq* of the Great gate is not there in the two structures and the upper niche in the two-tiered alcove flanking the *pishtaq* of the Great gate is blind in the case of the mosque (Fig. 5.10) and the *mihman khana* (Fig. 5.11). Another major difference between the Great gate and these two structures is the presence of the three domes, all in marble, in the latter.

The mosque and the guest house have a tank (*hauz*) in the courtyard fronting them. This was used for ritual ablution before prayers in the case of the former but had a purely ornamental purpose in the case of the latter. Likewise, both the structures have red sandstone dados or relief patterns of plants with blossoms in the lower part of the walls, surrounded by a wave-like design (Fig 5.12). These dados also get repeated in the mausoleum, though in marble. The interior of both these structures also have identical incised paintings adorning the space between the dados to the ceiling. They consist of white stylized floral and geometrical motifs against red background. These paintings are made in sgraffito technique whereby a red plaster is put on a white one and then the motifs are created by scrapping the upper red layer (Fig. 5.13). The mosque is however different from the *mihman khana* in some respects – it has a *mihrab*, or arched niche indicating the direction of the *qibla* wall/Mecca; a *minbar* or pulpit for *imam* or the leader of the prayer to deliver Friday sermon; and a *masqura* or a secluded compartment for the emperor. The floor of the mosque is also inlaid with patterns of prayer mats (Fig. 5.10a).

The Marble Platform and the Minarets

The mausoleum is placed on a platform completely faced with marble (Fig. 5.15) for architectural details. The platform is 19 feet high and 187 feet on each side. It is also called *kursi* or 'chair' in contemporary accounts as it symbolizes the platform on which the throne stands. This expression was mostly used for imperial mausoleums and signified the presence of the enthroned persons. The *kursi*, in turn, is placed over the *chabutara* or terrace.

The platform contains non-functional trefoil blind arches set in rectangular frames on all sides. It is approached by two concealed flight of stairs placed at the centre of the south side. The centre of the other three sides of the platform contain an oblong room flanked by square chambers and approached through small doors. These may have been used as rest rooms for tomb attendants or imperial visitors in the past. The plainness of surface decoration of the platform, concealed stairs and blind arches, as opposed to arched recesses in Humayun's tomb, have a purpose – they do not distract visitors' attention from the main building. The four corners of the platform are accentuated by the bases of the detached minarets (Fig. 5.16). Set in four corners of the mausoleum they enhance the principle of strict symmetry and provide a spatial reference frame to the central structure.[15] Considered favoured architectural symbols of Islam, the minarets also created a special aura around the mausoleum. In the words of Lahauri, they were 'like ladders to the foot of the sky'.[16]

It is here in Taj that free-standing minarets make their first appearance in Mughal architecture. In the case of Akbar's tomb at Sikandra, the circular and tapering minarets are attached to the roof of the South gate (Fig. 5.17). The towers attached to the tomb of Itmad-ud Daulah and the 'high minarets in five stages rising upto the height of about 100 feet at the corners of Jahangir's tomb further reinforced the idea of synthesizing minarets with Mughal buildings.'[17]

Made of curved marble blocks, the minarets at the Taj are tall, slender and tapering structures built in three stages connected with a spiralling staircase of 162 steps and surmounted by an octagonal *chhatri* with a *kalasha* finial or superimposed pots on the top of the dome (Fig 5.16). Each stage has a low balcony and railing supported by vaulted brackets. The minarets have deliberately been built to a slant so that if they ever collapse, they fall outwards – away from the mausoleum.

The Mausoleum

The mausoleum's design is inspired by the Timurid *hasht bihistht*, the concept of 'eight paradises' explained in Chapter 2, was first introduced in Humayun's tomb. It is square in plan with chamfered/rounded corners making it look like an irregular octagon, also known as a Baghdadi octagon. This irregular octagon is divided into nine parts by four intersecting construction lines. It follows a perfect cross-axial symmetry with the domed octagonal chamber in the centre and connected to rectangular *pishtaq* halls on the cardinal axes. For a rough idea, see Fig. 2.4 in the chapter on Humayun's tomb, though there are some differences between the two. Unlike Humayun's tomb, the corner chambers of the structure at the Taj are more complex – they move in towards the centre, remain within the outline of the chamfered square and form a square ambulatory, connected by short corridors, around the central chamber. This plan is repeated on the upper floor.[18]

The mausoleum rises over a plinth which carries stylized pattern of leaves with interlacing stems, symmetrically arranged in cartouches or carved design frames. Its exterior follows the same design and appearance as the Great gate and the mosque and *mihman khana* – a large *pishtaq* or a monumental arched niche flanked by two tiers of niches or alcoves which are like sub-*pishtaqs*. The *pishtaq* is set into a rectangular frame and highlighted by a triple rope moulding; marble inlay work in the spandrels; and a calligraphic band outline (Fig. 5.15). This calligraphy is absent in *mihman khana*, though. Some features, however, differentiate the design and appearance of the mausoleum from the other structures in comparison. The mausoleum is surfaced with superior material; white marble as opposed to red sandstone seen on the Great gate, the mosque and the *mihman khana*. Further, the corner octagonal towers or turrets surmounted by octagonal cupolas, found in the corners of the other three structures, are replaced in the mausoleum by chamfered or rounded corners with two-tiered alcoves.

The inner walls of the arched recess of the *pishtaq* are decorated with symmetrically arranged bands of multi-cusped blind arches and cartouches or interlacing designs set in rectangular frames. They have two doors, one above the other, filled with *jaalis* or perforated screens to allow light. The dados or lower walls of the *pishtaq*, ornamented with naturalistic motifs of plants with blossoms within inlaid frames, look superior to the low-relief leaf and stem carving in the cartouches in the plinth. The sub-*pishtaqs* are diminutive versions of the central *pishtaq* and carry the same surface embellishment. This arrangement is replicated on all sides of the mausoleum.

The features of the *pishtaq* on the exterior and its surface embellishment are also repeated in the interior octagonal domed hall in the lower of the two tiers of eight – the number eight is associated with eight spaces of the Quranic paradise – radiating niches called *nashiman* or seat separated by an inscriptional band of Quranic verses. There is one difference however – individual plants with blossoms in the dados or lower walls in the niches on the exterior are replaced with luxurious vases filled with flowers in the interior. The lower niches lying along the cardinal axes in the hall in the interior are transparent and fitted with perforated screens while those along the diagonal axes are solid rectangular doors with *jaalis*. The vault of the mausoleum is filled with *muqarna* – honeycomb shaped elements which are conclave, arched decorative motifs.

Mumtaz Mahal's cenotaph or 'empty tomb' is in the centre of the upper room while that of Shah Jahan lies to its west. These are replicas of the actual cenotaphs or tomb stones created over the two graves in the lower tomb chamber. The cenotaphs in the upper chamber are surrounded by an octagonal perforated marble screen with exquisite inlay work and delicate *jaalis*. The marble screen created an ambulatory passage around the cenotaph and was a new feature in domed tomb architecture. Set up in 1643, it replaced the original gold railing made by the goldsmith Bibadal Khan in 1633, on Mumtaz's second *urs*. Mumtaz's cenotaph in the upper chamber is decorated with Quranic inscriptions, naturalistic plants and hanging blossoms while the one in the lower chamber contains ninety-nine names of Allah, beautifully calligraphed in black marble and inlaid in white marble.

The mausoleum is topped by a bulbous dome – likened to the onion domes seen in the architecture of Bijapur – which rises on a high drum. The Taj's dome differs from its counterpart at Humayun's tomb in both concept and form. While the latter springs directly from the drum at its base, the one at Taj first incurves at the base, then curves out smoothly, and finally recedes smoothly in an inverted lotus, which had become a standard feature of structures described as Indo-Islamic.[19] At the top, lies a *kalasha* finial consisting of superimposed gilded pots surmounted by a crescent. Taj's dome is surrounded by four octagonal and domed pavilions or cupolas arranged on its diagonal ends. The roof terrace is outlined by a parapet with *guldastas*, or pinnacles carrying flower bunches, projecting from all angular points, as in the case of Humayun's tomb.

SURFACE DECORATION, PIETRA DURA AND CALLIGRAPHY

Surface decoration in the Taj Mahal is at its classic first. Three features deserve particular mention – geometrical and plant and flower motifs, marble inlay work, and calligraphy. In the earlier monuments of the Sultanate and the Mughal period, typical geometric patterns dominated surface decoration. In the case of the Taj, such motifs were mostly relegated to floors – on the platform in front of gateway, walkways of the garden, platform of the riverfront terrace, marble and sandstone platform of the mausoleum – and *jaalis* or screens. As opposed to this, plant and floral motifs appear on the base, lower walls or dados, spandrels or some upper parts of the buildings such as the Great gate, the mosque and *mihman khana* and the mausoleum.

The flower and plant motifs used for surface decoration symbolized perfect paradisiacal bloom and reinforced the larger concept of mausoleum as a paradisiacal garden house. The metaphor of gardens and its flowers also had a deeper imperial symbolism under Shah Jahan – it represented not only the emperor and his rule and governance but also his court and his family. Besides, the metaphor also had an extended political significance and served as an instrument of imperial propaganda for his chroniclers, who portrayed him as an 'erect cypress of the garden of the caliphate.' Under Shah Jahan's rule, it was said, 'Hindustan had become the rose garden of the earth.'[20] Vases filled with overflowing plants were not only important in Muslim cultures but also pointed to the ancient Indian symbol of prosperity and well-being – the *purna ghata* which symbolizes the 'vase of plenty'.[21]

Marble inlay is seen in the frames of the dados, spandrels of the pishtaqs and sub-pishtaqs, as well as the cenotaphs and railings of the major buildings at the Taj. The technique of inlaying marble with coloured or 'choice stones' is seen in the earlier Islamic monuments of Gujarat and Mandu. It is also seen in the *pishtaqs* and gates of Akbar's tomb at Sikandra. In the case of Taj Mahal, inlaying white marble with precious and semi-precious stones such as lapis, onyx, jasper, topaz, cornelian, and so on, is taken to its classic form. The technique of inlaying marble with precious and semi-precious stones is commonly called pietra dura (Fig. 5.18). It was first developed in Florence, Italy, during the 16th century.

Some scholars have suggested that the technique was introduced in the Mughal court by European lapidaries or artisans – few even credit Austin or Augustin de Bordeaux, a French lapidary known during Jahangir's time.[22] This has been opposed by others who say that the Florentine pietra dura is principally figurative and its only instance in Mughal architecture can be seen in the alcove or niche behind the emperor's throne in the Diwan-i Aam at the Red Fort in Delhi, which was constructed between 1643 and 1648.[23] The pietra dura work in the Diwan-i Aam depicts beautiful flowers, birds and animals. It also shows a representation of the Greek god Orpheus playing lute to animals.

Another set of scholars locate the inlaying technique within the larger indigenous tradition of *parchinkari*, in which the inlay work was originally done on metal (for example, artefacts from Bidri and Muradabad) and wood. In the case of the Mughals, they argue, the idea of the form and design is principally Islamic, and the motifs were borrowed from Persian examples. They underscore that the depiction of naturalistic flowery plants can be previously seen in Jahangiri miniatures. Marble inlays with images of plants with blossoms – affected by the choice of stones corresponding to the natural hues – validated the unrivalled standing of the Mughals in inlay work. The Mughals called this technique of inlaying white marble with precious and semi-precious stones *parchinkari*. An example of such an inlay, though with typically Islamic motifs, of flowers, cypresses, floral arabesques, vases and wine pots was first seen in the tomb of Itmad-ud Daulah. During Shah Jahan's time, it is argued, this indigenous technique of embedding marble with precious and semi-precious stones became a leading characteristic for surface decoration of distinguished palaces and tombs.[24]

H. Voysey, who did the first scientific study of the inlaid stones in 1825, wrote: 'A single flower in the screen around the tombs, or sarcophagi, contains a hundred stones, each cut to the exact shape necessary, and highly polished; and in the interior alone of the building there are several hundred flowers, each containing like a number of stones.'[25]

Surface decoration in the Taj takes a religious-spiritual dimension in the form of inscriptional bands of Quranic verses. The Taj, in fact, displays the largest inscriptional programme in the Islamic world. Calligraphed in black marble and inlaid in white marble, Quranic verses are inscribed on three of the four major buildings – the mausoleum, the great gate and the mosque. It has twenty-five Quranic inscriptions, of which fourteen are complete *suras* or chapters. In one way or another, all inscriptions deal with themes like the Day of Judgment, divine mercy and paradise for the faithful. The verses on the *darwaza-i rauza* directly identify the Taj with paradise.

It has been pointed out that even the acoustics of the Taj Mahal – the echo of sound in the dome of the tomb chamber – adds to the paradisiacal symbolism. 'We feel as if it were from heaven, and breathed by angels; it is to the ear what the building itself was to the eye' is how W. H. Sleeman, one of the early British observers of the Taj Mahal, described the effect in 1836.[26]

THE TAJ AFTER SHAH JAHAN

After shifting the capital from Agra to Shahjahanabad in 1648, Shah Jahan made just one visit to the Taj Mahal in 1654 to show his son Dara Shukoh the newly built Moti Masjid at Agra Fort.[27] In 1658, the emperor was deposed by his son Aurangzeb who held Shah Jahan captive in the Agra Fort till the latter's death in 1666. His coffin was taken down through the Shah Burj of Agra Fort, placed on a boat and carried to the 'illumined tomb' (Taj Mahal) where it was laid down in the lower tomb chamber next to his wife.

After Shah Jahan's death, the Taj temporarily faded from Mughal history. Scattered evidence points to some repairs under the Mughal emperor Aurangzeb and to the fact that it was raided by many, including the Sayyid Brothers in 1719, the Jats in 1761 and the British and others during the 1857 Rebellion. The Sayyid Brothers are supposed to have taken away imperial treasures, among them a pearl *chadar* (sheet) which originally covered the cenotaph of Mumtaz Mahal, while the Jats are believed to have taken away the doors. In various raids before and during the 1857 Rebellion, the Taj was also robbed of many precious and semi-precious stones that once adorned the surface.

The monument regained prominence once again during the colonial period. The East India Company gained control of north India towards the late 18th–early 19th century. In 1803, Lord Lake took control of Agra after the Second Anglo-Maratha War. With the British East India Company gaining political ascendancy in Delhi and Agra, Western travellers, artists and officials started visiting the Taj and other monuments in north India. The monument sometimes functioned as a guesthouse for officers and visitors or served to entertain 'British ladies and gentlemen'. While important guests would occupy the *mihman khana*, garden towers or tents pitched in the gardens, the soldiers or attendants would stay in the *jilaukhana*. Gradually, the Taj started featuring in 'Company drawings' or 'Company paintings' and in Orientalist depictions of India. Through the British, the Taj became known to the larger world. [28]

The British also made attempts to repair, restore and conserve the monuments, including the Taj – efforts which became more systematic after the formation of the Archeological Survey of India (ASI) in 1860–61. However, the formal monumentalization of the Taj began in the early 20th century, particularly under Lord Curzon.[29] Unlike his predecessors, who were obsessed with the mausoleum, Curzon focused on the entire complex including the gardens and the outer courts. A massive restoration project was undertaken, and it tried to:

> Accommodate Indian feelings and perceptions – permissions were granted to the local community to use the mosque and tomb space for religious/ceremonial purposes; a particular kind of 'Mughal' dress [white suits with a green scarf and a badge] was given to the attendants of the ASI at the Taj; and a decorated lamp [Saracenic style Mamluk lamp procured from

Egypt] was installed inside the main chamber of the tomb in order to show the intrinsic link between [the] Mughal past and the British present.[30]

This colonial politicization of the Taj was opposed by nationalist leaders, particularly Jawaharlal Nehru, independent India's first prime minister. For him, the sites popularly regarded as Indo-Islamic, especially the Taj Mahal, were 'a symbol of India's composite culture' and he 'worked hard to translate this interpretation of India's past into a serious policy discourse'. Accordingly, the Taj Mahal was 'declared a monument of national importance' and 'publicized as an official symbol of India's contribution to world heritage'. This 'official portrayal of the Taj purely as a "heritage site" and/or a symbol of "eternal love" got established as the most reliable and uncontested meaning of this building in later years'.[31]

The influence of the Taj Mahal went beyond the official discourse. As Ebba Koch points out, it has been used as a metaphor for excellence and deployed in advertisements to sell products that have barely anything to do with the tomb – from jewellery, teabags, Scotch whiskey and liqueur to beer. Whether it is the Tata Group of hotels in Delhi and Mumbai or Trump's Taj Mahal, the casino resort in Atlantic City, New Jersey, which closed in 2016, brands have been created based on the glory of the monument as a symbol of grandeur. Numerous restaurants across the world append Taj to their names to showcase their association with India. Besides, models of the Taj Mahal comprise the most popular souvenirs of India alongside marble plates, boxes and tabletops carrying the monument's characteristic pietra dura design.[32]

Ebba Koch also draws attention to instances of the world of music being influenced by the Taj – the rock-blues singer from

Massachusetts, Henry Saint Clair Fredericks, adopted 'Taj Mahal' as his stage name. 'Inside the Taj Mahal', Paul Horn's flute session recorded in 1968, became very popular as a work of new-age music and sold more than a million copies. In 1997, Greek musician Yanni staged a concert within the Taj premises despite strong opposition from the heritage enthusiasts. It received worldwide attention. The monument is a staple presence in Bollywood films and songs, popular histories and narratives of tour guides.[33]

The monument and its legacy have also led to political contestations and scams. Within the subcontinent, the politics of appropriation has led to polarization. P. N. Oak's writings have floated the theory that the Taj Mahal is not Mumtaz's tomb but an ancient Hindu temple palace of Lord Shiva then known as *Tejo Mahalaya*. The idea caught on with some Hindu-nationalist politicians, who reiterated the Hindu character of the monument and said that Shah Jahan usurped a part of temple land from the Hindu king Jai Singh. There have also been demands from Muslim politicians to hand over the tomb complex to the Sunni Waqf Board for the protection, conservation and management of the tomb complex.

In April 2015, a lawsuit was filed by six lawyers in the Agra Civil Court claiming Taj was a Shiva temple called *Tejo Mahalaya*. This claim was contested both by the Union culture ministry and the ASI. The former clarified in the Lok Sabha (in November 2015) that there was no evidence to suggest that the Taj Mahal was a Hindu temple of Shiva, while the latter, in a written reply to the court in August 2017, categorically stated that the monument was a tomb and not a temple.[34] While such ideas continue to be debated and contested, the mausoleum is fast being appropriated by the global community for different purposes. Replicas of the monument have been made in places such as China, Bangladesh, Malayasia, United Arab Emirates and even New Jersey. Moreover, the Taj has already made its way into the official list of the 'New Seven Wonders of the World', on the strength of more than 100 million votes, as an exemplar of global heritage throughout history.

HOW THE IDEA OF THE BLACK TAJ AND OTHER MYTHS CAME INTO BEING

Some myths and legends, floated by visitors, scholars and guides, have become ingrained in popular history and folklore surrounding the monument. Sometimes, they take precedence over academically researched narratives. These stories, as most guides would admit, makes the monument more interesting to the visitors.

One of the most common myths, emerging primarily from the West, was that the Taj Mahal was designed by a 'Western'/'foreign' architect. Foreign travellers to India suggested that such a grand architectural feat could not have been accomplished without the involvement of an external architect. Sebastian Manrique, the Spanish traveller who visited Agra in 1640–41, gave credit to the Italian jeweller and designer Geronimo Veroneo, while William Sleeman, who visited Agra in 1836, ascribed it to a Frenchman – Austin de Bordeaux. The theory of 'Western'/ 'European' involvement started circulating soon after the monument was unveiled to the world and one can hear its echoes, in some form or other, in the modern times as well. Scholars like W. E. Begley and Z. A. Desai point out that the 19th-century manuscript *Tarikh-i Taj Mahal* regards Isa Muhammad Effendi of Turkey as the architect of the monument. However, as we have discussed earlier in this chapter, contemporary sources indicate that the monument was designed by a collective of architects with a proactive emperor in the lead.[35]

More enduring than the myth of a foreign architect has been the story of the Black Taj Mahal. It continues to be narrated with interesting graphic details by some local guides. The idea of a second, rivalling Taj, the Black Taj, was first floated by Jean-Baptiste Tavernier, who visited Agra in 1640–41 and 1665. He reported that Shah Jahan wanted to build his own tomb in black marble on the opposite bank of river Yamuna in Mahtab Bagh ('Moonlight Garden') but his sons opposed the plan and Aurangzeb finally abandoned it.[36] The story caught on and became a part of the folklore surrounding the Taj. It was said that the emperor's black marble tomb on the left bank of the river was to serve as a counter-image to the white marble tomb of his favourite wife on the right bank. The two structures were to be linked by a bridge over the river. British army man and administrator Sleeman carried forward Tavernier's theory that Shah Jahan had started the construction of his own tomb on the opposite bank of Yamuna and that it was connected to the Taj Mahal by a bridge. He furthered the perception that the death of Austin de Bordeaux – who, Sleeman thought had designed the Taj – and the subsequent wars among Shah Jahan's sons prevented the completion of the Black Taj.[37]

The positioning of Shah Jahan's larger cenotaph to the west of that of Mumtaz Mahal, located in the centre of the upper tomb chamber, introduces an element of asymmetry to the otherwise perfect Taj. This also lent substance to the story that the emperor's burial was not originally planned in the Taj Mahal and that it was an afterthought.[38]

There is no historical evidence to support this claim of a Black Taj. Even archaeological excavations carried out in Mahtab Bagh in the 1990s (Fig. 5.19) did not reveal evidence of any such black marble tomb. Elizabeth B. Moynihan, a scholar specializing in gardens, clarifies that Mumtaz Mahal's tomb once stood between two *char baghs* (of Taj Mahal and Mahtab Bagh) separated by river Yamuna. When viewed from the riverfront pavilion on the opposite bank, the Taj gave the appearance of an ethereal tomb floating on sacred waters (Fig. 5.20). The mausoleum and its image united the two *char baghs* and symbolically stood at the centre of an ordered universe – the paradise ideal.[39]

Another popular myth is that Shah Jahan killed the architects and workers who built the Taj. Other versions mention that the emperor got their hands chopped off and their eyes gouged out or had them thrown into the dungeons of Agra fort, so that no one would be left to build a second monument like that. Other non-violent versions of this myth say that the emperor paid them handsomely and signed an agreement with them that they would never build a monument like that again. Taking away someone's ability to work in future also means 'chopping off the hands' in popular usage – this is how some guides explain the story. This story again has no historical basis and such tales are a part of folklore surrounding monuments in many cultures, including England, Ireland, Russia and parts of Asia.[40]

Finally, there is a tale related to Lord William Bentinck, who had apparently planned to demolish the Taj Mahal and auction the marble. His biographer, John Rosselli, clarified that this was never the case and the basis of this rumour was Bentinck's fundraising sale of discarded marble from Agra fort. Parts of marble facing and outer hall of the *hammam* (bath house) at Agra fort were taken down by Lord Hastings in 1815 and its marble columns with inlay work were scattered – two of them can still be found at the Taj museum. The marble facade and perhaps some columns were later auctioned by Lord Bentinck when he was the Governor General of India (1828–35). This gave rise to the rumours that he wanted to dismantle the Taj and sell it.

Such myths and legends have served to popularize the charm of Taj Mahal. They have, over a period of time, become an integral part of experiencing Taj Mahal. Deconstructing such myths and narrating how they came into being could perhaps be an equally interesting exercise for the guides and experience for the visitors.

TAJ MAHAL, 'GARDEN OF PARADISE': KEY INSIGHTS

Akbar's reign was marked by an amalgamation of architectural traditions of their Central Asian homelands and those regions in India that had recently been brought under the control of the Mughal empire. By Shah Jahan's time, the empire had become absolute and centralized like never before and his art and architectural projects speak of the centralized authority and hierarchy just like his court rituals.

The architectural style combining red sandstone and white marble, which first made its appearance in the Alai Darwaza in the Qutb Minar complex, passed through several stages – including Ghiyasuddin Tughlaq's tomb, Jamali-Kamali mosque, Qila-i-Kuhna Masjid and Humayun's tomb in Delhi; Jama Masjid at Fatehpur Sikri; and Itmad-ud Daulah's tomb in Agra – to reach its apogee in the Taj Mahal.

The Taj marks an evolution in tomb architecture in India from a simple square plan with a tentative dome first seen in the tomb of Iltutmish in the Qutb complex in Delhi to a complex tomb representing the 'Gardens of Paradise' through the Tughlaq period tombs with sloping walls and half domes to the Lodi-era octagonal tombs with semicircle domes to the Persianized Humayun's tomb with true double dome, *char bagh* and *hasht bihistht* plan to Itmad-ud Daulah's tomb built in white marble with minarets and pietra dura ornamentation to the Taj Mahal. One should try and see the monuments in this order to understand both the development of funerary architecture during the Sultanate and Mughal periods.

6

THE RED FORT

> ...There can be no other such strong Fort on the face of this universe – probably there is no such fort underneath the sky which glitters such as the sun and the moon in the firmament. Its structures are beyond imagination. Its every corner is dazzling and every direction full of heavenly gardens. It is in the form of heavens.

This is how Muhammad Waris, one of the chroniclers of the reign of Shah Jahan, described the Red Fort around the time of its construction in the 17th century.[1] More than 200 years later, James Fergusson, one of the leading architectural historians of the 19th century, also uses similar language to describe the Red Fort in his famous work *History of Indian and Eastern Architecture* (1876). He says: 'The palace at Delhi is, or rather was, the most magnificent palace in the east – perhaps in the world – and the only one at least in India.' The Fort continues to remain one of the iconic monuments of India.

Lal Qila, or the Red Fort, lies on the eastern edge of the old parts of Delhi along the Ring Road encircling the city, adjacent to the Salimgarh Fort. It was originally located on the banks of the Yamuna, which has shifted its course considerably since. Once a palace-fort, the Red Fort complex was built by the fifth Mughal emperor, Shah Jahan (r. 1628–58), as the citadel of his

DID YOU KNOW?

Shah Jahan sought to impart a paradisiacal symbolism to Red Fort by means of a water channel called *nahar-i-behisht* or 'Stream of Paradise' which flowed through important buildings of the palace-fort and through the principal streets and bazaars.

Do you know that the elevated seat of the emperor in the Hall of Public Audience is the only place in the palace-fort which has depictions of animate beings, otherwise considered un-Islamic? (see pages 239–40)

The Hall of Private Audience has an inscription endorsing paradisiacal symbolism of the place. It says 'If there be paradise on earth, it is this, it is this, it is this.'

Shahjahanabad had two imperial streets emerging from within the fort and running out into the city; one ran towards the iconic Chandni Chowk and the other towards the present Darya Ganj. Both were dotted with bazaars (see pages 246–47).

The iconic diamond Koh-i-Noor ('Mountain of Light'), now displayed as a part of the Crown Jewel collection at the Tower of London, once adorned the famous peacock throne of Shah Jahan and was kept in the Hall of Private Audience in the Agra Fort and Red Fort (see pages 241; 248)

Shah Jahan's peacock throne was taken to Iran by its ruler Nadir Shah. The throne became an insignia of the Iranian monarchy and, though the original one was lost soon, its reproductions continued to be made for the future kings (see page 248).

King George V and Queen Mary appeared before the people of Delhi during the Durbar of 1911 from a balcony attached to a river-facing octagonal tower of the Red Fort (see page 242)

Do you know that there was a Rangoon (Yangon, Myanmar) connection behind Red Fort becoming a site of India's Independence Day celebrations? (see pages 252–54) new imperial capital, Shahjahanabad ('the abode of Shah Jahan') in the 17th century. All Mughal buildings in the complex were built during Shah Jahan's reign with the exception of Moti Masjid (which was built by his son, Aurangzeb) and Zafar Mahal and Hira Mahal, constructed around 1840s, by later Mughal emperor Bahadur Shah Zafar. The palace-fort remained under varying degrees of Mughal control until around 1857 when it became the seat and symbol of a famous rebellion directed against colonial British power. With the suppression of the rebellion, the palace-fort and the city passed under the control of the British. The British company demolished a large number of buildings and created army barracks, hospitals, bungalows, administrative buildings, sheds and godowns inside the complex. Following India's independence from British rule, Red Fort became one of the most iconic representations of the country's Independence Day celebrations. It was declared a UNESCO World Heritage Site in 2007. The monument has been in news in the recent years for being adopted by the Dalmia Bharat group under the central government's 'Adopt a Heritage' scheme. It became the first corporate house in India's history to adopt a monument for maintenance and operations.

CIRCUMSTANCES LEADING TO THE CONSTRUCTION OF THE RED FORT IN DELHI

Known by several names at different points of time such as *Qila-i-Mubarak* ('Fort of Fortune'), *Qila-i-Shahjahanabad* ('Fort of Shahjahanabad') or *Qila-i-Mualla* (the 'Exalted Fort'), the Red Fort represents the pinnacle of Mughal palace-fort building activity. It also signifies the transfer of the seat of Mughal power from Agra to Delhi. Why did Shah Jahan shift the capital from Agra to Delhi? The most common view is that the scorching heat of Agra forced the emperor to look for a new capital. But there were other bigger reasons as well. The idea of distinguishing himself from his predecessors and leaving behind a monument as a testimony of individual glory and lasting fame was another reason behind the building of a new city and a magnificent palace-fort complex. This could not have been done in Agra as the city was too small for Shah Jahan's grand and ambitious building plans.[2] Located on the banks of the Yamuna, the city of Agra had developed as a long thin strip of inhabited land. It was fast getting eroded and some structures, particularly the ones on the riverbank, had already started collapsing. Further, the encroachments by mansions, shops and other buildings were congesting the streets and thoroughfares. Even the gates of the palace-fort at Agra had become small for the crowds that would assemble on the days of court audience or festivals and there had been instances of people getting killed or injured.[3]

Even Lahore was considered as a possible option for the new capital but it was ruled out because not only had the city become crowded but also its planning and layout were inherently jumbled and haphazard.[4] In 1639, Shah Jahan instructed his architects, engineers and astrologers to select a new site in a mild climate somewhere between Agra and Lahore. They finally narrowed on Delhi, which had remained the principal centre of Muslim rule in north India since the establishment of the Delhi Sultanate in the late 13th/early 14th century right until the beginning of the 16th century, when the Afghan rulers, the Lodis, shifted the capital to Agra. Delhi had also been an important religious-spiritual and pilgrimage centre housing tombs and graves of several holy men and Sufi saints, including Qutbuddin Bakhtiyar Kaki, Nizamuddin Auliya and Nasiruddin Chirag Dehlavi.

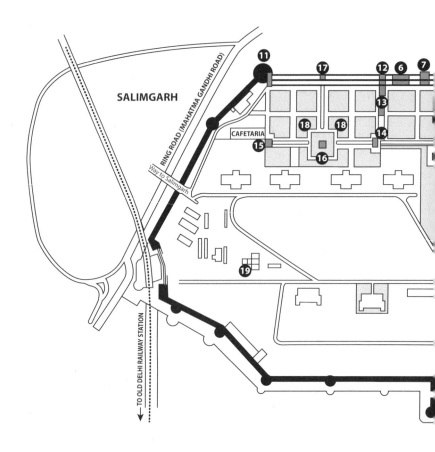

Site map of the Red Fort complex (based on Ebba Koch, Mughal Architecture, Second edition, New Delhi, 2014).

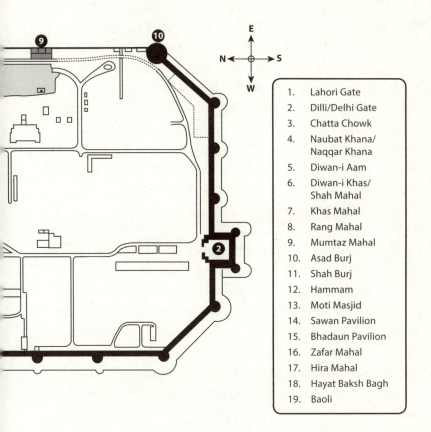

After several visits to Delhi and, discussions with Hindu astrologers, *ulama*, who were the Muslim religious scholars, and saints, Shah Jahan finally chose a site on the banks of river Yamuna between Firuzabad (the settlement established by Delhi sultan Firuz Shah Tughlaq) and Salimgarh Fort (built by Afghan ruler Sher Shah Suri's son Salim Shah).[5] The specific spot of the new capital — the right bank of the Yamuna lying to the south of the Salimgarh Fort — was regarded as auspicious in Hindu mythology. It was also believed to have been blessed by Lord Vishnu as a place where one could gain the knowledge of the Vedas (Hindu religious texts) by just taking a dip in the waters there. The spot was called *Nigambodhak*, meaning 'that which makes known the knowledge of the Vedas.'[6] Nigambodh Ghat still continues to be regarded as a holy site by the Hindus.

CONSTRUCTION

On April 29, 1639, at a time determined by imperial astrologers, the *subahdar* or Mughal governor of Delhi instructed the architects Ustad Ahmad and Ustad Hamid — both of whom had worked earlier on building the Taj Mahal — to begin the excavations for the new capital. Soon princes and high-ranking officials also ordered work on the land allotted for their *havelis* (mansions). Shah Jahan's historians inform us that the construction of imperial structures took place under three successive governors — Ghairat Khan, who organized the excavations and building material; Allah Vardi Khan, who got the river-facing palace walls erected; and, Makramat Khan, who supervised the construction of the walls, buildings and gardens of the palace-fort. After a period of nine years, on April 19, 1648, the Mughal emperor entered the Daulatkhana-i Khas/Diwan-i Khas, which was the 'Hall of Special Audience' through the gate fronting the river. Special celebrations were held

Fig. 6.1 The ramparts of the Red Fort from where the prime minister of India addresses the nation.

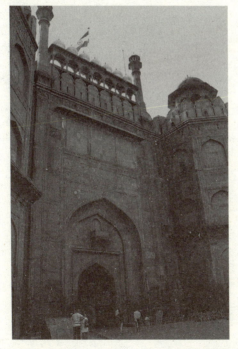

Fig. 6.2 The Lahori gate which still remains the public entrance to the palace-fort.

Fig. 6.3 The Delhi gate as seen from within the palace-fort.

Fig. 6.3a The elephants at the Delhi gate were removed by Aurangzeb but were later restored by Lord Curzon.

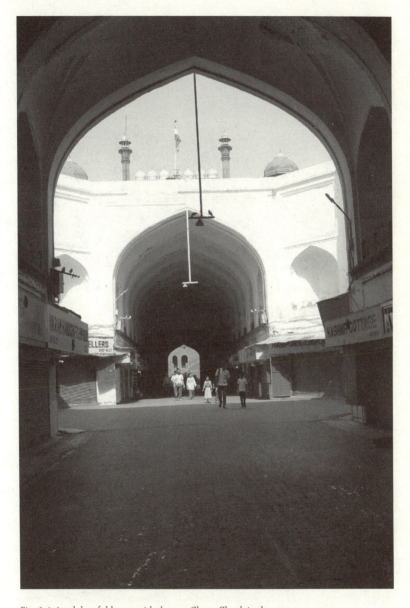

Fig. 6.4 Arcaded roofed bazaar with the open Chatta Chowk in the centre.

Fig. 6.5 Naubat Khana, *as seen from the Diwan-i Aam. Here,* music was played five times a day at chosen times.

Fig. 6.6 Inside view of the rectangular Diwan-i Aam, which is known for its seemingly flowing, engrailed arches.

Fig. 6.6a Marble canopy on the eastern wall of the Diwan-i Aam where the emperor sat and listened to the general populace.

Fig. 6.7 The Diwan-i Khas where the emperor met exclusive and select guests.

Fig. 6.7a Interior view of the Diwan-i Khas. The precious stones and metals on the walls and ceilings were looted during Nadir Shah's invasion and the 1857 rebellion.

Fig. 6.7b The Diwan-i Khas with the wide marble platform which once supported the famous peacock throne adorned with the Koh-i-Noor diamond.

Fig. 6.8 The marble screen, behind the engrailed arch, which separated the Tasbih Khana from the Khwabgah and contained the 'Scales of Justice'.

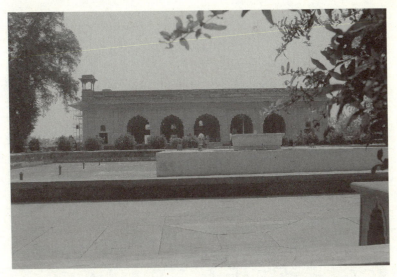

Fig. 6.9 The Rang Mahal derived its name from the painted interior. The two vaulted chambers on either end were popularly called Shish Mahal.

Fig. 6.9a Interior view of the Rang Mahal with the marble basin in the centre through which flowed the 'Stream of Paradise'.

Fig. 6.10 The Mumtaz Mahal, which was substantially modified after the 1857 rebellion.

Fig. 6.11 Red Fort from the side of river Yamuna. Left to right are the Rang Mahal, the Khas Mahal with the Muthamman Burj carrying the Jharokha and the Diwas-i Khas.

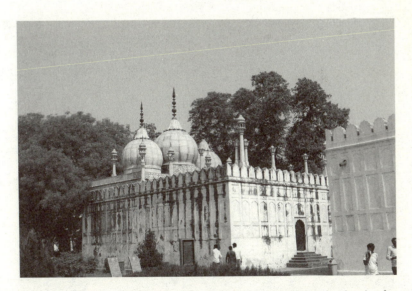

Fig. 6.12 The triple-domed Moti Masjid built of marble is the only building within the palace-fort erected by Aurangzeb.

Fig. 6.13 The Sawan pavilion at one end of the Hayat Baksh garden. In the background are barracks built by the British after the 1857 rebellion.

Fig. 6.14 Barracks built by the British after the 1857 rebellion.

Fig. 6.15 Built by Shah Jahan, the Jami Masjid (background) was the largest mosque in the Mughal empire. There used to be bazaar in the area connecting the mosque and the Delhi gate of the fort.

Fig. 6.15a The Red Fort, as seen from the eastern cloister of Jami Masjid.

on the occasion.[7] Singers were called from Iran, Turan, Kashmir and parts of northern India to feature at the ceremony alongside other performers. A special durbar was held in the Diwan-i Aam or the 'Hall of Public Audience'. Both these halls have been discussed in detail later in the chapter.

Diwan-i Aam was covered by a special embroidered velvet canopy – prepared in an imperial workshop in Ahmedabad – supported on four silver pillars and surrounded by a silver railing. Its roof wall and columns were decorated with brocaded velvet from Turkey and silk from China. The emperor sat on a special throne, enclosed by a gold railing, and distributed gifts and honours.

Diwan-i Khas was also ornamented with Persian carpets and brocades from Banaras and the famous peacock throne was installed in its centre. Other buildings were also decorated with carpets, Kashmiri shawls, brocade and velvet. A special verse was also inscribed on the occasion on the wall of Aramgah, the emperor's resting chambers.[8]

The palace-fort was built at a cost of around one crore (10 million) rupees then, half of which was spent on the construction of the palaces within. A stone-and-mud wall was also created in 1650 to enclose the city which collapsed during the following monsoons. Between 1651–58, a massive stone wall (27 feet high, 12 feet thick and 3.8 miles long) enclosing an area of 1,500 acres, was constructed around the palace-fort complex. It was punctuated by towers, bastions, gates and entryways.

DESIGN AND LAYOUT OF THE CITY AND THE PALACE-FORT
Comprehending the city of Shahjahanabad is an intriguing exercise and this has led to several models being suggested for the purpose of its location and plan. Some scholars argue that

like many other capital cities, such as Istanbul, Isfahan (Persia), Tokyo and Peking, Shahjahanabad was also the 'exemplar' of the sovereign city model – the 'capital of the patrimonial-bureaucratic empire', a type of state that characterized Asian empires from about 1400 to 1750. In such capitals, the structure and plan of the imperial household radiated outwards and served as a model for organizing the city and the empire.[9] Others have emphasized the connection between the physical structure and organization of the city and the contemporary legal system or Islamic law, broadly categorizing it as an 'imperial Islamic city'.[10]

While the nature of the city continues to be debated, there is no doubt that Shahjahanabad was one of the finest imperial capitals of the time. It had all the features of a great Mughal city: a palace-fort, enclosure walls, streets with squares, bazaars, mosques, gardens, imperial buildings, commercial neighbourhoods and industrial establishments, some within the palace-fort complex and others outside.

Historian Rana Safvi provides an exhaustive list of the thirteen *darwazas* (city gates) and fourteen wicket gates or *khidkis* (smaller entrances) of the imperial city of Shahjahanabad. On the northern wall of the city, the Kashmiri gate faced towards Kashmir. It was a site of action during the 1857 rebellion and suffered damages then. The western side had the Lahori gate facing towards Lahore, the Ajmeri gate facing towards Ajmer and the Kabuli gate facing towards Kabul. The southern side has the Turkomani and Delhi gates facing towards the Qutb-Mehrauli settlement which was then known as Delhi. Both the Delhi and Turkomani gates still survive. The Delhi gate was also sometimes mentioned as the Akbarabadi gate as it also faced Akbarabad or Agra. Towards the east and facing the river were the gates named Rajghat, Khairati, Calcutta (probably a later nomenclature) and Nigambodh.[11]

The city gates enclosed two main imperial streets. The principal street, running from east to west, originated in the palace-fort and ran through its Lahori gate to Chandni Chowk and then onto Fatehpuri Masjid (also called Fathpuri Masjid). The second street, running from north to south, ran through the Delhi/Akbarabadi gate of the palace-fort to the Delhi/Akbarabadi gate of the city and contained the Faiz Bazar or the 'Bazaar of Plenty'.

The historian Stephen Blake points out that the planning of Shahjahanabad combined both Hindu and Islamic influences. The street plan apparently borrowed its design (in part) from ancient Hindu Sanskrit texts on 'rules of architecture', the *vastu sastras*. Manasara, a *vastu sastra* dating 400–600 CE, lists a semi-elliptical plan, *karmuka* (bow-shaped) particularly suited for sites fronting a river or seashore. In the case of Shahjahanabad, the north-south road connecting Kashmiri (towards north) and Delhi gates (towards south), including Faiz Bazar, represented the bow string. The streets running south to east connecting Turkomani and Ajmeri gates with the Lahori gate, and north to east connecting Mori and Lahori gates, along with the outer wall of the city, represented the curved shaft of the bow. Chandni Chowk stretching from Lahori gate of the city to Lahori gate of the fort represented the arm of the archer. The most auspicious spot, the juncture of two main streets, was occupied by the palace-fort.[12]

The Islamic influence – derived from the *Rasail* or Epistles of a group of Iranian Shi'i scholars, *Ikhwan al-Safa* ('Brothers of Purity') written during the 10th and the 11th centuries – traditionally understood a city in terms of human anatomy. Applied to Shahjahanabad, the Chandni Chowk, which was the central bazar, represented the backbone. It originated at the palace-fort, the head; ran towards the heart – Jami Masjid, the congregational mosque also known as Jama Masjid, 900 metres to the west of the palace-fort; and exited at Kashmiri gate. The smaller streets represented the ribs and other structures – the shops, sarais (rest houses), baths, etc developed in proximity to the skeletal centre. The three principal structures – the palace-fort, Jami Masjid and Chandni Chowk respectively faced, ran or opened into the west, the direction of the Muslim holy land Mecca. The Walled City, another name for Shahjahanabad, symbolized the cosmos and the eight large gates, the four cardinal directions and the four gates of heaven.[13] The mixed character of the plan also reflected the nature of the city. It was 'a predominantly Hindu city governed by Muslims, the capital of a Muslim dynasty in an overwhelmingly Hindu subcontinent.'[14]

The Palace-Fort

Shah Jahan's building plans at his first imperial seat at the Agra Fort were limited by the pre-existing structures and the layout of the complex. His experimentations at Agra Fort could therefore be improvised and perfected only in the later palace-forts of Lahore and Shahjahanabad. The one in Shahjahanabad was planned in the form of a giant oblong irregular octagon, called *muthamman baghdadi*, an idea we encountered first in the chapter on Humayun's tomb, and was built on a grid of squares. The Shahjahani ideal of bilateral symmetry could be executed without obstruction in Shahjahanabad's Red Fort as it was an altogether new creation. However, the idea of a perfect geometrical planning was relaxed in practical execution to accommodate some structures, such as the Salimgarh fort on the north-east.[15]

The palace-fort complex was organized along three axes. The private and semi-official axis – consisting of the pavilions and halls belonging to the emperor and the imperial women – lay along the riverfront. This private axis was met at right angles by a public east-west axis which ran through the courtyard of the

Diwan-i Aam, the *jilaukhana* (open forecourt), the covered Chatta Bazar, Lahori gate and beyond into the city. There was a third north-south axis, which ran parallel to the private axis and passed through the *jilaukhana*, the Delhi gate and beyond. This contained an open bazaar and the imperial stables.[16]

The irregular octagonal shape of the palace-fort has its two longer sides in the east along the river and the west towards Jami Masjid. The riverfront section contained important royal buildings and pavilions. Like his earlier projects, Shah Jahan sought to impart a paradisiacal symbolism to the architectural complex in Shahjahanabad by means of a water channel called *nahar-i-behisht* or 'Stream of Paradise'. This channel originated in the Shah Burj or the 'King's Tower' – where water was drawn from the river by means of a device called *shutrugulu* which means camel's neck; water flowed internally through pools and fountains of buildings along the eastern wall of the palace-fort and, finally out into the gardens, pavilions and other areas.

The walls of the palace-fort were punctured by four large gates, two wicket gates or small entrances and twenty-one towers out of which seven were round and fourteen octagonal. The palace-fort complex together with the Salimgarh Fort occupies an area of 121 acres. The wall of the palace-fort covers a perimeter of 2.41 kilometres. It ranged in height from 60 feet (18 metres) along the river to 75 feet (33.5 metres) on the landward side. Likewise, the walls ranged in width from 45 feet at the base to 30 feet at the top. The walls, bastions and most other structures were built of red sandstone brought upstream on the Yamuna from Fatehpur Sikri, near Agra – and hence the name 'Red Fort'.

There were four large gateways to enter the palace-fort, only two of which are still in use: the imposing three-storey Lahori gate and the Delhi gate. The latter – used by Shah Jahan for his visits to Jami Masjid – is similar in layout and appearance to the Lahori gate but is also known for the two life-sized stone elephants on its either side (Figs. 6.3 and 6.3a). Shah Jahan had built statues of a pair of elephants as symbolic guards to both these gates. His son and successor, Aurangzeb (r. 1658/66–1707), considered such statues sacrilegious and had them demolished early in his reign. Later, the British Viceroy Lord Curzon had new statues of elephants installed at the Delhi gate in 1903 as part of a restoration plan. Lying under the Muthamman Burj, the river-facing octagonal tower projecting from the emperor's living quarters, was the third gate called Khizri. This was used by the emperor as a private entrance. The fourth gate opened near the Salimgarh fort. Besides, there were two small entrances (both closed now) – one in the north-east, between Salimgarh gate and Shah Burj called the Water gate, and the other on the southeast side near Asad Burj and Jahanara's apartments.

STRUCTURES/BUILDINGS WITHIN THE PALACE-FORT
Lahori and Delhi Gate

The Lahori gate (Fig 6.2) remains the main public entrance to the palace-fort. The pointed arched entrance has *kanguras* or ornamental bands or merlons on the parapet topped by a row of domed marble pavilions between slender minarets – like the ones found at the Buland Darwaza at Fatehpur Sikri and the Great gate at the Taj Mahal. It is flanked by octagonal towers with sandstone domes and marble finials. Since 1947, prime ministers of India have made Independence Day speeches from the ramparts adjacent to this gate (Fig. 6.1).

Aurangzeb added barbicans to the original Delhi and Lahori gates and made the latter the headquarters of the *qiladar* or fort commander. Shah Jahan, then imprisoned by Aurangzeb in Agra

Fort, reportedly wrote to his son about the barbicans saying: 'You have made the fort a bride and set a veil before her face.'[17] Some historians say that Aurangzeb built the great wall in front of the Lahori gate to save his nobles the trouble of having to bow constantly as they walked the entire length of Chandni Chowk into the fort. Mughal court etiquette under Shah Jahan required them to bow whenever they were in the view of the emperor.[18] Most however argue that the wall was built to strengthen the outworks of the structure.

The walls were surrounded by river Yamuna on the eastern side and, by a large moat on the other three landward sides. On the riverside, a strip of sand separated the walls of the palace-fort from the river. Here, people gathered to have a glimpse of the emperor every morning, a practice which came to be known as *jharokha darshan*. We have already discussed the evolution of *jharokha darshan* in the chapter on the Agra Fort. Later in the day, elephant fights were held. Inspection of the imperial troops was also held here. The moat on a landward side was a huge one, 75 feet wide and 35 feet deep, and was filled with water and crocodiles to protect the imperial household. Beyond the moat, were located three gardens – *Buland* (Lofty), *Gulab* (Rose) and *Anguri* (Grape) – which served as a green buffer between the palace-fort and the city. There was also large square, between the Lahori gate of the Fort and the intersection of two principal streets, where troops of Rajput *mansabdars*, or nobles, standing guard were reviewed.

Chatta Bazar and Naqqar Khana

After entering the Lahori gate, which now forms the public entrance, one comes to a vaulted arcade, or a covered bazaar earlier known as *bazaar-i musaqqaf*, wherein 'saqqaf' means roof. Contemporary sources also point to one *bazar-i sarbaz*, a covered market, which is difficult to trace now. Roofed bazaars were very common in Iran and West Asia but unusual in India. This is a double-storey structure with arcaded shops at both levels. Earlier, there were shops on sides of the street too. Here, merchants of Delhi sold luxury goods to the imperial household and nobles such as gold, silverware jewellery, gems, brocades, velvet, silk, and such other material. The ceiling of the bazaar was once adorned with beautiful paintings which are being restored by the Archaeological Survey of India (ASI). Now, the shops here mostly sell souvenirs. In the middle of the bazaar is an octagonal court known as Chatta Chowk with an open roof that allows air and light to enter the area (Fig. 6.4).

Going past the covered bazaar, one reaches a three-storey sandstone building called Naubat Khana or Music Gallery, also called Naqqar Khana or Drum House (Fig. 6.5). This was where ceremonial music and drum was played five times a day and the arrival of the emperor and other dignitaries was announced as well. After the suppression of the 1857 rebellion, this building housed British officers stationed at the fort. The Indian War Memorial Museum now occupies its upper storey. Between Naqqar Khana and Chatta Chowk lies an open square forecourt, *jilaukhana*, on the sides of which were small rooms for officials connected with the daily guard. It is in the *jilaukhana* that the people attending daily audience – ministers, bureaucrats, senior nobles and others – waited. Only the princes could go beyond this point on their horses; all others had to dismount here.

Public Buildings
Diwan-i Aam
The Naqqar Khana leads to the 'Hall of Public Audience'. Known as the Diwan-i Aam or *Chihil Sutun*, this 'Forty-pillared Hall', was

closely modelled on its earlier counterpart in the Agra Fort. Rectangular in shape, this striking red sandstone building is open on three sides with a courtyard in front. The series of apartments and arcaded galleries that once stood around the structure were destroyed by the colonial administration after the 1857 rebellion.[19]

The structure is an arcaded one consisting of nine engrailed/multi-cusped arches, known as the iconic Shahjahani arches, supported by double columns. Divided into three aisles, the hall has twenty-seven bays (Fig. 6.6). The ceiling and the columns were originally shell-plastered in ivory white with gilded stucco work. The white plaster for the building came from a special stone quarried from Gujarat. The arcaded hall was once decorated with heavy velvet and satin curtains and Persian carpets. Set against the centre of the eastern wall is a marble canopy known as the *Nashiman-i-Zill-i-Ilahi* or the 'Seat of the Shadow of God', a clear reference to the exalted status of the Mughal emperor (Fig. 6.6a). This canopy with fluted or baluster columns, which is also seen at Agra Fort, had inlays of pietra dura – precious stones on marble; and a Bengal-styled curved circular roof called *bangla* over the emperor's throne. Here, Shah Jahan sat and listened to complaints and suggestions from the general populace and deliberated upon routine military, administrative and financial matters. A railing separated him and the common people. Below the throne lies a marble dais decorated with semi-precious stones, which was used by the *wazir*, or the prime minister. The wall behind the emperor's throne was ornamented with beautiful black marble panels of Florentine pietra dura work, said to have been executed by European lapidaries, primarily Florentine artist Austin de Bordeaux. Some others are of the opinion that this formed a royal gift to the Mughals. They depict beautiful flowers along with birds and animals. This is the only place in the entire palace which has depictions of animate beings, otherwise considered un-Islamic. Art historian Ebba Koch says this seat was conceptualized as a copy of the throne of Solomon, the Quranic prophet-king and the ideal ruler in Islamic thinking.[20] This symbolism was further reinforced by another panel at the top of the wall showing representation of the Greek god Orpheus playing lute to animals, including a hare, a leopard and a lion. It denoted the ideal rule of Shah Jahan 'whose justice would make the lion lie down with the lamb and, in the human world, free the oppressed from their oppressors.'[21]

Semi-private/Private Buildings
Diwan-i Khas

To the east of the Diwan-i Aam and along the riverfront is the Diwan-i Khas, known as Shah Mahal, or King's Palace, during Shah Jahan's time. The location of this building, deep within the living quarters of the imperial family, indicates its special, private character. This rectangular chamber was used only for exclusive and private gatherings. Built of pure white marble, it is one of the most elegant buildings in the palace-fort. Its roof has pillared canopies at the corners (Figs. 6.7 and 6.7a). The chamber has engrailed arches resting on a set of 32 piers with square shafts. The lower walls were studded with agate, pearl and other precious stones while the upper portion had fruits and flowers painted in colourful and intricate designs. *Takht-i-Taus*, the famous peacock throne with the iconic Koh-i-Noor ('Mountain of Light') diamond embedded in its canopy once stood in the centre of the room, on a wide marble platform (Fig. 6.7b). The throne is mentioned in contemporary sources and is depicted in Mughal miniature paintings. Copies of these miniature paintings are now available in Indian, European and American art museums. The *Takht-i-*

Taus was inscribed as the 'throne of the just emperor' and built around 1634, when Shah Jahan was based at Agra. It was kept in the Diwan-i Khas of Agra Fort before the emperor shifted his court to Shahjahanabad. On special occasions involving larger audience, the throne could also be carried to the Diwan-i Aam. Known to be one of the most splendorous thrones ever made, the *Takht-i-Taus* carried a representation of two golden peacocks studded with diamonds, rubies, emeralds and other precious stones and the birds carried a string of pearls in their beaks. The throne was built at twice the cost of the Taj Mahal then.

The *nahar-i-behisht* flowed right through the centre of the Diwan-i Khas, adding to the beauty of the place. The paradisiacal theme of the palace-fort is further underlined in the couplet, popularly attributed to the poet Amir Khusrau, inscribed by Prime Minister Sadaullah Khan on the building wall: 'If there be paradise on earth, it is this, it is this, it is this.' The Diwan-i Khas directly experienced events connected with fluctuating fortunes of Delhi – whether it was Shah Jahan's exclusive gatherings or the surrendering of the peacock throne by emperor Muhammad Shah to Nadir Shah (1739) or the blinding of emperor Shah Alam by Rohilla chief Ghulam Qadir (1788) or the crowning of Bahadur Shah as the emperor of Hindustan during the 1857 rebellion and the pronouncement of his exile when the rebellion was suppressed.

Emperor's living quarters and the Imperial Harem

The Diwan-i Khas was connected with a platform to the emperor's living quarters called the Khas Mahal or 'Special Palace'. This composite palace consisted of a set of three marble apartments through which the *nahar-i-behisht* flowed: a beautifully carved building inlaid with precious stones called the Aramgah or Khwabgah which represents 'Resting Chambers'/'Chamber of

Dreams' flanked by the Tasbih Khana or 'Chamber for Counting Beads for Private Prayers' and the Tosha Khana or 'Robe Chamber'. The Tasbih Khana was a set of three rooms facing the public Diwan-i Khas where the emperor met his special nobles. This apartment was separated from the central Khwabgah by a marble screen containing a representation of the 'Scales of Justice' – another symbolism to depict the just rule of Shah Jahan – suspended over a crescent amidst stars and clouds (Fig. 6.8). 'Scales of Justice' as a motif is also repeated in the miniature paintings of Shah Jahan's time.

The 'Robe Chamber', also known as the Badi Baithak or the 'Large Sitting Room', faced the private Rang Mahal where the queens resided. It had painted walls and ceiling and a perforated screen. The octagonal domed tower, Muthamman Burj, protruded from the eastern wall of the Aramgah. French physician and traveller Francois Bernier, who visited parts of the Mughal empire between 1650s and 1660s, talks about a small river-facing tower which is 'covered with plates of gold in the same manner as the towers of Agra (Fig. 6.11); and its azure apartments were decorated with gold and azure, exquisite paintings, and magnificent mirrors.'[22] The tower's five sides overlooking the river had marble screens on four sides and a *jharokha* or balcony in the centre from where Shah Jahan gave *jharokha darshan* – a practice borrowed from Hindus whereby the emperor appeared before his subjects every morning. In 1808, Mughal emperor Akbar II added a small balcony to this tower. It was from this balcony that King George V and Queen Mary appeared before the people of Delhi during the Durbar of 1911. After 1857, the original copper gilding of the dome of the tower was replaced with lime plaster.

Next to and south of the Khas Mahal lies the Imtiaz Mahal or 'Palace of Distinction', popularly called the Rang Mahal or 'Palace of Colours' either because of its coloured interior or its function as a pleasure pavilion (Fig. 6.9). Muhammad Salih, Shah Jahan's court chronicler, says 'in lustre and colour it is far superior to the palaces in promised paradise.'[23] This formed the largest palace of the Imperial Harem and of the fort complex as well. This private palace had a huge courtyard, which separated it from the public Diwan-i Aam, with canals, fountains and gardens inside. Its garden had a huge monolithic marble basin in the courtyard which was uprooted by the British after the 1857 rebellion and taken to Queen's gardens. It was later brought back and reinstalled when the Red Fort was being decorated for the imperial durbar or the Delhi Durbar of George V in 1911.[24]

The basic plan of Rang Mahal consists of a large central hall with smaller vaulted chambers on either end. It had a facade of five engrailed arches set on marble piers with square shafts. The ceiling of the central hall was originally built of silver and, in the words of Salih, was 'gilded and ornamented with golden flowers.'[25] During the times of the later Mughals, weak and impoverished, this silver ceiling was first replaced with copper, as its silver was used to mint coins, during the reign of Farrukh Siyyar (r. 1713–19) and, then by wood, during the time of Akbar II (r. 1806–37). The central hall was divided into fifteen bays formed by intersecting arches. The *nahar-i-behisht* flowed through this structure, north to south, through an exquisite marble basin in the center originally provided with an ivory fountain (Fig. 6.9a). The eastern wall of the palace has five perforated windows or *jaalis* through which the royal ladies watched the elephant fights on the banks of Yamuna. The walls carried precious stones adorning the beautiful inlay work. These stones were literally wrested out after the suppression of the 1857 rebellion and the palace was also used as an officers' mess.[26] The vaulted chambers on either end of the hall were adorned with wedges of mirrors embedded in the ceiling. These apartments are popularly called Shish Mahal or the 'House of Mirrors' because of the mirror effect they produced.

Beyond the Rang Mahal, lies the Mumtaz Mahal (Fig. 6.10) or the 'Distinguished Palace' which was the palace for women or the Zenana Mahal. This building till recent years housed the Fort's Archaeological Museum. The space between Rang Mahal and Mumtaz Mahal was earlier occupied by another building connected with the Imperial Harem – the Chhoti Baithak or the 'Small Sitting Room', also known as Khurd Jahan or the 'Little World'. Destroyed by the British after 1857, this was a green haven with fountains and pools. Mumtaz Mahal was very similar in design to the neighbouring Rang Mahal – shaded with *chajja* or sloping stone projections to protect it from the sun and rains on the exterior, gilded *chattris* or domed pavilions on the roof, and covered with white-shell lime plaster.[27] Meant for leading royal ladies or princesses, this palace consists of six apartments divided by arched piers. The piers and lower portions of the palace were made in marble while the walls were decorated with stucco work, paintings, marble inlay and gilding. After the 1857 rebellion, this palace was converted into a prison and later Sergeants' Mess. Between Mumtaz Mahal and Asad Burj or the 'Lion Tower' were living quarters for women of the imperial household. Small gardens laid around central pools dotted the courtyard. Asad Burj formed the south-eastern corner of the palace-fort. It is said that the *nahar-i-behisht* once fed a step well near this tower before joining the Yamuna.

Other Structures

North of the Diwan-i Khas lay the *hammam* or royal baths which were used by the emperor for bathing and exclusive meetings.

It is a three-chamber structure built of marble and its floors and dados or decorations on the lower wall were inlaid with coloured stones. While the central chamber was used as a dressing room, the other two were for hot- and cold-water baths respectively. At the north-eastern corner of the palace-fort and along the riverfront, lay another octagonal tower, the Shah Burj or imperial tower. Like its southeastern counterpart, Asad Burj, this tower was a three-storeyed structure. However, its dome was destroyed during the 1857 rebellion.

North of the Diwan-i Khas was the marble Moti Masjid or the 'Pearl Mosque' built around 1659 for exclusive private use of the emperor (Fig. 6.12). This is the only building that Aurangzeb erected within the palace-fort. The mosque is now closed to the public. The main imperial mosque, the Jami Masjid, was located outside the palace-fort. Shah Jahan ordered the construction of Jami Masjid, as the congregational mosque in 1650. It was built on a hillock called Bhojala Pahari at the cost of 10 lakh rupees then (Figs. 6.15 and 6.15a). The emperor took special care to ensure that the mosque was built on a plinth higher than that of his residence and its pulpit remained higher than the royal throne.[28]

The northern sector of the imperial quarters in the palace-fort was occupied by the gardens, primarily the Hayat Baksh Bagh or the 'Life Bestowing Garden' and the Mahtab Bagh which means the 'Moonlight Garden'. The Hayat Baksh Bagh was designed like a paradise garden with tanks, fountains, tunnels, pavilions and all the other structures typical of a Timurid *char bagh*, the four-fold garden. It had a rectangular pool in the centre where emperor Bahadur Shah Zafar built a red sandstone palace called Zafar Mahal in 1842. At the north and south ends of this garden stood two identical pavilions (Fig. 6.13) named after the monsoon months of the Hindu calendar: *Sawan*, the fourth month of the calendar, and *Bhadaun*, the fifth month. Most of this garden was destroyed under British occupancy and what one sees now is the structure as restored by Viceroy Lord Curzon during 1904–11. To the west of this garden lay the Mahtab Bagh, where now stand three-storeyed barracks built to house the British army (Fig. 6.14).

On the east of the Hayat Baksh Bagh lies a small marble pavilion called Hira Mahal or *baradari* – a recreational pavilion with twelve arches, three on each side – built by emperor Bahadur Shah Zafar. A similar pavilion called, Moti Mahal, existed on its north but was removed after the British occupation of the fort

STREETS AND BAZAARS OF THE CITY AND PALACE-FORT

The palace-fort was characterized by rectangular buildings laid out in a symmetrical arrangement with intersecting thoroughfares. The two imperial streets, which also served as thoroughfares and bazaars, emanated from within the palace-fort and went beyond into the city. They intersected at right angles in the forecourt outside Naqqar Khana or the 'Drum House'.

The principal imperial street, running from east to west, began at Rang Mahal and ran through the Lahori gate of the Fort to Fatehpuri Masjid. This street was in turn divided into three bazaars separated by two squares. The first, lying between the Lahori gate and the *chowk* of the Kotwali Chabutra or the 'City Magistrate's Platform', was called Urdu Bazar or the 'Bazaar of the Royal Camp'. The second part, commissioned by Shah Jahan's daughter Jahanara Begum, extended from the Kotwali Chabutra to the octagonal Chandni Chowk or the 'Silver Square' and was called Ashrafi Bazar denoting the 'Moneychangers' Market' or Jauhari Bazar, the jewellers' market. It had a *hammam*, a *sarai* or rest house and a garden (Bagh Sahibabad) near it. The final section, from Chandni Chowk to Fatehpuri Masjid, was called Fatehpuri

Bazar. The *nahar-i-behisht*, bordered by shaded trees, ran through the middle of the bazaars. The imperial street is being restored as a part of a redevelopment plan.

The second street, in the north-south direction, stretched from the Akbarabadi/Delhi gate of the fort to the Akbarabadi gate of the city and housed the market known as the Faiz Bazar, around the modern Daryaganj area. As in the case of the first street, a stream from the *nahar-i-behisht* ran through the middle of this bazaar.

There was also a small bazaar that connected Jami Masjid and the palace-fort. This was inhabited by dancing girls, medicine men, jugglers, storytellers and astrologers.

RED FORT AFTER SHAH JAHAN

The fortunes of the palace-fort started dwindling after the death of Aurangzeb in 1707, the process of disintegration of the large Mughal empire had already set in during his reign. The post-Aurangzeb phase of Shahjahanabad witnessed battles for succession, rise of ambitious nobles and kingmakers, invasions from abroad, attacks by regional powers and natural calamities. However, the city and the court also experienced artistic and cultural efflorescence during some periods. Muhammad Shah (r. 1719–48), one of the later Mughal emperors, patronized Urdu language as well as musical performances particularly *qawwali*, spiritual music sung by Sufis, and *khyal*, a kind of Indian classical vocal music. Paintings of Holi (festival of colours) celebrations of his period are quite well known.

In 1739, Nadir Shah, the Turk ruler of Iran, crossed Afghanistan and Punjab and defeated the Mughals at Karnal, located around 120 kilometres from Delhi. In the subsequent display of power, Nadir Shah's name was proclaimed as the sovereign in the *khutba*, the sermon during the congregation

Friday noon prayers, in the mosques of Shahjahanabad. Nadir Shah also got Muhammad Shah to receive him at the palace-fort where he symbolically returned the throne to the defeated Mughal emperor. On March 22, 1739, infuriated by some minor attacks on his army, Nadir Shah ordered a massacre of citizens of Delhi and witnessed the barbarity sitting on the roof of the Sunehri Masjid near Chandni Chowk. He also plundered the palace-fort and the city and carried away a booty with an estimated value of 700 million rupees, including the peacock throne and the iconic diamond, Koh-i-Noor. The throne was brought to Iran. Nadir Shah died in a campaign against Kurdish tribesmen in 1747. In the ruckus that followed, the tribesmen dismantled the throne and distributed the precious stones and metals amongst themselves. The peacock throne however became the insignia of the Iranian monarchy and its reproductions continued to be made for later rulers including those from the Shah and Qazar dynasties. One of these reproductions is apparently housed at Topkapi Palace, Istanbul. The Koh-i-Noor, on the other hand, changed several hands before coming under the possession of the British. From Nadir Shah the diamond passed on to one of his lieutenants, Ahmad Shah Durrani (also known as Ahmad Shah Abdali). Later, Shah Shuja Durrani, a descendant of Ahmad Shah Durrani, gave the diamond to Maharaja Ranjit Singh, the ruler of Punjab, for helping him win back the throne of Afghanistan. After the British conquest of Punjab in 1849, the Koh-i-Noor finally passed into the hands of the British. It currently forms a part of the Crown Jewel collection displayed at the Tower of London.

Meanwhile, the destroyed Mughal city and the plundered empire were further weakened by the raids – by powers like the Marathas, the Sikhs, the Jats, and the Gurjars as well as the Rohillas and Afghans – between mid to late 19th century. The Marathas captured Delhi in 1759 to lose it to Ahmad Shah Durrani, the Afghan ruler who succeeded Nadir Shah, in the Third Battle of Panipat (1761). They recaptured the city in 1771, made Mughal emperor Shah Alam their pensioner, and stationed Maratha troops in the palace-fort. Some scholars say that the Marathas took down and melted the ceiling of Diwan-i Khas, made in silver and inlaid with gold, and used the metal to make coins then worth 23 lakh rupees. The wooden ceiling one sees now in the structure was painted by the British in 1911, around the time of the Delhi Durbar. Later, the Rohilla chief Ghulam Qadir captured Shah Alam (r. 1759–1806) in 1788 and imprisoned him in Salimgarh Fort. He asked the emperor to show the place where Mughals hid their treasures. When the impoverished and helpless emperor failed to show any such place, an infuriated Ghulam Qadir blinded him and dug up the floors of the Diwan-i Khas looking for hidden treasures. The Marathas soon regained their control over the city and the palace-fort and Shah Alam became their puppet again.

The Mughal Empire as an imperial raj or a political entity ceased to exist in the 1750s. But the 'imperial' aspect of the emperor and his distinctive social status as the foremost resident of Delhi ensured that his position remained central to the identity of the city and the palace-fort even after the British occupation.[29] In 1803, Lord Lake defeated the Marathas near Patparganj in Delhi and gained control of the Ganga-Yamuna plains and the Delhi–Agra region. Administratively, the city of Shahjahanabad became a part of the North-Western Provinces and was governed from Agra. A British Resident was stationed in Delhi. He started functioning from the building known as Dara Shukoh's Library. This is a building on Lothian Road in present-day Delhi, on the right bank of the Yamuna close to the imperial palace, and is named after Aurangzeb's eponymous elder brother. There are plans to open a second Partition Museum in Dara Shukoh's Library.

The early decades of the 20th century, described as the 'English Peace', were also the period of the 'Delhi Renaissance'. This period was characterized by the writings of literary greats such as Mirza Ghalib, Hakim Momin Khan, and Sheikh Ibrahim Zauq; the intellectual endeavours of the faculty at the Delhi College and its English Institute; and the coming into circulation of printing presses and newspapers. This intellectual and cultural efflorescence was disrupted by one of the most serious challenges to the British colonial rule, the rebellion of 1857.

The year 1857 witnessed armed revolts in parts of central and northern India, leading to a loss of British control over these regions. Recent research shows that the rebellion was more widespread than thought earlier. It began with a mutiny of sepoys but soon acquired a civil and popular character in parts of northern India. The rebel sepoys showed a tendency to converge or congregate at Delhi. The Red Fort thus emerged as a focal point for the rebellion. Under pressure from the rebels and his own princes, the reluctant eighty-two-year-old Mughal emperor, Bahadur Shah Zafar (r. 1837–57), became the titular leader of the rebellion.

The palace-fort soon became the seat of the rebel power and, Bahadur Shah a symbol of the rebellion. There were attacks on Europeans, Christians and those connected with the British government. British officers and army took refuge in the forested ridge around Delhi University and waited for reinforcements from Ambala. Once the British army started gaining control of the city, it went on an offensive against both Hindus and

Muslims. Most residents of Shahjahanabad were driven out. They took shelter in areas around the Qutb and the Nizamuddin. The ousted residents could not re-enter the city before the following year. Mosques were also taken over. After September 1857, the British forces unleashed a reign of terror that saw indiscriminate shootings, court martials and summary hangings. Meanwhile, Bahadur Shah escaped the Red Fort via Yamuna and took refuge in Humayun's tomb. He was soon arrested by the British forces along with three princes. The latter were killed on the way back near the Delhi gate by Major William Hodson. Bahadur Shah returned to Red Fort as a prisoner of the British. He was tried in the Diwan-i-Khas in 1858, and exiled to Rangoon, Burma (now Yangon, Myanmar), on October 7.

British officials were not content with deporting the emperor and killing his descendants. They also unleashed their anger on the palace-fort which had been the citadel of power during the 'Great Indian Rebellion'. More than two-thirds of the inner structures were destroyed. Henceforth, structures in the palace-fort served as quarters for the British garrison and the famed Diwan-i Aam as a hospital. The buildings south of the Diwan-i-Khas were found to be 'of little architectural interest' and were declared suitable for troops. Most jewels, precious stones and artworks of the Red Fort had already been looted during Nadir Shah's invasion. The aftermath of suppression of the rebellion saw further looting. Several existing Mughal structures were demolished, including the harem courts and gardens to the west of Rang Mahal, the royal storerooms and kitchen to the north of Diwan-i Aam and the Mahtab Bagh. New structures including army barracks, hospitals, bungalows, administrative buildings, sheds and godowns soon came up in the palace-fort complex. The rebellion also ended the rule of the East India Company, and an act passed in the British Parliament in August 1858 made Queen Victoria the sovereign head of British India.

HOW RED FORT BECAME A SITE OF INDIA'S INDEPENDENCE DAY CELEBRATIONS

The exiled Mughal emperor Bahadur Shah Zafar and his family lived in complete obscurity in Rangoon till the end of the 19th century. Here, the emperor not only lived but also died in obscurity. There was curiosity about how the Mughal emperor spent his last days in exile, but the colonial administration ensured that no definite news of the Mughal family became available to the public in the 1930s and 1940s.[30] However, the 1857 rebellion and its heroes continued to remain important in public memory and the growing nationalist imagination. Almost a century after 1857, the memory of Bahadur Shah Zafar and Red Fort emerged on the horizon again in the years preceding the independence of India. It was the setting up of the headquarters of the Indian National Army's (INA) provisional government at Rangoon in January 1944 that brought memories of the seemingly forgotten Mughal emperor back in the public domain.

The INA was originally formed in Southeast Asia to secure India's independence from the British rule. It was supported by Japan which formed one of the Axis Powers, along with Germany and Italy, fighting against the Allied formation of Britain, France, Russia and the USA. With Rangoon emerging as the base, many leaders of the Azad Hind Fauj or INA visited the city. During his stay at his base in Rangoon, the leader of the INA, Subhash Chandra Bose, popularly known as Netaji, reportedly visited the shrine that had come up around the unmarked grave of Bahadur Shah Zafar at the beginning of the

20th century. Interestingly, it was the latent memory of the suppression of the 1857 rebellion that threw up the idea of Red Fort as the most prominent non-colonial structure in the capital of the British Indian empire.[31]

Netaji soon linked this forgotten icon of the 1857 rebellion and the Red Fort with his struggle for India's freedom. Historian Amar Farooqui observes that on becoming the supreme commander of the INA, he gave the famous slogan *Chalo Dilli* ('March to Delhi') and exhorted his soldiers to continue to fight till the British are driven out of Delhi, the national flag flies over the Viceroy's House (now the official home of the President of India), and the Azad Hind Fauj holds the victory parade in the Red Fort.[32] His famous call *Chalo Dilli* floated the idea of the recapture of the fort: '[O]ur task will not end until our surviving heroes hold the victory parade on the graveyard of the British empire, at the Lal Quila, the Red Fort of ancient Delhi.'[33]

The INA was eventually defeated after two disastrous campaigns – in Imphal in India and Mount Popa in Burma. Netaji's disappearance from Singapore, where he had gone after the INA reverses, as yet remains unexplained. INA surrendered. After the surrender, around 20,000 INA soldiers were interrogated and transported back to India. However, the most committed of the soldiers of the INA were court-martialled and put on public trials. The British colonial government hoped to expose the horrors perpetrated by the INA men during the public trial and turn public opinion against them.[34] The most celebrated of these trials was one that involved the three INA officers, namely Colonel Shah Nawaz Khan, Colonel Prem Kumar Sahgal and Colonel Gurbaksh Singh Dhillon. They were housed in the *baoli* (step well) complex at the Red Fort in Delhi during the period of the trial. For this purpose, the chambers within the *baoli* complex were converted into a prison. This *baoli* predates the Red Fort but was integrated in the design.

The colonial administration had clearly miscalculated. The trial, on the contrary, resulted in a massive nationwide outrage for their release. There were many factors behind the mass anger, including the fact that the trial took place at the Red Fort, the 'most authentic symbol of British imperial domination.'[35] The nationwide campaign for the release of the INA officers further reinforced the public perception of the former Mughal palace-fort as the symbol of anti-colonial resistance.[36] Finally, in August 1947, the first Prime Minister of India, Jawaharlal Nehru, raised the Indian national flag above the Lahori Gate of the Red Fort. Nehru's speech made a special mention of Netaji, regretting his absence on the occasion. The act of replacing the British flag with India's national flag, a day after the swearing in of independent India's first cabinet on August 15, led to the reclamation of the Red Fort for the nation.[37]

THE STATELY PRESENCE OF THE RED FORT: KEY INSIGHTS

The Red Fort also signifies the re-establishment of Delhi as the preferred imperial seat of India after a gap of almost 150 years (excluding Humayun's short-lived city in the Purana Qila), once the Lodis had shifted the capital to Agra at the beginning of the 16th century. Releasing the symbolic and strategic importance of Delhi, the British also chose to build their last imperial capital in the city and called it New Delhi. With the coming into being of New Delhi, the Walled City or Shahjahanabad became known as Old Delhi.

Red Fort formed the pinnacle of Mughal fort building activity. Built as the palace-fort of a newly established Shahjahanabad, it marked an improvisation of the Agra Fort and also included two Timurid-style four-fold gardens within the complex.

The emergence of Red Fort as the headquarters the 1857 rebellion and Bahadur Shah Zafar as its leader, long after the Mughals had passed their prime, shows how the Mughals, Delhi and the Fort still remained symbolic centres of power. The Indian National Army trials of 1945 reinforced the memory of the former Mughal palace-fort as the symbol of anti-colonial resistance and intensified the freedom struggle against the British.

AUTHOR'S NOTE

'Why is it so difficult for a common person to get a good historical essence of monuments?' My friend and companion, Manisha, asked this question some years ago during our visit to the ancient city of Mandu in Madhya Pradesh. This was soon after an entertaining tour of the surrounding monuments, soaked in folklore and mythology, accompanied by a friendly local guide. 'Well, you could read books on the monuments and their history to understand such sites better,' I had responded, and the conversation ended there. However, the question struck roots inside me, for I knew she seldom asks such simple ones. Upon further thinking, I was able to uncover layers to her loaded and timely query. It had also been posed to someone who had studied history for a long time, had completed a PhD in the discipline and had taught undergraduate students at a reputed university for almost a decade.

I am fond of experiencing heritage and culture, so after Mandu, I continued to visit other monuments with different tour guides. I started to correlate the knowledge gathered from the guides with the scholarly works I had read on the subject. I must, however, confess that despite a background in history, I had always found the technicalities of architecture, which remains one of the key concerns of academic books about monuments, intimidating. But with further groundwork and intense readings, these books finally started making some sense to me. I also researched a lot of websites on monuments that are designed for tourists. It was shocking how many of them carried the same generic information, sometimes verbatim, other times with minor modifications. There was a huge gap between the narratives in the academic books and the ones presented by tour guides and websites. The gap, I realized, impacted the way historical knowledge was disseminated at ground level which resulted in distortions.

During those days, my friend Nilanjan Sarkar had gifted me a book on the history of architecture and heritage sites. That was a timely gift, *dost*. Thank you for the many conversations we subsequently had on monuments/artefacts and history and your generosity in arranging articles and readings. I read and re-read a lot of books and essays on architecture, monuments and history. The more I read on the subject, the more I began to appreciate the intensity of Manisha's question. I realized there were multiple, complex questions embedded within what seemed a simple query. It led me to a chain of questions pointing to disturbing gaps between the formation of academic knowledge of monuments (and by extension, their history) and its eventual consumption by the lay public, which rarely has a formal background in history, but also those who study history or related disciplines.

It is possible to read about monuments from several sources, including books, journals, magazines and online platforms. However, a visit to a monument – or even museums –constitutes a unique experience. It forms a site where people are face to face with tangible historical objects, artefacts and buildings. It is a place where people come closest to experiencing history, as opposed to reading about it. For the foreign tourists, they offer significant insights into the idea of India. For domestic tourists, who are somewhat familiar with Indian history, the monuments are sites where they can re-brush their historical knowledge. For those with a formal background in history, such visits are occasions to connect the dots and plug gaps in their knowledge. In my experience, even some of the country's best universities do not follow an applied approach when it comes to teaching history on a day-to-day basis. For the general public, a first-hand encounter with historical sites opens an entirely new world of meanings and possibilities. In any case, people come back with ideas or impressions of the monument's history after the visit. But the depth or profundity of that experience depends on the knowledge one has of the site or gathers there. Monuments are not just about architecture and builders – they also contribute to a larger understanding of the concerned dynasties and empires, and the related historical periods.

In all categories of visitors discussed above, the knowledge gained/imparted at the heritage sites is critical to their understanding and experience of the monument and its connected history. In the case of general public or foreign visitors and even those with a basic idea of history, the knowledge is predominantly attained from the narratives of tour guides, who are mostly trained at travel and tourism institutes (and rarely by trained historians or heritage experts). For the tour guides, creating an interesting narrative is key as they are mainly concerned with providing an enjoyable experience to the visitors. Most of them are not trained well enough to explain the intricacies of history offered by the monument. They are largely unaware, perhaps also unmindful, of the dangers their embellished narrations pose for the public understanding of history. Tourists who want a more informed view of the site either read in advance or look for guidebooks available at the physical publication counter of the site. Regrettably, there are few good books on Indian monuments, available outside of the Archeological Survey of India (ASI) circles. Most of them are primarily suited for an academic audience. Although the ASI tour guides available at the site are informative and provide a basic outline of the monuments, the technical details are sometimes intimidating for non-specialists. It is deeply unfortunate that the content of these guidebooks is not periodically updated; in fact, oftentimes, the research is quite dated. This book shows how our understanding of heritage sites – or certain aspects of them – has been significantly modified by recent research, which is missing from the primers on heritage sites.

To make the visits to the monument enjoyable and meaningful for visitors, one needs to tread a knowledge terrain somewhere between the narratives of the tour guides and the seemingly 'dry' guidebooks and academic publications. A new, perhaps different, kind of knowledge positioning is required which can help budding academics/researchers negotiate the intricacies and layers of a relatively untapped source, provide an effective framework through which such sites can be experienced by the non-academic, general public and serve as a critical medium for the involved agencies and guides in communicating historical knowledge. That is how this book was born. It aims to address the lacuna between the knowledge produced in academic settings and its eventual consumption at ground level. The task was always going to be a challenging considering the number of factors, such as language, upon which depends the effective transmission of knowledge. For the purposes of this book – and the series – I have tried to position academic knowledge in an inclusive, accessible way. Bringing together updated research from interdisciplinary sources, including history, archaeology, art history, architecture, heritage studies, the book presents them in the tradition of public history, making complex academic research available to the public with due sensitivity to the traditional methods of historical research. Such a knowledge positioning also needs to constructively engage with elements of folklore, legends, stories and popular history; hence, rather than being dismissive, I tried to explore how these elements gradually become a part of the 'historical' experience. My training further helped me add a critical component to the narrative about the making of a heritage site – its afterlife. What happened to the monuments once their primary builders left the scene? This does not figure in most existing accounts. Events, anecdotes or stories about their afterlife sometimes give new meanings to monuments, which become dominant frameworks through which they can be understood or experienced.

I first tested this idea in a series of articles in *Frontline* magazine and *Wire.in*. I am indebted to *Frontline* and its editor-in-chief, R. Vijayasankar, for publishing those pieces. The chapters on the six individual world heritage sites in this book were originally published in *Frontline*. I am thankful to the magazine for the permission to use them here. Adding substantially to the original articles, I have revised and restructured them. I am also grateful to *Wire.in* and Chitra Padmanabhan for publishing my articles and for allowing me to use that content. Chitra, your editorial interventions made the pieces more meaningful for a wider public, thank you so much. I wish to acknowledge that some sections of the book, particularly the stories towards the end of the chapters on Qutb Minar, Red Fort and Taj Mahal, borrow from and build on the essays published on *Wire.in*.

The responses I had received on sharing my *Frontline* and *Wire.in* pieces on social media were very encouraging, and my small world of heritage started growing. I was able to reach out to heritage experts, archaeologists, historians but, more importantly, to nonspecialist heritage enthusiasts. This book benefited enormously from the comments and suggestions I received from several of them. I also made some great friends over social media and had the opportunity to meet many of them in person. Whether on questions of heritage or on the process of knowledge formation or on the world of writing and publishing, I have tremendously gained from and enjoyed the conversations with Ranbir Singh, Arthur Needham, Debotri Dhar and Paul Stremeur. Ranbir Singh also gave me useful tips and helped me with the readings.

Lately, the coming-into-being of several YouTube channels, blogs and heritage walks, together with a renewed appetite for biographical films, documentaries and TV series related to history and historical fiction, show there exists a much bigger audience with a growing interest in monuments and their surrounding histories. But these changes also reiterated my conviction to explore a differential positioning for this book – it had to lie somewhere between 'serious' academic history and a 'more appealing' history; one that responsibly, but interestingly, engages with both the knowledge domains.

This idea of an academic–public interface for the study of monuments, the cities in which they are located and their larger geocultural connections nourished from my engagements with the popular media. Opportunities to feature on television programmes and documentaries – and the responses to these programmes – further convinced me of a much bigger public constituency beyond the scholars of history, archeology, architecture or heritage studies. I am indebted to Rajya Sabha TV, especially Rajat Kain, who is extremely well read in heritage and history, NDTV 24X7 and News18 networks for inviting me on their platforms. The Literary Society of the IAS Association, Rajasthan, invited me for my first-ever Facebook live session which was attended by a much larger audience than I could have thought of. The questions and comments from the audience, by both specialists and non-specialists, were critical in sharpening the final section of some of the chapters. I am grateful to the IAS Association of Rajasthan and Mugdha Sinha for offering me their platform. Thank you, Mugdha, for your thoughtful and perceptive questions – they made me think deeper.

The book has been further shaped from the comments or suggestions from or discussions I have had with Himanshu Prabha Ray, S. A. Nadeem Rezavi and Mayank Kumar. They also helped me with readings. Nadeem Sa'ab has been generous in sharing my pieces on online history platforms. Mayank encouraged me to locate the work within the larger context of the writing and teaching of history. I am indebted to Sohail Hashmi for taking time out to go through a large part of the book, with so much attention and sensitivity, especially through such difficult times. Thank you, Hashmi Sa'ab, for your feedback. My conversations with Amar Farooqui, Biswamoy Pati, Shreedhar Lohani, A. Raghuramaraju, Kaiser Haq, Swadhin Sen, S. P. Verma, Sudhir Chandra, John S. Hawley, Arjun Dev and Prasun Chatterjee at various stages also contributed to the making of the book. Aakash Chakrabarty's suggestions for pitching my work to a wider audience and his inputs remain crucial to the formation of this book.

Many old friends and well-wishers have enthusiastically supported the new turn in my research and writings; I would like to thank Roland Chojnacki, Alok Kumar, Surinder Jodhka, Chandan Sinha, Akshaya Mukul, Parimala Rao, Pankaj Jha, Jayabrata Sarkar, Krishnan Unni, Seema Sinha, Nandini Panda, Indrani Sen, Ishrat Alam, Ashwani Kumar, Param, Chitta Panda, Ahona, Sanjeev Roy, Amrit, Maneesh Prasad, Tuktuk Ghosh, Raziuddin Aquil, Tapti Roy, Kamlesh Mohan, Wijesinghe Wije, Atul Tripathi, Shoma

Munshi, Sangeetha Menon, Pranav Chaudhury, Tushar Upadhyay, J. P. Singh, Sanjay Kumar, Sanjeev Sinha, Amit Kumar, Lata Singh, Abha T. Gandhi, Jyoti Atwal, Neeraj Sahay, O. P. Singh, Rajesh Kumar, Ruchika, Reeta Raj, Tarika, Rowena Saket, Mona Sedhwal, Sujata, Amitabh Sharma, Kamal Nijhawan, Rohit Shankar, Hema Chauhan, Priyanka Thakur, Reena Laisram, Renu Goel, Sonia Roy, Rajiv Bhagat, Rajat Chhabra, Haimanti Dey, Amit Prasad and Sanjay 'Buchchi'. Bunny, Shashi Narayan, Monika and Nayana were at my side whenever I ran out of enthusiasm. They gently prodded me along and ensured I remain glued to the book. *Bahut shukriya!* Ojas, Manju, Shilpa, Khushal and Sarika do not know how big a support they have been in the writing of this book. The lunchtime addas with the teammates at my current office has always expanded the horizons of my thought process and their role goes much beyond the conceptualization of this book – a big thank you, people. You always rock!

There are some friends who, like my family, are a part of all my scholarly pursuits. Thank you, Amitabh, Sumit, Dvivedi, Amit, Moon, Ravindra, Rajan, Rajat, Anupam, Atish, Sandeep, Amarendra, Rajiv, Chandan, Madhukar, Bauwa Singh, Osama, Kamal and Titu for always encouraging me with your usual warmth. A big shout-out also for my mother, my sisters, Amit, Jignasa, Sanjay and the supportive next generation – Vishy, Vartika, Mittan, Mayank, Nishtha, Shubhangi, Mohnish, Amrit and Reyan, besides Prishu, Veer and Aaru – for being strong anchors in my life and projects. I feel especially privileged to have two affectionate and caring souls – Ravi Sinha and Satish Chandra – always by my side. Reyan has dealt with my obsessions patiently, accompanied me on various field trips, helped me with photographs and happens to be my tech guru. Though I am unable to acknowledge and express it frequently or adequately, I must say it feels really good to grow with you, Reyan. And thank you, Manisha, for asking that important question.

I am grateful to my publisher, Pan Macmillan India, for agreeing to publish this book with enthusiasm. Thank you, Prasun, for initiating this project and skilfully seeing it through to the proof stage; Teesta, for supporting it at a crucial juncture; Isha, for carefully going through the proofs and dexterously steering the book through its crucial final stages; and Rajdeep, for always being accessible and helpful. Two other people are directly associated with the making of the book – my friend and former colleague, Misha Chakravarty Oberoi, for designing the cover and Pratap jee (Pratap Narayan of Vertex Design), for drawing the site maps of the six world heritage sites and two illustrations.

Finally, I wish to state that this book was written purely in the capacity of an independent researcher and the content of the book or views expressed in it do not, in any way, represent the views of any organization I have worked for in the past or my current employers. It's a purely personal exercise.

ENDNOTES

MONUMENTS, CITIES AND CONNECTED HISTORIES

1. Upinder Singh, *Ancient Delhi* (Second edition), Oxford University Press, New Delhi, pp. 89–90.
2. Ibid., pp. 93–94.
3. Ibid.
4. Ibid., p xxii.
5. Ibid., p. 90. Two inscriptions belonging to the 13th century were found respectively in a step well near Palam village and on a stone tablet in Sonepat near Delhi; and, two from the 14th century were found respectively at Sarban village (in New Delhi near Raisina Road) and Naraina in west Delhi.
6. This is recorded in a 12th-century inscription found in a small town called Bijholia in Rajasthan.
7. Ibid., p. 98.
8. The slaves of this region were owned by their masters who themselves might have been of such origin. They could be acquired, bought and inherited. They were bought for domestic service, for company or for their special skills. Skilled slaves were valued more and could rise to higher offices and become commanders and rulers. Instead of a master-servant relationship, the slaves often had a relation of father-son or family with their masters and were thus called *bandagan* or 'member of the group'. Often, when they became part of the core group of the ruler, who was like their father or leader of the group, the slaves began to be given the honourable mention of

bandagan-i-khass and entrusted with special military and administrative responsibilities.

9. For details, see Sunil Kumar, *The Emergence of Delhi Sultanate*, Permanent Black, Ranikhet, 2007, p. 291.

10. Some scholars, on the other hand, argue that the excavations conducted in 1990s indicate that Lal Kot's enlargement took place much later in the 14th century under the Turks.

11. Historian Cynthia Talbot has recently argued that Prithviraj Chauhan's association with Delhi – based on legends, poetic narratives, and chronicles composed long after his death – may be more of a myth than reality and that it is possible that he never entered the city despite conquering it. Catherine Asher adds another layer of complexity to this association saying Lal Kot possibly served as a military garrison to the Chauhan capital Ajmer, rather than being the capital itself. For details, see Catherine Asher, *Delhi's Qutb Complex: The Minar, Mosque and Mehrauli*, Marg, New Delhi, 2017, p. 23.

12. Ibid.

13. Vidya Dehejia, *Indian Art*, Phaidon, New York, 1997, p. 252.

14. Finbarr Barry Flood, 'Appropriation as Inscription: Making History in the First Friday Mosque of Delhi' in Richard Brilliant and Dale Kinney eds, *Reuse Value: Spolia and Appropriation in Art and Architecture from Constantine to Sherrie Levine*, Routledge, London and New York, 2016, pp. 121; 128.

15. For details see Sunil Kumar, *The Present in Delhi's Pasts*, Three Essays Collective, Gurgaon, 2011 (second revised edition), pp. 23–38.

16. Richard H. Davis, *Lives of Indian Images*, Motilal Banarsidass, Delhi, 1999, pp. 122; 137–38; Romila Thapar, Harbans Mukhia and Bipan Chandra, *Communalism and the Writing of the Indian History*, People's Publishing House, Delhi, 1969, pp. 14; 31; Richard M. Eaton, 'Temple Desecration in Pre-Modern India', *Frontline*, December 22, 2000, pp. 65–66.

17. Rana Safvi, *Where Stones Speak: Historical Trails in Mehrauli, the First City of Delhi*, Harper Collins, NOIDA, 2015, p. 33.

18. Finbarr Barry Flood, 'Appropriation as Inscription', p. 135.

19. Sunil Kumar, *Delhi Sultanate*, p. 221.
20. Ibid., pp. 236–37.
21. Ibid., pp. 238–98.
22. For details, see Ibid., pp. 233–36.
23. Percival Spear, *Delhi: A Historical Sketch*, Oxford University Press, Bombay (Mumbai), 1945, pp. 9–10.
24. M. Athar Ali, 'Capital of the Sultans: Delhi during the Thirteenth and Fourteenth Centuries', in R. E. Frykenberg, ed. *Delhi though the Ages*, Oxford University Press, New Delhi, 1986, pp. 28–29.
25. Spear, *Delhi*, p. 18.
26. Athar Ali, 'Capital of the Sultans', p. 29.
27. Asher, *Delhi's Qutb Complex*, p. 79.
28. R. Nath, *Agra and its Monuments*, The Historical Research Documentation Programme, Agra, 1997, p. 4.
29. cited in Ibid., p. 4.
30. Ibid., p. 5.
31. Ibid.
32. For details, see Ibid., pp. 4–5.
33. K. K. Trivedi, *Medieval City of Agra*, Primus Books, Delhi, 2018, p. 12.
34. Ibid., p. 13.
35. Ibid., pp. 8–12.
36. Ibid., pp. 16–17.
37. Nath, *Agra and its Monuments*, p. 5.
38. Spear, *Delhi*, p. 21.
39. Harbans Mukhia, *The Mughals of India*, Blackwell Publishing, Malden, 2004, pp. 2–3.
40. Ibid., p. 4.
41. Ebba Koch, *The Complete Taj Mahal*, Thames and Hudson, London, 2012, p. 24.
42. Ibid., p. 29. For details regarding translation of Babur's autobiography, see Koch's book.
43. Richard M Eaton, *India in the Persiannate Age: 1000–1765*, Allen Lane, New Delhi (Indian edition), pp. 215–16.

44. For details of Akbar's rule from each capital, see Michael H Fisher, *A Short History of the Mughal Empire*, I B Tauris, London and New York, 2016, pp. 108–40.

45. Ibid., p. 109.

46. Cited in Koch, *The Complete Taj*, p. 29.

47. Trivedi, *Medieval Agra*, p. 122, footnote 8.

48. Ibid., pp. 105–06.

49. Ibid.

50. Ibid., p. 33.

51. Ibid., pp. 33–55.

52. Syed Ali Nadeem Rezavi, *Fathpur Sikri Revisited*, Oxford University Press, New Delhi, 2013, p. 15.

53. Ibid., p. 2.

54. Michael Brand and Glen Lowry cited in Fisher, *A Short History*, p. 117.

55. For details of Akbar's policies at Sikri, see Fisher, *A Short History*, pp. 117–31.

56. Eaton, *India in the Persiannate Age*, pp. 238; 242.

57. Ebba Koch, *Mughal Architecture*, Primus Books, Delhi, 2014 (revised edition), p. 70.

58. For details, see Trivedi, *Medieval Agra*, pp. 138–39.

59. For details regarding the development of garden city under Jahangir, see Koch, *The Complete Taj*, p. 29–30.

60. Trivedi, *Medieval Agra*, p. 123, footnote 16.

61. cited in Koch, *The Complete Taj*, p. 30.

62. Ibid., p. 30. Sohail Hashmi points out that Aaram Bagh – which later became known as Ram Bagh – was the first Mughal garden in India and was originally constructed by Babur. The pavilions and the underground basements were constructed in the time of Jahangir. A massive marble slab placed outside the garden by the Archaeological Survey of India contains the details of the fruit-bearing trees and flowering shrubs that Babur got from Kabul for planting at the garden (email communication).

63. Trivedi, *Medieval Agra*, p. 106.

64. Koch, *The Complete Taj*, p. 28.
65. Trivedi, *Medieval Agra*, p. 114.
66. Ibid.
67. Ibid.
68. Ibid.
69. Ibid., p. 56.
70. Ibid.
71. Ibid., pp. 84–88.
72. Ibid., p. 56.
73. Ibid., pp. 80–81.
74. Ibid., pp. 124–125, footnote 32.
75. Ibid., pp. 124, footnote 31.
76. Ibid., pp. 107–08.
77. Ibid., pp. 108; 112, for details.
78. Ibid., p. 109.
79. cited in Koch, *The Complete Taj*, p. 23.
80. Ibid.
81. Ibid., pp. 32–33, for details of gardens under Shah Jahan.
82. Ibid., p. 33. For details of the poem as well as translation and copyright of this and other portions cited from the book, please see Koch's volume.
83. For a detailed analysis of the ways in which Shah Jahan formalized imperial power, see Fisher, *A Short History*, pp. 167–71.
84. Ibid., p. 167–70.
85. Koch, *The Complete Taj*, p. 32.
86. Trivedi, *Medieval Agra*, p. 106.
87. Ibid., p. 107.
88. Stephen Blake, *Shahjahanabad: The Sovereign City in Mughal India 1639–1739*, Cambridge University Press, Cambridge, 2002, p. 186.
89. Ibid., p. 187.
90. Ibid., p. 185.
91. For details regarding the development of local markets, see Trivedi, *Medieval Agra*, p. 111.

92. Ibid.
93. Blake, *Shahjahanabad*, p. 187.
94. Trivedi, *Medieval Agra*, p. 111.
95. Ibid., p. 113.
96. Ibid., p. 151.
97. Blake, *Shahjahanabad*, p. 30.
98. Ibid., pp. 55–58. This has details on bazars and suburbs.
99. Ibid., p. 67.
100. Koch, *The Complete Taj*, p. 33.
101. Ibid.
102. For details of the debate, see Blake, *Shahjahanabad*, p. 102.
103. Ibid., pp. 102–03.
104. For details regarding the later Mughals, see Fisher, *A Short History*, pp. 212–18.
105. Spear, *Delhi*, p. 39.
106. Ibid., p. 40. I have changed the expression a bit here, based on a feedback I received from Sohail Hashmi. The meaning or translation remains unchanged. Spear uses the expression 'Az Delhi to Palam, Badshahi Shah Alam.'

CHAPTER 1: THE QUTB MINAR AND ITS MONUMENTS

1. Taken from *Selections of the Travels of Ibn Batuta* translated and edited by H. A. R. Gibb. Cited in Michael Alexander ed. *Delhi and Agra: A Traveller's Reader*, Robinson (Little Brown Book), London, 1987, p. 26.
2. Catherine Asher, *Delhi's Qutb Complex: The Minar, Mosque and Mehrauli*, Marg, New Delhi, 2017, p. 23
3. Vidya Dehejia, *Indian Art*, Phaidon, New York, 1997, p. 250.
4. Finbarr Barry Flood, 'Appropriation as Inscription: Making History in the First Friday Mosque of Delhi' in Richard Brilliant and Dale Kinney eds, *Reuse Value: Spolia and Appropriation in Art and Architecture from Constantine to Sherrie Levine*, Routledge, London and New York, 2016, p. 122.

5. Dehejia, *Indian Art*, p. 255.

6. *Qutb Minar and Adjoining Monuments*, Archaeological Survey of India, New Delhi, p. 41.

7. For details see Asher, *Delhi's Qutb Complex*, pp. 38–39.

8. Ibid., pp. 39–40.

9. Rana Safvi, *Where Stones Speak: Historical Trails in Mehrauli, the First City of Delhi*, p. 55.

10. Michael D. Willis, *The Archaeology of Hindu Ritual: Temples and the Establishment of the Gods*, Cambridge University Press, Cambridge, 2009.

11. Flood, 'Appropriation as Inscription', p. 136.

12. Asher, *Delhi's Qutb Complex*, p. 23.

13. For details see Sunil Kumar, *The Present in Delhi's Pasts*, Three Essays Collective, Gurgaon, 2011 (second revised edition), pp. 33–35.

14. Safvi, *Where Stones Speak*, p. 62.

15. Flood, 'Appropriation as Inscription', pp. 135–38.

16. For details, see Sunil Kumar, *The Emergence of Delhi Sultanate*, Permanent Black, Ranikhet, 2007, pp. 226–27.

17. Flood, 'Appropriation as Inscription', p. 135.

18. Asher, *Delhi's Qutb Complex*, p. 61.

19. Ibid., pp. 45–46.

20. *Qutb Minar and Adjoining Monuments*, p. 41.

21. Dehejia, *Indian Art*, p. 258.

22. Anthony Welch et al, 'Epigraphs, Scripture, and Architecture in the Early Delhi Sultanate', *Muqarnas*, Vol.19, No. 1, 2002, p. 29.

23. Asher, *Delhi's Qutb Complex*, p. 53.

24. Ibid., p. 24.

25. Flood, 'Appropriation as Inscription', p. 134.

26. Ibid., pp. 135–36.

27. Asher, *Delhi's Qutb Complex*, p. 59.

28. Safvi, *Where Stones Speak*, p. 68.

29. Asher, *Delhi's Qutb Complex*, p. 62.

30. Ibid., pp. 74–75.

31. Kumar, *The Present in Delhi's Pasts*, p. 7.
32. Ibid., p. 35.
33. Ibid., pp. 23–24.
34. David Lelyveld, 'The Qutb Minar in Sayyid Ahmad Khan's Asar us Sanadid', in Indra Sengupta and Daud Ali eds. *Knowledge Production, Pedagogy, and Institutions in Colonial India*, Palgrave Macmillan, New York, pp. 151–52.
35. For details see Kumar, *The Present in Delhi's Pasts*, endnote 1, p. 40.
36. Ibid., pp. 5–7.

CHAPTER 2: HUMAYUN'S TOMB

1. Ebba Koch, *Mughal Architecture*, Primus Books, Delhi, 2014 (revised edition), pp. 42–43.
2. https://www.nytimes.com/2002/09/29/magazine/on-the-verge-a-mughal-splendor-regained.html; accessed on May 31, 2020.
3. Koch, *Mughal Architecture*, p. 42.
4. Ibid., p. 54.
5. S. A. A. Naqvi, *Humayun's tomb and Adjacent Monuments*, Archaeological Survey of India, New Delhi, 2002, p. 30.
6. Koch, *Mughal Architecture*, p. 36.
7. Ibid., p. 36.
8. Naqvi, *Humayun's tomb*, p. 30.
9. Koch, *Mughal Architecture*, p. 42.
10. Glenn D. Lowry, 'Humayun's Tomb: Form, Function, and Meaning in Early Mughal Architecture', in *Muqarnas*, Vol. 4, No. 1, 1987, p. 145.
11. For details, see Ebba Koch, *The Complete Taj Mahal*, Thames and Hudson, London, 2012, p. 85.
12. Ibid., p. 85.
13. https://www.ft.com/content/c3c94f3a-de19-11e0-a115-00144feabdc0; accessed on September 27, 2020.
14. Koch, *The Complete Taj*, p. 85.

15. Ibid., p. 86
16. Ibid.
17. Ibid., p. 42.
18. Naqvi, *Humayun's tomb*, p. 52.
19. Koch, *The Complete Taj*, p. 24.
20. Ibid.
21. Naqvi, *Humayun's tomb*, p. 54.
22. Narayani Gupta, *Lets Explore Humayun's Tomb*, Archaeological Survey of India, New Delhi, 2011, p. 44.
23. Ibid., p. 61.
24. Koch, *Mughal Architecture*, p. 44.
25. Ibid., pp. 44–45.
26. Ibid., p. 44.
27. Ibid., p. 45.
28. Lisa Golombek, 'From Tamer Lane to the Taj Mahal', in Monica Juneja ed. *Architecture in Medieval India: Forms, Contexts, Histories*, Permanent Black, Ranikhet, 2008, p. 323.
29. Ibid., p. 324.
30. Ibid.
31. Ibid., p. 325.
32. Ibid.
33. Lucy Peck, *Delhi: A Thousand Years of Building*, Lotus (Roli Books), New Delhi, p. 161.
34. Gupta, *Lets Explore Humayun's Tomb*, p. 64.
35. Naqvi, *Humayun's tomb*, p. 43.
36. Ibid.
37. Ibid., 41.
38. Gupta, *Lets Explore Humayun's Tomb*, p. 47.
39. Swapna Liddle, *Delhi: 14 Historic Walks*, Westland, New Delhi, 2011, p. 138.
40. Archaeologist Y. D. Sharma cited in Naqvi, *Humayun's tomb*, p. 66.
41. Peck, *Delhi: A Thousand Years*, p. 154.

42. Liddle, *Delhi*, p. 141.

43. *First Report of the Curator of the Ancient Monuments in India for the year 1881–82*, Government Central Branch Press, Simla, 1882, p. 27.

44. Michael Alexander ed. *Delhi and Agra: A Traveller's Reader*, Robinson (Little Brown Book), London, 1987, p. 90.

45. R.V. Smith, historian and chronicler of Delhi, cited in https://www.hindustantimes.com/delhi/when-families-from-pakistan-took-refuge-in-delhi-tombs/story-AZA20NHVJ46F9W1zhBrvLL.html; accessed on May 18, 2020.

46. For details of the restoration, see https://www.akdn.org/project/humayuns-tomb-conservation-completed; accessed on May 18, 2020.

47. Ibid.

48. Ibid.

49. https://scroll.in/article/808636/the-ruination-of-ruins-how-we-destroy-our-future-by-disregarding-our-past; accessed on September 26, 2020.

50. https://m.mid-day.com/amp/articles/dont-make-statements-contrary-to-well-established-facts-historians-to-leaders/15879186; accessed on May 31, 2020.

51. personal communication; first reproduced in Shashank Shekhar Sinha, 'Magnificent Mausoleum', *Frontline*, Vol. 35, No. 14, July 7–20, 2016, p. 85.

52. Ibid.

53. Ibid.

CHAPTER 3: THE AGRA FORT

1. Ebba Koch, *Mughal Architecture*, Primus Books, Delhi, 2014 (revised edition), p. 60.

2. Cited in Ebba Koch, *The Complete Taj Mahal*, Thames and Hudson, London, 2012, p. 66.

3. Michael H. Fisher, *A Short History of the Mughal Empire*, I B Tauris, London and New York, 2016, pp. 111–112.

4. R. Nath, *Agra and its Monuments*, The Historical Research Documentation Programme, Agra, 1997, p. 40.

5. For details see, Koch, *Mughal Architecture*, pp. 53–54.

6. Ibid.

7. Nath, *Agra and its Monuments*, p. 37.

8. Ibid., p. 39.

9. Ibid., pp. 37–38.

10. Nath, *History of Mughal Architecture* (Vol. II), Abhinav Publications, Delhi, 1985, p. 119.

11. Ibid., pp. 119 and 127.

12. Koch, *Mughal Architecture*, p. 54.

13. Nath, *History of Mughal Architecture* (Vol. II), p. 125.

14. Ibid., pp. 133–34.

15. Koch, *Mughal Architecture*, p. 55.

16. Nath, *History of Mughal Architecture* (Vol. II), pp. 133–134.

17. William G. Klingelhofer, 'The Jahangiri Mahal of the Agra Fort: Expression and Experience in Early Mughal Architecture', *Muqarnas*, Vol.5, No 1, 988, p. 164.

18. Ibid., for details see pp. 165–168.

19. Ibid., p. 168

20. Koch, *Mughal Architecture*, p. 109.

21. W. H. Siddiqi, *Agra Fort*, Archaeological Survey of India, New Delhi, 2008, p. 53.

22. Nath, *Agra and its Monuments*, p. 56.

23. For details, see *History of Mughal Architecture* (Vol. IV, Part I), Abhinav Publications, Delhi, 2005, pp. 172–73.

24. Koch, *The Complete Taj*, p. 69.

25. Nath, *Agra and its Monuments*, pp. 63; 65.

26. Koch, *The Complete Taj*, p. 69.

27. Nath, *Agra and its Monuments*, p. 51.

28. Koch, *The Complete Taj*, p. 69.

29. Ibid., pp. 68–69.

30. Ibid., p. 68. See the page for details of other decorative motifs.

31. Fisher, *A Short History*, p. 111.
32. Koch, *Mughal Architecture*, p. 110.
33. Ibid.
34. Nath, *History of Mughal Architecture* (Vol. IV, Part I), pp. 198–199.
35. For details, see Koch, *Mughal Architecture*, pp. 118–123.
36. Ibid., p. 123.
37. Nath, *Agra and its Monuments*, p. 66.
38. For details, see Romila Thapar, *Somanatha: The Many Voices of a History*, Penguin Books, New Delhi, 2004 pp. 169–201. The following paragraphs list some elements of the story.

CHAPTER 4: FATEHPUR SIKRI

1. Lucy Peck, *Fatehpur Sikri: Revisiting Akbar's Masterpiece*, Lustre Press/ Roli Books, New Delhi, 2014, p. 2.
2. For details see, Syed Ali Nadeem Rezavi, *Fathpur Sikri Revisited*, Oxford University Press, New Delhi, 2013, p. 56; pp. 213–15.
3. S. A. A. Rizvi, *Fatehpur Sikri*, Archaeological Survey of India, New Delhi, 2002, p. 8.
4. Rezavi, *Fathpur Sikri*, p. 2.
5. Fisher, *A Short History of the Mughal Empire*, I. B. Tauris, London and New York, 2016, p. 117.
6. Ebba Koch, *The Complete Taj Mahal*, Thames and Hudson, London, 2012, p. 84.
7. Ibid., pp. 84; 89.
8. R. Nath, 'Sources and Determinants of the Architecture at Fatehpur Sikri', in Monica Juneja ed. *Architecture in Medieval India: Forms, Contexts, Histories*, Permanent Black, Ranikhet, 2008, pp. 565–66.
9. Rezavi, *Fathpur Sikri*, p. 33.
10. Ebba Koch, *Mughal Architecture*, Primus Books, 2014 (revised edition), p. 55.
11. Ibid., pp. 56–58. For details see the following paragraphs.
12. Koch, *The Complete Taj*, p. 94.
13. Nath, 'Sources and Determinants...' p. 568.

14. For details see, Rezavi, *Fathpur Sikri*, p. 28.
15. Ibid., p. 28.
16. Ibid., p. 119.
17. Koch, *Mughal Architecture*, pp. 58–60.
18. For details, see Rizvi, *Fatehpur Sikri*, pp. 26–27.
19. Catherine Asher, *The New Cambridge History of India: Architecture of Mughal India*, Cambridge University Press, Delhi, 1992, pp. 62–63.
20. Rezavi, *Fathpur Sikri*, p. 62.
21. Ibid., 72; Koch, *Mughal Architecture*, p. 57.
22. Rezavi, *Fathpur Sikri*, pp. 70–72.
23. Ibid., p. 61.
24. Ibid., p. 64.
25. Rizvi, *Fatehpur Sikri*, p. 46.
26. Rezavi, *Fathpur Sikri*, p. 65.
27. Divya Narayanan, 'Cultures of Food and Gastronomy in Mughal and post-Mughal India', Inaugural Dissertation, University of Heidelberg, Heidelberg, 2015, pp. 40–41, http://archiv.ub.uni-heidelberg.de/volltextserver/19906/1/Pub_Diss_Narayanan_07.12.2015_F.pdf; accessed on June 05, 2021.
28. Rezavi, *Fathpur Sikri*, p. 88, footnote 61.
29. Rizvi, *Fatehpur Sikri*, p. 40.
30. Ibid., pp. 40–41.
31. https://timesofindia.indiatimes.com/lucknow-times/Was-there-ever-a-Jodha-Bai/articleshow/1984130.cms; accessed on May 23, 2020.
32. Ibid.
33. Rezavi, *Fathpur Sikri*, p. 92.
34. Koch, *Mughal Architecture*, p. 56.
35. Rizvi, *Fatehpur Sikri*, p. 66.
36. Peck, *Fatehpur Sikri*, p. 113.
37. J. F. Richards,' The Formulation of Imperial Authority under Akbar and Jahangir', in J F Richards ed. *Kingship and Authority in South Asia*, Department of South Asian Studies of the University of Wisconsin, Madison, 1978, pp. 255–71.

38. Rezavi, *Fathpur Sikri*, p. 157.
39. Ibid., pp. 153–54.
40. Ibid., p. 154.
41. Ibid., p. 151.
42. Ibid.

CHAPTER 5: THE TAJ MAHAL

1. Koch, *The Complete Taj Mahal*, Thames and Hudson, London, 2012, p. 20.
2. Ibid.
3. Ibid., pp. 97–100.
4. Som Prakash Verma, *Taj Mahal*, Oxford University Press, New Delhi, 2012, pp. 27–28.
5. Koch, *The Complete Taj*, p. 215.
6. Ibid., p. 6.
7. Ibid.
8. Ibid., p. 100.
9. W. E. Begley and Z. A. Desai, *Taj Mahal, The Illumined Tomb: An Anthology of Seventeenth Century Mughal and European Documentary Sources*, Agra Khan Program for Islamic Architecture, Cambridge, 1989, p. 195.
10. Koch, *The Complete Taj*, pp. 134–135.
11. Wayne Begley, 'The Myth of the Taj Mahal and a New Theory of its Symbolic Meaning', *Art Bulletin*, Vol. 61, No. 1, March 1979, pp. 7–37.
12. Verma, *Taj Mahal*, p. 68.
13. Koch, *The Complete Taj*, p. 96.
14. Ibid.
15. Verma, *Taj Mahal*, p. 49.
16. Koch, *The Complete Taj*, p. 180.
17. Verma, *Taj Mahal*, p. 49.
18. Koch, *The Complete Taj*, p. 155.
19. Verma, *Taj Mahal*, pp. 45–46.
20. Koch, *The Complete Taj*, p. 224.
21. Ibid., p. 219.

22. Ebba Koch, *Mughal Art and Imperial Ideology: Collected Essays*, Oxford University Press, New Delhi, 2001, pp. 76–77; H Hosten, 'European Art at the Mughal Court', *Journal of Uttar Pradesh Historical Society*, Vol. 3, No. 1, 1922, pp. 128; James Fergusson, *History of Indian Architecture*, John Murray, London, 1891/1910, p. 588.

23. Verma, *Taj Mahal*, p. 71.

24. Ibid., p. 72.

25. cited in Koch, *The Complete Taj*, p. 92.

26. Ibid., p. 228.

27. Ibid., p. 101.

28. Ibid., pp. 233; 237.

29. https://theprint.in/opinion/sangeet-som-taj-mahal-narratives/12711/; accessed on May 25, 2020.

30. Ibid.

31. Ibid.

32. Koch, *The Complete Taj*, pp. 247–48.

33. Ibid., p. 248.

34. https://timesofindia.indiatimes.com/city/agra/for-the-first-time-asi-tells-court-taj-is-not-a-temple-but-a-tomb/articleshow/60224065.cms; accessed on October 19, 2020.

35. https://thewire.in/communalism/taj-chronicles-tracing-attempts-appropriate-history; accessed on 18 October, 2020.

36. Koch, *The Complete Taj*, p. 249.

37. W. H. Sleeman, *Rambles and Recollections of an Indian Official*, Oxford University Press, Karachi, 1973, p. 385.

38. Koch, *The Complete Taj*, p. 170.

39. Elizabeth B. Moynihan, *Paradise as a Garden in Persia and Mughal India*, George Braziller, New York, 1979, pp. 131–32.

40. Koch, *The Complete Taj*, p. 250.

CHAPTER 6: THE RED FORT

1. Syed Ali Nadeen Rezavi, '"The Mighty Defensive Fort": Red Fort at Delhi under Shah Jahan: Its Plan and Structures as described by

Muhammad Waris', *Proceedings of Indian History Congress*, 71st *Session*, Indian History Congress, 2010–11, p. 1,111.

2. Stephen Blake, *Shahjahanabad: The Sovereign City in Mughal India 1639–1739*, Cambridge University Press, Cambridge, 2002, p. 27

3. Ibid.

4. Ibid., pp. 27–28.

5. Rana Safvi, *Shahjahanabad: The Living City of Old Delhi*, HarperCollins, NOIDA, 2019, pp. 6–7.

6. Swapna Liddle, *Chandni Chowk: The Mughal City of Old Delhi*, Speaking Tiger, New Delhi, 2017, p. 5.

7. For details, see Blake, *Shahjahanabad*, p. 31.

8. Ibid.

9. Ibid. pp. 183–221.

10. Eckart Ehlers and Thomas Krafft, 'Islamic Cities in India' in Eckart Ehlers and Thomas Krafft eds., *Shahjahanabad/Old Delhi*, Manohar, New Delhi, 2003; B. S. Hakim, *Arabic-Islamic Cities: Building and Planning Principles*, KPI, London, 1986.

11. Safvi, *Shahjahanabad*, pp. 94–96.

12. Blake, *Shahjahanabad*, p. 32–33.

13. Ibid., pp. 34–36.

14. Ibid., p. 36.

15. Ebba Koch, *Mughal Architecture*, Primus Books, Delhi, 2014 (revised edition), pp. 110–11.

16. Ibid., p. 111.

17. cited in Y. D. Sharma, *Red Fort*, Archeological Survey of India, New Delhi, 2009, p. 24.

18. Percival Spear, *Delhi: Its Monuments and History*, Oxford University Press, New Delhi, 2008 (third edition), pp. 1–2.

19. Safvi, *Shahjahanabad*, pp-25–26.

20. Koch, *Mughal Architecture*, p. 112.

21. Ibid., p. 112.

22. cited in Sharma, *Red Fort*, p. 54.

23. Ibid., p. 46.

24. Safvi, *Shahjahanabad*, p. 78.
25. cited in Sharma, *Red Fort*, p. 47.
26. Safvi, *Shahjahanabad*, p. 81.
27. Sharma, *Red Fort*, pp. 44–45.
28. Safvi, *Shahjahanabad*, p. 116.
29. Amar Farooqui, *Zafar and the Raj: Anglo-Mughal Delhi, c. 1800–1900*, Primus Books, Delhi, 2013, pp. 4–7.
30. Ibid., p. 194.
31. Ibid., p. 193.
32. Ibid.
33. Ibid.
34. Sekhar Bandyopadhyay, *From Plassey to Partition and After: A History of Modern India*, Orient BlackSwan, New Delhi, 2015 (Second edition), p. 427.
35. Ibid., p. 428.
36. Farooqui, *Zafar and the Raj*, pp. 193–94.
37. Ibid., p. 193.

INDEX

Abdarkhana (or 'Water Store' or 'Girl's School') 176, 177, 178
Afsarwala mosque and tomb 100, 120
Agra xiii, xv, xvii–viii, xix–xxxiii, 24, 25–30, 32–64, 67, 102, 106–07, 112–13, 123, 128, 130, 131, 134, 141, 145, 151, 153, 154, 158, 164–66, 170, 186–87, 189, 190, 193, 195, 198, 201, 204, 215–16, 219, 222, 226–27, 232, 235, 236, 241, 242, 249, 254–55 (Agra's strategic location in relation to Delhi 37; and Agrasena and Agarwals 26; and Krishna and Kamsa 26; as a cultural centre 59; becomes 'Wonder of the Age' 52; decline of Agra 63; development as a commercial hub 38; development of the city 59; Europeans and Christian habitations 51; gardens under Shah Jahan 53; local business communities 58; Lord Krishna and Ugrasena 26; Mahmud Shah's attack on the fort 27; Maithan 51; markets 61; mystery behind the origin of the name 26; mythological connections 26; Padritola 51; shift of capital to Shahjahanabad 59; trade 38; under Delhi Sultanate xxiv; why and how Agra became the capital of the Delhi Sultanate 28–29)
Agra Fort xiii, xv, xvii, xxv, xxviii, xxix, xxxii, 27, 32, 34, 36, 37, 43, 45, 54, 55, 63, 64, 128–57, 167, 174, 181, 190–91, 198, 199, 201, 215, 221, 225, 234, 237, 239, 241, 255 (1857 rebellion and the fort 128; Akbari Mahal 129, 137–39; Amar Singh gate 135, 137; Anguri Bagh complex 141, 154; attacks by Jats and Marathas 146; Bangla-i-Darshan or 'Imperial

Viewing Pavilion' 142; Bangla of Jahanara 142; British military garrison 154; Chandni Chowk 61, 62, 98, 225, 233–34, 246, 248; circumstances leading to the construction of fort complex 131–34; design and layout 135–36; Diwan-i Aam 135, 136, 138, 149–51, 154; Diwan-i Khas 147–49, 153; gates of the fort 136; Jahangiri Mahal 129, 137, 138–45, 157, 167; Machchli Bhawan or 'Fish Palace' complex 135, 145, 147, 149, 152; Nagina Masjid 152, 181; Panchmahal (or 'Chaharsuffa') 175, 177; Somnath Gate 154–55, 156; under Akbar 130; under Aurangzeb 146, 153; under Rajputs and Lodis 130; under Shah Jahan 130)

Agra gate 170, 171

Ahmad Shah Durrani or Ahmad Shah Abdali 153, 248, 249

aiwan 173–74

Ajmer gates 170

Ajmeri gate 232–33

Akbar xxi, xxiv, xxvi, xxvii, xxviii, xxxi, 35–37, 39–47, 51, 52, 53, 56, 61–63, 100, 102–03, 106, 108–09, 113, 121, 127–45, 148, 151–52, 157–61, 164, 165–66, 169–98, 204, 209, 213, 222, 232, 233, 243, 247 ('Jaipur Map of Agra' 38; administrative reforms 38, 39; Agra as capital city 39; and building of Agra Fort 37; and development of Agra as a riverfront city 37; and Humayun's tomb 36; and Second Battle of Panipat 35; and Shaikh Salim Chishti 40–42; and shift of the capital to Fatehpur Sikri 41–44; early years 35; rule from for capitals 35–36)

Akbari Mahal 129, 137–39 (part of Bengali Mahal 137–39)

Alai Darwaza 20, 71, 76, 92, 93, 94, 98, 108, 117, 222 (architecture of 92; construction of 92; Quranic verses 93)

Alai Minar 3, 19, 71, 76, 92 (and Qutb Minar 94; construction of 92)

Alauddin Khalji xxi, xxiii, xxv, 3, 18, 23, 75, 79, 91, 93–94, 108 (and Alai Darwaza 19–20, 92; and Alai Minar 3; Alauddin Khalji's madrasa 94; Alauddin Khalji's tomb 71; and Mongols 18, 92; and the Qutb complex 19–20; and Siri 19; extensions to Qutb mosque 92; his conquests 22; reforms and regulations 18)

Alauddin Khalji's madrasa 94. See also Alauddin Khalji.
alcove 202, 207, 210, 213
Amanat Khan 195
Amar Singh gate 135, 137 (at Agra Fort 135; story behind the name 137)
Anguri Bagh 141, 142, 144-45, 147
Anguri Bagh complex 141, 154 (Bangla-i-Darshan or 'Imperial Viewing' 142; Bangla of Jahanara 142; Khas Mahal 141, 142)
Anup Talao (or 'Peerless Pool') 172, 175, 176 (and Kapur Talao 175)
Arab Sarai 100, 119, 120
Aramgah or Khwabgah or 'Resting Chambers'/'Chamber of Dreams' (at Agra Fort 142; at Red Fort 231, 241–42)
arch xv, 17, 46, 62, 70, 75, 77, 79, 80, 81, 85, 89, 90, 92, 94, 108, 111, 112, 115, 116, 119, 120, 137, 140, 142, 144, 146, 148, 149, 150, 170, 182, 184, 202, 203, 206, 208–10, 236, 239, 240, 243 (corbelled arch 80; Hindu temples 97; under Sumerians and Romans 70, 79)
Arjumand Banu Begum (or Mumtaz Mahal) 192, 200, 203, 204, 211, 215, 220

Asad Burj or 'Lion Tower' 244–45
Ashrafi Bazar (or 'Moneychangers' Market' or Jauhari Bazar or the jewellers' market) 246
Astrologer's Seat 173
Aurangzeb xxi, xxii, xxix, 56, 63–65, 121, 128, 135, 146, 153, 157, 201, 215, 220, 226, 236, 237, 245, 247 (and Deccan 65; and the decline of the Mughal empire 66; at Agra Fort 146; Aurangzeb and Red Fort 65; and imprisonment of Shah Jahan 153; and joint stock trading corporations 66; meeting with Maratha king Shivaji 153; rise of European 68)
Austin de Bordeaux 213, 219, 220, 239
ayina bandi or *ayina kari* 146

Babur also known as Zahiruddin Babur xxv, 30, 31–34, 41, 55, 100–02, 107, 110, 113, 128, 131, 141, 161, 188, 268 (and Agra 32; and *char bagh* or fourfold garden 33; and Ibrahim Lodi 31–32; at Ferghana Valley and Kabul 31; Babur's tomb at Kabul 33; First Battle of Panipat and conquest of north India 31; raids in Hindustan 30)

INDEX 285

Badshahi Darwaza 184
Bahadur Shah Zafar 226, 245, 246, 250, 252, 255
Bahlol Lodi 24, 25
Balban, also known as Ulugh Khan or Ghiyasuddin Balban 16–18, 75, 91 (and Afghans 17, 24, 25, 31, 35; and Ganga–Yamuna doab 7, 17, 28, 29; and Ghayaspur 17; and Mongols 16; Balban's tomb 17)
baluster column 149, 239
bangla 239
Bangla of Jahanara 142 (*bangladar/bangla* 142)
Bangla-i-Darshan or 'Imperial Viewing Pavilion' 142 (*bangladar/bangla* 142)
baoli (at Fatehpur Sikri 188, 189; at Red Fort 253–54)
Barber's tomb 100, 121
barbicans (at Agra Fort 135; at Red Fort 236–37)
Battle xxv, xxx, 4, 6, 7, 9, 27, 31, 32, 35, 41, 67, 75, 81, 101, 103, 128, 130, 135, 153, 161, 188, 247, 249 (Battle of Khanwa 41; First Battle of Panipat 31, 32; First Battle of Tarain 4, 6; Second Battle of Panipat 35; Second Battle of Tarain 7, 9; Third Battle of Panipat 67)

bazaars 57 (and Shahjahanbad/Red Fort 225, 232, 238, 246, 247; and Taj Ganj 201)
Bibadal Khan 192, 211
bilateral symmetry (at Taj Mahal 193, 199, 206, 207)
Birbal's House 178, 180
Black Taj 219–20
Bu Halima garden 119
Buland Darwaza 44, 165, 169, 183–85, 203, 236 (and conquest of Gujarat 165)

calligraphy (at Qutb Complex 77, 81, 84, 89; at Taj Mahal 210, 212, 214, 215)
caravanserais 49, 193, 194, 201
cenotaph 211, 213, 215, 220
chabutra (or terrace) 200, 246
Chahar Suq 170
chajja 41, 95, 108, 118, 140, 142, 145, 147, 150, 152, 180, 182, 244
Chalo Dilli ('March to Delhi') 253
Chandni Chowk xxix, 61, 62, 98, 225, 233–34, 246, 248
char bagh xv, 33, 46, 53, (and Agra/Agra Fort 131, 144; and Babur 33; and Humayun's tomb 113–14; and Red Fort 245; and Taj Mahal 196, 200, 204, 221, 223; and tomb garden 107–08;

286 DELHI, AGRA, FATEHPUR SIKRI

Itmad-ud Daulah's tomb 53; under Akbar 46)
Chatta Bazar 235, 237
chattris 57, 108, 112, 117–19, 121, 136, 140, 142, 147, 182, 202, 244
Chauhan 1–3, 4, 6, 12, 74, 75, 76, 83 (Prithviraja Chauhan (also known as Prithviraja III or 'Rai Pithora' 1, 4, 6, 12; Vigraharaja IV (also known as Visala Deva) 4)
Chini ka Rauza/'Chinese Tomb' 56
Chhoti Baithak or 'Small Sitting Room' 244
coins 2, 3, 45, 50, 173, 243, 249 ('Dilliwala' or 'Dhillika' 3; Bull and Horseman 2, 3, 45, 50)

dados 146, 148, 207, 210, 211, 212, 213, 245
Daftarkhana (or Secretariat or Records Office) 167, 174, 175
Dak Bungalow 170
darwaza and *khidkis* 232
Daulatkhana-i Aam or Diwankhana-i Aam (at Fatehpur Sikri 171–72)
Day of Judgment 215
Delhi (a part of Hariyanaka country, Dhilli 2; Ahmad Shah Abdali 66; and English East India Company 48, 50, 63; and 1857 rebellion 23, 64, 67; attacks by Nadir Shah and Third Battle of Panipat 67; Dhillika 2, 3, 4; end of Mughal rule 66; imperial *durbars* 68; Maratha attacks 66; Renaissance 77; transfer of power from East India Company to British Crown 67; under the Rajputs 2–6; Yoginipura 3)
Delhi College 250
Delhi Durbar 243, 249
Delhi gate (or Akbarabadi gate) 232, 247, 251 (at Agra Fort 135–36)
Delhi Renaissance xxx, 67, 250
dhilli killi 1, 2, 4
Diwan-i Aam or 'Hall of Public Audience' 43, 54, 213 (and *Chihil Sutun* or Diwan-i Khas (or Jewel House) 171; at Agra Fort 135, 136, 138, 149–51, 154; at Fatehpur Sikri 167, 170–71; at Red Fort 231, 239–43, 251; carved pillar in 172; circular platform 172; connection with the concept of *Chihil Sutun* or Forty-pillared Hall in Iran 150–51; evolution of 149–50; layout and architecture 135–36; Forty-pillared Hall 129, 238)
Diwan-i Khas or 'Hall of Private Audience' 43, 45 (at Agra Fort 147–49, 153; at Fatehpur Sikri 163, 168, 171–74; at Red Fort 30–31, 240–42, 244–45, 249,

251; layout and architecture 149–50)

domes xv–vi, 15, 57, 70, 77, 79, 80, 85, 86, 90, 92–95, 108, 110, 112, 115, 117–18, 121, 124, 136, 137, 140, 142, 145, 150, 152, 166, 177, 182–84, 194, 202, 207, 209–12, 222–23, 236, 242, 244, 245 (also bulbous dome 211; under Romans 70, 79)

double dome 112, 117, 121, 124, 127, 223 (and finial 118; evolution of 117)

East gate (or 'Fatehabadi Darwaza') 201

Faiz Bazar (or 'Bazaar of Plenty') 233, 247

Fatehpur Sikri xiii, xv–xix, xxxi–ii, 10, 35, 36, 40–44, 128, 131, 142, 157, 158–90, 195, 198, 204, 222, 235, 236 (Aankh Michauli 172; Abdarkhana 176, 177, 178; Agra and Sikri 41; and Akbar's policies 43; and carpet-making and indigo-manufacturing 186, 190; and Jodha Bai's kitchen 159, 179; and Muhammad Shah Rangila 187; and Shaikh Salim Chishti 161; and the influence Shaikh Salim Chishti 41; and water shortage 188; Anup Talao (or 'Peerless Pool') 172, 175, 176; Astrologer's Seat 173; Babur and Sikri/Shukri 41; Badshahi Darwaza 184; Birbal's House 178, 180; Buland Darwaza 44, 165, 169, 183–85, 203, 236; capital shifts from Lahore to Agra 44; *Chahar Suq* 170; change of capital from Agra to Fatehpur Sikri 185; circumstances leading to the establishment of a new capital at Sikri 161, 164–65; Daftarkhana (or Secretariat or Records Office) 167, 174, 175; Dak Bungalow 170; decline of Fatehpur Sikri 185; design and layout 166, 168–69; Diwan-i Aam 167, 170–71; Diwan-i Khas 163, 168, 171–74; Gujarati influence on architecture 167; Hakim's Baoli 189; Hauz-i Shirin (or 'Sweet Tank') 171, 176; Hawa Mahal (or the 'Wind Palace') 179; Hiran Minar 170, 187; Hospital 159, 176; Ibadat Khana 43, 165; Imperial Complex 170; Imperial Harem (or Haramsara or Shabistan-i-Iqbal) 169, 171, 174, 176, 241, 243; inspiration from Timurid or

Mughal encampment 168;
Jamaat Khana (or 'Tomb of
Islam Khan') 183; Jami Masjid
165, 169, 181, 182, 198,
203; Jodha Bai 159, 179, 180;
Mariam's House (or Sunhara
Makan) 175–77; masjid-
dargah complex 159–60;
Shaikh Salim Chishti's tomb
169; shift of capital to Lahore
185; Sikri under Akbar 185,
190; Sikri under Babur 161;
Stone Cutters' Mosque 181;
Treasury 173–74, 176; Turkish
Sultana's Chamber/Palace/
Pavilion 172; under Jahangir
187; under Shah Jahan 187)
Fatehpuri Masjid (also Fathpuri
Masjid) 201, 233, 246
finial (and Humayun tomb complex
117, 118, 120, 121, 126; and
Red Fort 236; and Taj Mahal
209, 212)
Firuz Shah Tughlaq 22, 23, 60,
230 (and canals and water
bodies 62; and disintegration
of the Delhi Sultanate 22; and
Firuzabad 22, 23, 24; and two
Ashokan pillars 23)
Forty-pillared Hall 129, 238

Gardens of Paradise xv, xvi, (at
Humayun's tomb 101, 113–
14; at Taj Mahal 193, 200, 202,
205, 222)
Ghazni gate or 'Somnath gate' 12,
154–55 ('Proclamation of the
Gates' by Lord Ellenborough,
connection with First British-
Afghan War 155; how gates of
the mausoleum of Mahmud of
Ghazni reached Agra Fort 155)
Ghiyasuddin Tughlaq xxiii, 20,
222 (and curse of Nizamuddin
Auliya 20–21; and Tughlaqabad
20; Tughlaqabad Fort 20)
Ghulam Qadir 241, 249
Ghuri (also known as Muhammad of
Ghur, Shahabuddin Muhammad,
Muizuddin Muhammad bin
Sam or Muhammad Ghuri)
xxii, 4, 6, 7, 14, 18, 75, 85, 89
(and Prithviraja Chauhan 6; and
Punjab 4, 5, 6, 8, 9, 15, 17, 24,
31, 35, 44, 52, 65; conquest of
Delhi 7)
Great gate (at Taj Mahal or *darwaza-i
rauza*) 202–03
guldastas 112, 184, 203

Hakim's Baoli 189
Hamida Banu Begum (or Mariam
Makani) 35, 102, 177, 180,
187
hammam 43, 109, 111, 129, 145,
147, 148, 160, 188, 189, 221,

244, 246 (at Agra Fort 145; auction of its parts by Lord William Bentinck 148)
hasht bihistht (or concept of 'eight paradises') xv, 53 (and Humayun's tomb 112, 114–15, 127; and Taj Mahal 209, 223 (evolution of the plan 114–15; Mughals and muthamman baghdadi 115)
Hathi Pol gate (or 'Elephant gate') (at Agra Fort 135–36; at Fatehpur Sikri 154, 170)
Hauz-i Shirin (or 'Sweet Tank') 171, 176 (and Ganga water 176)
Hawa Mahal (or the 'Wind Palace') 179
Hayat Baksh Bagh or 'Life Bestowing Garden' 245, 246
Hessing's tomb or 'Red Taj Mahal' 154
Hindu 11–14, 21, 26, 28, 39, 43, 47, 51, 70, 74, 77, 78, 81–82, 85, 89, 97, 103, 108, 112, 123, 129, 143, 155, 156, 159, 165, 167, 172, 177, 178–80, 198, 218, 230, 233–34, 242, 250
Hinduism 1, 175, (and art forms 77)
Hira Mahal 226, 246
Hiran Minar 170, 187
Hospital 159, 176
Humayun xxiv, xxv, xxvi, 32, 34–36, 60, 100, 101–03, 106–07, 110, 115, 118, 121, 128, 131, 157, 254 (and Babur 32; and Dinpanah 102; and Koh-i-noor or 'Mountain of Light' diamond 32; circumstances prevailing during his reign 101–03; death at Sher Mandal 103; death from Sher Mandal 35; defeat by Sher Shah and exile 34; Dinpanah or the 'Refuge of the Faithful' 34; Humayun Nama 115)
Humayun's tomb xiii, xvii, xxiv, xxvi, xxxi–iii, 10, 24, 36, 98, 99–127, 144, 184, 198, 208, 209, 211, 212, 222, 223, 234, 251 (Afsarwala mosque and tomb 100, 120; and 1857 rebellion 122; and Akbar's architectural style 109; and Bahadur Shah Zafar 250, 252, 255; and funerary architecture in Islam 109, 110; and partition of India 123; and the revival of Delhi Sultanate architectural style 107; Arab Sarai 100, 119, 120; Barber's tomb 100, 121; Bu Halima garden 119; circumstances leading to the construction of 100–103; design and layout 111; inspiration from emperor's

wooden boat palace 115; Isa Khan's tomb and mosque 100, 118; modern restoration and related debates 124; name of architects 101, 107; stones used 112; tomb garden 111; tomb garden after Akbar 121; who built it 106)

Ibadat Khana (or the 'House of Worship') 43, 165

Ibrahim Lodi xxv, 31–32 (and Babur 32; and Badalgarh fort 32, 37; and First Battle of Panipat 32)

Iltutmish 12, 14, 15, 16, 19, 28, 75, 79, 80, 83, 85, 87–92, 95–96, 222 (and Aibek's death 14–15; and Delhi as capital city 16–17; and extensions to the congregational mosque and Minar 88–89; and Iron Pillar 83; and the foundational inscription in the congregational mosque 91; circumstances prevailing during his reign 87–88; death and weaker sultans 16–18; Delhi as 'Sanctuary of Islam' or *Qubbat al-Islam* 15–16; migrations from Central Asia 15, 52)

Iltutmish's tomb 71, 89, 90–92 (and Sultan Ghari 89; construction of 89; design 90; Quranic verses 91; use of squinches and pendentives 90)

Imperial Harem (or Haramsara or Shabistan-i-Iqbal) 169, 171, 174, 176, 241, 243 (and Rajput queens 168, 178, 180; Rajput architecture 167, 168, 179)

Independence Day xv, xxxii, 225, 226, 236, 252

Indian National Army (also INA Trials) 253, 255

iron pillar 1, 2, 70, 71, 78, 82–84 (at the Qutb complex 78, 82, 84; composition of pillar 84; debates regarding original location 86–88)

Isa Khan's tomb and mosque 100, 118

Islam xv, 5, 6, 7, 8, 10, 11, 15, 17, 19, 40, 61, 70, 74, 76, 77, 80, 81, 84, 85, 87–89, 93, 95–98, 109, 110, 112, 116–18, 129, 146, 157, 164, 164, 180, 194, 208, 213, 214, 232, 233, 240 ('Hindu–Muslim conflicts' 13; Abbasid court and cultural exchange 4, 15, 53; and 'clash of religions' 13; and Arab, 7–11; and Arab Muslim merchants 7; and art forms 77; and conquest of Sindh 8; and domes 110; and Muslim settlements 24, 57; and Pratiharas Rashtrakutas 8; and

Sufis 7, 8, 9, 40; and tombs 110; Indo-Islamic architecture 11)
Islamic 5, 8–12, 13–15, 25, 36, 42, 74, 76–79, 81, 84, 88–90, 96, 102, 109, 112, 116–17, 129, 151, 156, 159, 164, 165, 167, 202, 212–13, 214, 217, 225, 232, 233, 240
iwan 142

jaalis or perforated screens 93, 95, 108, 116, 183, 206, 210, 211, 212, 243
Jahanara Begum 55, 62, 64, 142–44, 146, 151, 236, 246 (her palace at Agra Fort 144; Jami Masjid 151)
Jahangir xxi, xxvii–xxix, 26, 42, 44–48, 50–53, 55, 57, 65, 113, 120, 129, 134, 137–45, 148, 151–52, 157, 164, 166, 167, 178, 180, 187, 201, 204, 209, 213, 214 (and Akbar's tomb at Sikandara 46; and development of Agra as a commercial hub 46; and development of Agra as a riverfront city 44–45; and gardens 46; emperor's black throne 45; in Allahabad 54; Nur Afshan garden 46; Nur Jahan 52; rise of Itmad-ud Daulah and family 52)
Jahangiri Mahal 129, 137, 138–45, 157, 167 (architectural styles 139, 157; functionality 139; Hauz-i Jahangiri or 'Jahangir's bath' 138; part of Bengali Mahal 138)
Jalaluddin Khaji (and Kilokhari Palace) 18
Jamaat Khana (or 'Tomb of Islam Khan') 183
Jami Masjid (or Jama Masjid or Masjid-i Jami) 13 (and Agra 136, 152; and Fatehpur Sikri 163, 165, 169, 181, 182; and Qutb complex 78; and Shahjahanabad 233, 234, 235, 236, 245, 247; and Taj Mahal 198, 203)
Jawaharlal Nehru 217, 254
jharokha darshan 65, 129, 143, 144, 145, 174, 237, 242 (at Agra Fort 143; Darshaniya sect 144; evolution of 143)
jilaukhana (forecourt) xvi, 200–02, 216, 235, 238
Jodha Bai 159, 179, 180 (and Jodha Bai's kitchen 159, 179; Jodha Bai's Palace 167, 178, 179; legend of Jodha Bai 180)

Kabuli gate 232
kalasha 78, 81, 209, 212
kanguras 184, 236

karmuka 233
Kashmiri gate 232–34
Khas Mahal or 'Special Palace' (at Agra Fort 141, 142; at Red Fort 241)
khawasspuras (or residential courtyards) 200–01
Khizri gate 135, 145, 153, 236
khutba 247
Khwabgah (at Fatehpur Sikri 167, 172, 173, 174, 175, 177; at Red Fort 241–42)
Koh-i-Noor ('Mountain of Light') diamond xvi, 32, 66, 225, 240, 248

Lahori gate 232, 233–37, 246, 254
Lal Kot xxiii, xxvi, 3, 12–14, 19, 22, 70, 74, 75, 77, 83, 92, 98 (and Anangpal II 3, 12; and Prithviraja Chauhan 1, 4, 6, 12; and temple destruction under Turks 5, 13, 14, 51; and the Rajputs 74; congregational mosque and Qutb Minar 1, 13, 16, 42, 44, 61; Qila Rai Pithora (see above); under the Turks 75). See also Qila Rai Pithora.
Lodis xx, xxiv, xxv, xxxi, 28, 29, 32, 118, 128, 129, 130, 227, 254 (and Delhi Sultanate 22; Sharqis of Jaunpur 25)

Lord Curzon 123, 154, 170, 216, 236, 246
Lord William Bentinck 221–22

Machchli Bhawan or 'Fish Palace' complex 135, 145, 147, 149, 152 ('throne terrace' 147; and Diwan-i Khas 147; *hammam* 147; Jahangir's black throne 149)
Mahmud of Ghazni xxii, 5, 129, 155, 156 (and Ghazni 12, 24, 37; and Persian language and culture 5, 8, 10, 46; Ghaznavid conquest of Punjab and Multan 5, 6; raids in India 6)
Mahtab Bagh (or 'Moonlight Garden') 55–56, 220, 245, 246
mahzarnama 182
Makramat Khan 194, 230
Marathas xxi, xxix, xxx, 45, 63–67, 129, 130, 138, 153, 187, 219, 248, 249
Mariam Zamani 42, 178
Mariam's House (or Sunhara Makan) 175–77
mausoleum (or tomb) xxvi, 16, 36, 42, 53, 55, 75, 80, 100, 101, 106, 109, 110–11, 114, 116, 118, 121, 126, 127, 146, 155, 191, 193, 194, 198, 200, 202, 204, 205, 207, 208–16, 221

INDEX   293

Mecca 66, 77, 106, 119, 151, 181, 208, 234
mihman khana (or 'guest house') 193, 200, 202, 206, 210, 216
mihrab 90, 95, 116, 151, 207
Mina Bazar 152, 181
Mina Masjid ('Gem Mosque' at Agra Fort 152)
minaret(s) xvi, xxxii, 14, 46, 69, 70, 74, 78, 84–89, 92, 94, 152, 172, 206, 208–09, 223, 236
minor Haramsara 181
Mir Abdul Karim 194
mosques xxv, 1, 8, 12–16, 20, 22, 25, 30, 32, 33–34, 41, 44, 61, 65, 70, 71, 88, 98, 107, 109, 134, 151, 152, 158, 161, 181, 182, 194, 198, 200, 202, 206, 207, 208, 210, 212, 214, 216, 222, 232, 248, 251 (at Agra Fort 134; Jami Masjid 61; Mina Masjid (or 'Gem Mosque') 152; Moti Masjid (or 'Pearl Mosque') 152; Nagina Masjid 152; Qutb Mosque or *Arhai din ka jhompra* 13)
mosque-shrine complex 160, 168, 169, 181–82
Moti Masjid (or 'Pearl Mosque') 65, (at Agra Fort 133, 152, 154, 215; at Red Fort 226, 229, 245)

Mughals xviii, xx, xxi–iv, xxx, 2, 10, 40–42, 45, 48, 59, 67, 69, 98, 100, 107–10, 113–15, 118, 121–23, 127, 129, 130, 136, 139, 143, 146, 147, 153, 155, 157, 158, 166, 189, 190, 192, 198, 200, 204, 214, 239, 243, 247, 249, 255 (and Mongols 30, 34; connections with Changez Khan and Timur 24, 30, 31; relation with Chaghtais 30)
Muhammad bin Tughlaq xxi, xxiii, xxiv, 21, 22, 85 (and creation of co-capital in Devagiri 21; and death of Ghiyasuddin Tughlaq 20–21; and decline of the Sultanate 22; and expansion of Delhi Sultanate 21; and Jahanpanah or 'The Refuge of the World' 21; Bijay Mandal 22)
Muhammad Waris 224
Mumtaz Mahal xxviii, 55, 143, 152, 191, 192, 193, 196, 200, 203, 204, 211, 215, 220, 221, 244 (first burial in a garden in Zainabad 192; in Burhanpur 192; second burial 194)
muqarna 84, 211
Muslims xxiii, xxv, xxviii, xxxi, 5, 8–11, 13, 15–16, 25, 28, 43, 47, 60, 70, 79, 80–83, 87,

88, 90, 94–98, 123, 155, 165, 167, 178, 180, 182, 213, 218, 227, 230, 234, 251
muthamman baghdadi 115, 234
Muthamman Burj 236, 242 (and evolution of *ayina bandi* or *ayina kari* or glass-art technique 146; and *jharokha darshan* at Agra Fort 143; at Agra Fort 145; at Agra Fort and Jahangir's 'chain of justice' at Agra Fort 145; Shish Mahal or 'Mirror Palace' 145–47, 157)

Nadir Shah xxx, 66, 225, 241, 247, 248–49
Nagina Masjid 152, 181
nahar-i-behisht or 'Stream of Paradise' 225, 235, 241, 243, 244, 247
Naqqar Khana (or Drum House or Naubat Khana or Music Gallery) 237–38, 246
nashiman 211 (at Taj Mahal)
Nashiman-i-Zill-i-Ilahi or the 'Seat of the Shadow of God' 239 (at Red Fort)
naubatkhana (or *baradari* or Jal Mahal ('Water Palace') 205 (at Agra Fort 137)
Nigambodh Ghat 230

pachisi board 173, 187 (at Fatehpur Sikri)

palace-fort xvi, xxix, xxxii, 22, 23, 42, 57, 60–62, 103, 128, 224, 225–27, 230, 231–37, 240–41, 244, 245–55
Panchmahal (or 'Chaharsuffa') 175, 177
paradise xxxii, 46, 90, 93, 110, 112–15, 192, 202, 203, 204, 209, 211, 215, 221, 241, 243, 245
paradise tomb garden xxxii, 112, 127, 204 (and evolution of tomb garden 123; Quran and 'Garden of Paradise' 113–14; walled garden 101)
pavilion 20, 45, 46, 53, 57, 62, 70, 79, 85, 86, 103, 108, 111–13, 115–17, 121, 128, 139, 140–42, 143, 147, 154, 160, 163, 166–71, 175, 176, 179, 182, 184, 200, 202, 205, 212, 221, 234, 235, 236, 243–46
Peacock Throne (also known as *Takht-i-Taus*) 240, 241
pietra dura (or *parchinkari*) 145, 150, 212, 213, 217, 223, 239 (marble inlay work, 210, 212)
pishtaq 142, 151, 152, 182, 183, 184, 202, 207, 209, 210, 213

qibla 77, 208
Qila Rai Pithora (*also see* Lal Kot)

Quran 8, 43, 81, 85, 90, 93, 101, 110, 113, 114, 119, 120–21, 182

Qutb complex xxv, xxvi, xxxi, 1, 3, 9, 12, 13–16, 17, 19, 70, 71, 75, 76, 80–82, 86–88, 91, 92, 94, 98, 117, 127, 222 (Alauddin Khalji's madrasa 94; Alauddin Khalji's tomb 71; circumstances leading to the construction of the complex 71–74; design and layout 76; the complex after Alauddin Khalji 70; tomb of Imam Zamin 71; under Alauddin Khalji 91; under Iltutmish 83)

Qutb Minar xiii, xv, xvii, xviii, xxxi, 1, 3, 9, 14, 16, 19, 22–23, 60, 69–98, 108, 177, 222, 260 (and Syed Ahmad Khan 84; and Turks 12; construction of 84; contested history 84; original name and function of the Minar 86; repairs to the Minar 85–86; Smith's Folly 86)

Qutbuddin Aibek 5, 7, 12, 14, 15, 28, 60, 75, 76, 78, 79, 81, 82, 83, 85–92 (and Ganga–Yamuna doab 7, 17, 28, 29; and Iltutmish 12, 15–16)

Quwwat al-Islam, also known as congregation mosque or Qutb mosque 13, 71, 75, 76, 95–97. *See also* Masjid-i Jami, Delhi's first Friday mosque (and arabesque 77, 81; and iron pillar 78; and Syed Ahmad Khan 96; and the stone screen 78; connection with 'Qubbat al-Islam' or 'Dome/Sanctuary of Islam' 87, 96; construction of 95; extensions under Alauddin Khalji 92; extensions under Iltutmish 88; how the name of the congregational mosque changed 87; original name 94; pillared galleries and the courtyard 77, 78, 88; pillars from Rajput temples 78)

Quwwat al-Islam 13. *See also* Qubbat al-Islam.

Rajputs xxii, xxiii, 2, 3, 4, 7, 11, 14, 24, 31, 39, 41, 43, 47, 49, 53, 57, 65, 70, 74, 75, 77, 129, 130, 161 (Chauhan 1–3, 4, 6, 12; in north India 74, 77, 87, 88, 94, 96, 98; Tomar 1, 2, 3, 12)

Rang Mahal or Imtiaz Mahal or 'Palace of Distinction' 42, (at Fatehpur Sikri 164; at Red Fort 242–44, 246, 251)

Rangoon (now Yangon) 122, 225, 251, 252, 255 (deportation Bahadur Shah Zafar 226, 245,

246, 250, 252; grave of Bahadur
Shah Zafar 252; INA provisional
government 252)
Rebellion of 1857 xxx, xxxii, 23,
64, 67 (and Agra Fort 128,
154, and Fatehpur Sikri 187–
88; and Humayun's tomb 122;
and Red Fort 226, 232, 238,
239, 241–45, 250, 251, 252,
253, 255; and Taj Mahal 215)
Red Fort or Lal Qila or Qila-i-
Mubarak ('Fort of Fortune') or
Qila-i-Shahjahanabad ('Fort of
Shahjahanabad') xiii, xv–xxxiii,
3, 12, 37, 54, 61, 65, 67, 74,
86, 98, 122, 128, 144, 194,
213, 224, 225, 228, 234,
237, 239, 241, 243, 245, 247,
249, 251–55, 242 (Salimgarh
Fort 60, 224, 230, 234, 235,
236, 249)
red sandstone and white marble
(combination) xv, 127, 195,
198, 222
riverfront terrace 45, 55, 141,
148, 194, 200, 204, 206, 212
Red Fort xxix, xxx, xxxi, xxxii,
xxxiii, 37, 67, 194, 213,
224–55 (Chatta Bazar 235,
237; Hayat Baksh Bagh or 'Life
Bestowing Garden' 245, 246;
Hira Mahal 226, 246; *Sawan* and
Bhadaun pavilions 245, 246)

Salimgarh Fort 60, 224, 230, 234,
235, 236, 249
sarai xxviii, 49, 58, 62, 71, 95,
119, 234, 246
Sawan and *Bhadaun* pavilions 245, 246
Scales of Justice 242
Shah Alam xxx, 183, 241, 249
Shah Burj or the 'King's Tower' (at
Agra Fort 145, 215; at Red Fort
235, 236, 245)
Shah Jahan xx, xxiv, xxvii–viii, xxix,
xxxi, 3, 37, 48, 52, 53, 54–57,
191–94, 198, 201–06, 211,
213–15, 220, 222, 224–27,
234–37, 239, 240–43, 246,
247 ('Chini ka Rauza'/'Chinese
Tomb' 56; accession 53; Agra
as a cultural centre 59; and
development of Agra city 57;
building activity at Agra Fort 54;
court rituals 55; development of
markets 57; gardens in Agra 55;
imprisonment by Aurangzeb
64; Jahanara Bagh 55; *katra* 58;
Mahtab Bagh 55; *mandi* 67; new
capital at Shahjahanabad 59;
peacock throne 65; Rajwara 57;
sarai 58; Tajganj 58; Taj Mahal
53–54)
Shahjahanabad or Qila-i-Mualla (the
'Exalted Fort') xxiv, xxix, xxix,
xxx, xxxi, xxxii, 23, 24, 54, 59,
60–63, 64–65, 67, 98, 151,

19, 215, 225, 226, 234 (and 1857 rebellion 238; and shift of capital from Agra 225; Ashrafi Bazar 246; Chandni Chowk 61; construction of 230–31; decline of Agra 63; Faiz Bazar (or 'Bazaar of Plenty') 233, 247; Fatehpuri Masjid (also Fathpuri Masjid) 201, 233, 246; gardens 72; imperial and commercial streets 61; inaugural celebrations 247; Jami Masjid 61; layout and design 231–32; reasons for shift of capital from Agra to Delhi 59; Red Fort or Qila-i-Maula 61; under Aurangzeb 236; under Bahadur Shah Zafar 236; under Shah Jahan 234–35; under the British 236; Urdu Bazar or 'Bazaar of the Royal Camp' 246)

Shahjahani Mahal (at Agra Fort 138, 141)

Shaikh Salim Chishti xxi, xxvi, xxx–iii, 10, 40, 41–42, 86, 127, 159, 161, 164, 169, 181, 183, 186, 188, 190 (and Salim or Jahangir 187)

Shaikh Salim Chishti's tomb 169

Shish Mahal or 'House of Mirrors' xvi (and evolution of *ayina bandi* or *ayina kari* or glass-art technique 146; at Agra Fort 145, 146, 147, 157; at Red Fort 244)

Shutrugulu 235

Sikandara 25, 45, 46, 58, 63, 204 (Akbar's tomb 46)

Sikander Lodi 25, 28, 75, 94, 117 (and Bagh-i Jud or Lodi Gardens 25; and repairs of Qutb Minar 25; and shift of capital to Agra 63)

Siri xxiii, 18, 20, 21, 22, 76, 92 (and Alauddin Khalji 19; discovery by Alexander Cunningham 18)

Smith's Folly 86

South gate 111, 201

Stone Cutters' Mosque 181

stone screen in Qutb complex 92 (and arabesque 77, 81; and corbelled arch 80, 81; and Quranic verses 90; calligraphy 77, 81, 89; Iltutmish's extensions 88)

Subhash Chandra Bose 252

Sufis xix, xxi, xxiii, xxv, xxvi–vii, xxxii, 7–9, 10, 40, 41, 59, 60, 86, 87, 127, 164, 173, 181, 183, 227, 247 (and India 8; Bakhtiyar Kaki 9, 10, 32; Khwaja Muinuddin Chishti xxi, xxvi, xxvii, 8, 9, 10, 40–42, 50, 86, 127, 159, 161, 164, 168–69, 181, 183, 188, 190; mystical powers of 9; orders or *silsilahs* 8, 9; Shaikh Nizamuddin Auliya 9; Shaikh Salim Chishti xxi, xxvi, xxx–iii, 10, 40, 41–42, 86, 127, 159, 161, 164, 169, 181, 183, 186, 188, 190; Sufis as intercessors or protectors 9; the Chishtis and the Suhrawardis 8, 9, 40)

sulh-i kul 43, 165

Sunehri Masjid 248

tahkhana (or underground chamber at Taj Mahal) 206

Taj Ganj 194, 200

Taj Mahal xiii, xv, xvii, xxvii, xxxi–iii, 33, 51, 53–55, 58, 63–65, 98, 100, 127–29, 146, 148, 187, 191–223, 230, 236, 241, 260 (and 'Company Paintings' 216; and advertisements 217; and Aurangzeb 215; and Curzon 216; and East India Company 216; and folklore 219; and Jawaharlal Nehru 217; and music 217–18; and popular history 219; and the British 215; architects of 194; architecture of 199; architecture symbolism 199; Black Taj 219–20; *char bagh* at 200; construction of 194–99; corporate brands 217–19; Great gate (or *darwaza-i rauza*) 202–03; layout and design 199–201; location on Yamuna bank 194; Mahtab Bagh (or 'Moonlight Garden') 55–56, 220, 245, 246; *mihman khana* (or 'guest house') 193, 200, 202, 206, 210, 216; site selection 193; symbol of excellence 217; trees and plants at 204)

Tansen's Baradari 170 (at Fatehpur Sikri)

Tasbih Khana or 'Chamber for Counting Beads for Private Prayers' 242

Tejo Mahalaya 218

Third Battle of Panipat xxx, 67, 157, 249

Todarmal Baradari 189

Tomar 1, 2, 3, 12, 74, 75, 76, 82 (Anangapala (also known as Bilhan Deo) 2, 3; Anangpur 2, Suraj Pal 3; Surajkund 2, 3; Anangpal II 3, 12; Anangtal 3, 24)

tombs xxv, xxxii, 10, 30, 32, 36, 60, 62, 70, 89, 90, 100, 110, 116, 118, 123, 124, 161, 200, 202, 204, 214, 223, 227 ('Chini ka Rauza' 56; Akbar's tomb 26, 45, 46, 63; Alauddin's tomb 29; Babur's tomb 34; Balban's tomb 17; Barber's tomb 37; Humayun's tomb 10, 24; Iltutmish's tomb; Itmad-ud

Daulah's tomb 53, 56; Lodi-era tombs 32; or 'Red Taj Mahal' 51; Taj Mahal 11, 58, 63)

Tomb of Imam Zamin (at Qutb complex 94)

Tosha Khana or 'Robe Chamber' or Badi Baithak or 'Large Sitting Room', 242

Treasury 173–74, 176

Turkish Sultana's Chamber/Palace/ Pavilion 159, 172

Turkomani gate 232

Turks xx, xxii, xxxi, 2, 4–7, 10, 11–14, 18, 30, 70, 75, 76, 77, 78, 85, 98 (Abbasid Caliphate 4; and Arabic and Persian learning 5, 8, 10, 46; and art and architecture 10–11, 59; Central Asia 4, 5–7, 10, 13, 15, 30, 37; emergence of 4; Ghaznavid 4–6; Samanids 5; Sufis and trade 41–44; Turkish conquest of north India 8–10; Turks and Islam 5–7)

Urdu Bazar or 'Bazaar of the Royal Camp' 246

urs (Mumtaz Mahal's urs and the construction of the Taj 194, 211)

Ustad Ahmad Lahauri 194, 230

Ustad Hamid 230

waqf or endowment 201

West gate or 'Fatehpuri Darwaza' 201

Yamuna (River) xxii, xxiv, xxv, xxvi, xxvi–xxxii, 7, 17, 20, 22–24, 28, 29, 33, 34, 37, 44, 47, 55–58, 60, 62, 84, 100, 103, 111, 112–13, 115, 128, 128, 135, 136, 142, 145–46, 148, 191–93, 196, 205–06, 220, 221, 224, 227, 230, 235, 237, 243, 244, 249–51

Zafar Mahal 226, 245 (at Red Fort)

Zenana Mahal 244 (at Red Fort)